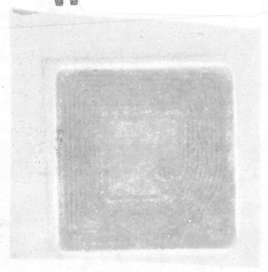

JAMES WALVIN

PASSAGE TO BRITAIN

Immigration in British History and Politics

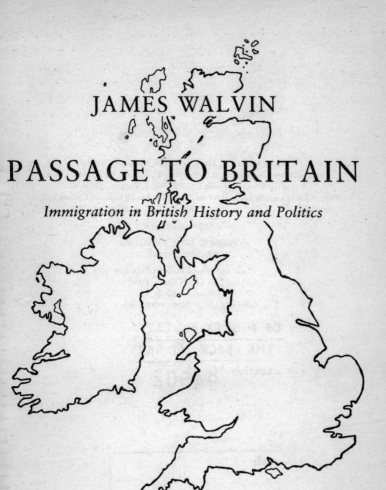

Penguin Books
in association with
Belitha Press

Penguin Books Ltd, Harmondsworth, Middlesex, England
Penguin Books, 40 West 23rd Street, New York, New York 10010, U.S.A.
Penguin Books Australia Ltd, Ringwood, Victoria, Australia
Penguin Books Canada Ltd, 2801 John Street, Markham, Ontario, Canada L3R 1B4
Penguin Books (N.Z.) Ltd, 182–190 Wairau Road, Auckland 10, New Zealand

First published 1984

Copyright © James Walvin, 1984
All rights reserved

Made and printed in Great Britain by
Richard Clay (The Chaucer Press) Ltd
Bungay, Suffolk
Set in 10/12 pt Monophoto Sabon

To the memory
of
Peter Sedgwick

Contents

Preface

This book has been written to accompany the Channel Four TV series 'Passage to Britain'. It covers many of the issues raised in that series but the following book is an autonomous study. I am once more grateful to a number of colleagues and friends for their help. Martin Pick encouraged me to write the book and later provided many helpful ideas and criticisms. I benefited greatly by working with David Cohen. The editorial staff at Penguin were most helpful in transforming my original manuscript into book form. I am also deeply grateful to Ann Wong for typing the manuscript. But my greatest debt is to Steve Fenton who offered a detailed and severe criticism of my original draft. The book which emerged is, whatever its shortcomings, much better because of his efforts.

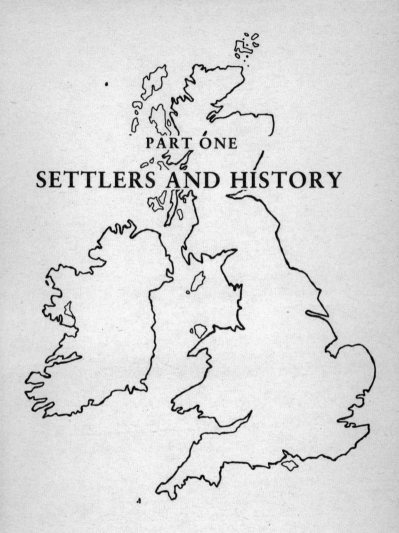

PART ONE

SETTLERS AND HISTORY

Introduction

Few political and social topics have aroused such passionate arguments as those which have centred on the complex matters of immigration and race in Britain over the past quarter of a century. The development of substantial communities of people from those areas of the world which became known as the 'New Commonwealth' unquestionably changed a number of the salient features of urban life in a large number of British towns and cities. To a marked degree, the arguments about the pros and cons of immigration resolved themselves increasingly into a debate (though that word is too cool and too rational adequately to describe the fiercer and more passionate arguments) about colour and race. Arguments about immigration and race so often hinged upon a series of assumptions about the people migrating to Britain, assumptions which had grown over the many years when Britain had been the world's pre-eminent imperial power and had been able in large measure to rule the waves by virtue of her own buoyant economic power. By the time non-white immigration into Britain had reached such levels that Parliament felt obliged to restrict it (in 1962), it was, however (and not coincidentally), abundantly clear that Britain was a nation in retreat from her earlier pre-eminence. We know, it is true, that this decline in British power had long been in progress; some historians have even traced its roots back to the years of the late nineteenth century.

However long-term this decline, it became unavoidably clear by the late 1950s, more especially, and as we shall see later, in the immediate aftermath of the Suez fiasco in 1956. It is true, however, that Britain's changing world role was not easily accepted by large numbers of British people of all sorts and conditions. One aspect of global and economic pre-eminence was the fierce commitment to

British superiority on the part of the British people, with of course the inevitable exceptions. Brought up from childhood days to accept unquestioningly that Britain and her empire had created and directed many of the world's finest social and political achievements, it was, naturally enough, very difficult for British people to accept the evidence of Britain's decline. More difficult still was the fact that the retreat from international power coincided with the years of unparalleled material prosperity of the late 1950s. As ever more Britons acquired those material artefacts which, though initially luxuries, were soon to be viewed as essentials, people could be forgiven for imagining that their country was still an ascendant power.

Some measure of the transformation which has overtaken Britain in the last quarter of a century can be seen in the words of national politicians. Whereas in 1959 the Prime Minister could tell the British electorate that they had 'never had it so good' (a materialistically crude view of an undoubted social fact), by 1983 the national political debate had changed utterly in tone, direction and outlook. By the early 1980s the political arguments centred around how to get ailing Britain better. Few politicians could deny, whatever their prognosis for the future and however different their ideologies, that Britain was in a serious economic and social decline. The political arguments, notably at the 1983 election, were about how best to arrest and reverse that decline. The optimism of Harold Macmillan, uttered only a generation before, had been shown to be glib and deceptive, just as its contemporary critics had always argued.

This book is not, however, about the decline of Britain. But unless we place the following study firmly in the context of the transformations in Britain's economic and international standing, it will be difficult fully to grasp the tensions and uncertainties exhibited by the British when confronted by yet another social upheaval: immigration into Britain itself. The British had to come to terms first with the existence of immigration and then the development of significant ethnic communities in British cities at a time of major social and political readjustment. Indeed, part of the following argument is that immigration into Britain is in large measure a function of Britain's changing global role; the difficulties of adjustment by the British were compounded by the visible evidence of foreign (i.e. 'coloured') settlement in Britain itself. For many people, the rapid growth of black and Asian communities provided the very evidence and proof of Britain's demise. The extreme right has, for instance, consistently argued that immigrants are the cause of Britain's woes. The truth of the matter is, of course, more confused and it is part of the purpose of the following book to offer an analysis of recent immigration into Britain which seeks to locate these demographic changes in their broader, global and social setting.

It would be quite wrong to imagine that immigration to Britain is uniquely a question of 'coloured' immigration, or that it is a feature solely of the post-war world. There has been a large-scale migration of white people to Britain in recent years – from North America, Europe and Australasia. More central still to this book's case is the broader historical setting. Indeed the author's main ambition is to place the study of recent immigration within its fuller historical setting, by suggesting the longevity and persistence of foreign settlement in Britain. This is not to claim there is nothing new about the recent experience of immigration for there clearly is; rather it is that the history of Britain has been affected, and in some respects shaped, by the settlement of outside people in a way which is largely ignored.

It is furthermore important to remember that the British experience is one of a genuinely global movement of peoples. The human make-up of one society after another has been unalterably changed by the ebb and flow of human migrations, as people fled from poverty or persecution or were lured by the prospects of happier or more prosperous conditions elsewhere. From imperial Rome – its population a remarkably heterogeneous human reflection of the far-flung imperial possessions – through to present-day Europe, imperial and post-imperial powers attract armies of migrants. German *gastarbeiter*, French *pieds-noirs*, these and more are a reminder of how widespread is the movement of peoples.

This book is primarily a work of history, although the second section concerns itself with what may be regarded as contemporary history. When writing about the recent past the author has, naturally, depended on the work not of other historians but of large numbers of British social scientists whose researches continue to throw light on the field of immigration and race-relations. By training, social scientists tend to be more acutely aware of the problems of definitions and of categories than historians. This is especially true in this particular field where, to put it simply, the very terms we use are matters of political sensitivity and personal delicacy. An example is the use of the word 'immigrant'. Although it has an obvious objective and non-pejorative meaning, it is unquestionably used clumsily, indiscriminately and sometimes offensively by the British to describe not merely *every* non-white person who has settled in Britain, but also their children. One can readily see why a person born and bred in, say, Hackney or Bradford, should feel aggrieved at being called an immigrant. It is part of the false polarization which has marred the political debate about immigration that the debate is generally presented as a crude contrast of immigrants and the British. Similarly, it has been argued that to speak of the 'host' British society is to obscure the complex reality of the world into which immigrants settle. They settle, for instance, into a particular (normally working-class) community in a specific part of a city. In a society fractured by social class, some have claimed that to speak of the 'host' society is to ignore the crucially determining force of social class. Throughout this book, the term 'host society' is used, as is the term 'immigrant'; both are employed in their obvious, descriptive senses. When inappropriate they are not used.

It is not my aim to write a book which will satisfy all the definitional doubts of researchers in the field, but to make sense of this difficult and complex topic for a wide and interested readership. Nor do I intend to perpetuate any of the myths or misunderstandings which have for so long characterized our discussions about immigration and race. I am, however, painting with a broad brush: a style which will not appeal to everyone. For those attracted to the finer points, the short bibliography related to each chapter, to be found at the end of the book, should provide greater satisfaction.

The book is concerned primarily with Britain. It is, as will become clear, written from an English viewpoint but I have sought not to commit the English historian's vice of writing Britain when meaning England. Let us begin, however, with a particularly English focus.

I

A Nation and Immigrants

The English in many respects have an acute sense of their own history. Across the face of the country there flourish a myriad organizations, groups and classes actively pursuing the study of history: local history, family history, military history, regional history – indeed, antiquarian studies of all conceivable sorts and conditions. It is an interest which feeds upon that wealth of surviving English artefacts and documentation – parish records, graveyards, census data, private and corporate materials of all types; an interest which provides a ready-made lecture circuit across the country for historians and peripatetic practitioners of the art. From September to June, local libraries and information centres are rarely without their lists of forthcoming historical lectures and events; visiting academics, coach-trips to an ancient monument, a grubbier afternoon at a recovered industrial archaeological site – even trips down Roman or Victorian sewers. The English obsession with things historical is quite extraordinary; it forms a sharp contrast with the aridity of public interest in the U.S.A. – unless it is in the form of viewing figures for a normally ersatz TV drama.

This English historical interest is so potent that it has become the target of powerful commercial interests, more especially in the media. Historical series occupy regular slots on both TV and radio. And for those unable to afford increasingly expensive books, historical topics are often available in cheap weekly or monthly parts. There is, then, little doubt that history is alive and well, being read about, listened to and practised by untold thousands of people, and all in addition to whatever formal instruction is received in schools. It is abundantly clear that the English are profoundly interested in, and extremely knowledgeable about, their own history.

We need to consider carefully what kind of history the English like. There has been, it is true, an extraordinary outflowing of social history in the past twenty years. One result of this is that professional and amateur historians are now interested in aspects of history which would have been derided or dismissed only a generation ago. Notwithstanding this interest, it is important to remind ourselves of the *lacunae* in the historical awareness of many people. It is as interesting and revealing to consider what the English in general do *not* know, are not aware of, or show little interest in, as it is to know their main historical preoccupations.

Take for example the interest in the empire and, more especially, in British India. Not only is this preoccupation primarily with the *British* – as opposed to the Indian – aspects of that history, but it is generally perceived of, and conveyed as, a virtuous and praise-worthy venture. So too, to take another specific example, is the history of the abolition of the slave trade. Rarely in popular imagery is there evidence of the other side of that story; of oppression, cynicism and self-interest. Perhaps it is to be expected that an ex-imperial power should dwell on the obvious glories and splendours of its imperial past rather than the manifold injustices doled out over the centuries to subjected peoples. But this and many other historical perceptions depend ultimately on a view of Britain itself; a view which largely sees a nation whose history has been shaped by good intentions, even-handedness and fairness. Such a view, however, is very recent indeed, stemming in the short-term from concepts of 'fair play' which originated in the nineteenth century. Rarely however do people stop to consider the fuller ramifications of their country's history.

It is also uncommon to consider what is meant by 'England' and the 'English'. It is widely assumed that the basic human stock of England – white Caucasian – has been a settled and relatively homogeneous stock since time immemorial. A mere glance at people's names will provide an impressionistic image of the human diversity which goes to make up the English people. The great number of Irish, Welsh and Scottish names scattered among the English people is a simple reminder of the ancient, and continuing, flow of people from the 'Celtic fringes' to the urban centres of English life. Long before the advent of major immigration from distant colonies, it was perfectly clear that England provided a home (however unwelcoming in many ways) for migrants from the poorer reaches of the British Isles. Even *The Times* noted this fact, as early as 1867:

... there is hardly such a thing as a pure Englishman in this island. In place of the rather vulgarized and very inaccurate phrase, Anglo-Saxon, our national denomination, to be strictly correct, would be a composite of a dozen national titles ...

No better illustration of this phenomenon could be provided than the royal family. In many respects it epitomizes England: a distinctive institution which has extraordinary popular appeal and which is jetted around the globe as ambassador for the country at large. It is also a family of varied European extractions and has, over the centuries, traditionally been so. England has had French, Scots, Dutch and German monarchs. Monarchical consorts were, if anything, even more varied: Victoria's husband was German; the present Queen's was born in Greece. And yet it is hard to think of any institution which is considered more English than the royal family. Of course it could reasonably be countered that, by definition, royalty is an international phenomenon (as their regular friendly and family reunions clearly show). Yet this is only one, albeit a minor, illustration of a general phenomenon, of the degree to which the English have more varied national and ethnic roots than is often imagined.

Since the Second World War foreign settlement in England has been largely an issue of colour, although to state the case so boldly is to minimize the unusually large *white* settlement during this time. One result of this has been the widespread assumption that immigration and immigrants are non-white. It is also true that there have been certain periods in English history when settlers in England were noticeable for their colour: eighteenth-century ex-slaves or Indians and Chinese in the nineteenth century. By and large, however, earlier generations of settlers to England were *not* unmistakably marked by colour or racial difference. This meant, at its simplest, that they and their offspring could more easily conform to the customs and styles demanded by the host society. Non-white people, whatever their skills, economic success, religions or accents, could never lose their colour. Debates about, and objections to, non-white settlers have so often, then, centred on the immutable fact of colour.

And yet, even when settlers were racially indistinguishable from the host society, they often stimulated a range of hostile responses from the hosts, who complained, among many things, of their smell, their family habits, their propensity to crime, their poverty, their sexuality, the cheapness of their labour and even their eating habits. Indeed it seems to be a common characteristic of antipathy to settlers that it derives in large measure from a host of contemporary problems, many, if not most of which, are put down to the settlers themselves. Urban poverty, cheap labour, filthy housing, disruptive children, crime: all these and an apparently endless litany of offences have, in greatly differing historical English contexts, been imputed to immigrants and settlers. It is often perfectly true that these and other problems are indeed the lot of immigrant groups. But it is equally true that the problems are not always of their own making.

First, however, we need to look at the length of foreign settlement in England. In fact, whole epochs of English history are presented by historians in historical categories which unmistakably point to the phenomenon of foreign settlement or conquest: England under the Romans, the Vikings, the Normans, the Tudors, the Hanoverians, the House of Orange. The Roman armies which settled in Britain consisted not so much of Romans themselves, but of a varied collection of subjects from throughout the widely scattered Roman empire – from Gaul, Spain, Germany, the Balkans, Asia Minor and Africa. Naturally enough, the more remote the epoch the more difficult it is to tease out firm conclusions from sparse evidence. This becomes less of a problem when we study the impact of the Normans, largely because, in the Domesday Book of 1086, the historian has been left with extraordinarily rich documentation about contemporary people, law and economy. The Norman Conquest was unusually effective, even to the point of relegating the English language to a secondary role. And it also had the effect of forging links between England and France which were to last – in the form of territorial claims, warfare and dynastic squabbles – until the reign of Elizabeth I. And throughout the intervening centuries Frenchmen were common visitors, advisers and the like in metropolitan and provincial English life.

Among the most notable settlers in the Middle Ages were the

Jews, allowed in from France after the Conquest because of their financial resources and abilities, virtues which successive English monarchs mercilessly exploited for their own plans – for conquest, adventure or simply administration. By the early thirteenth century, the Jews had come to occupy an influential, and prosperous, position, financing large parts of monarchical government, and living under the special protection of the monarch. Indeed so powerful had they become, despite successive predatory royal attacks on their money, that two clauses of Magna Carta (1215) were specifically devised to curb their powers. In fact other money lenders to medieval monarchs were also foreigners, notably Flemish and Italian. But it was towards the Jews that popular and political antipathy was periodically directed for varied reasons of envy, malice, self-interest or straightforward hatred. In 1189–90 there were fearsome anti-Jewish pogroms in half a dozen towns (most savage in York) which effectively ended Jewish contemporary prosperity. They were expelled in 1290.

The late medieval English economy was characterized by the dominance of certain key foreign groups. Merchants from the Hanseatic towns controlled important sectors of imports and exports. Flemings, long dominant in woollen exports, were in decline by the late Middle Ages. But it was the Italians who were the most prosperous and influential of all foreign merchants in the thirteenth and fourteenth centuries, as the name Lombard Street reminds us. Like the Jews before them, the Italians financed monarchical ventures in return for royal protection. But even that was not sufficient to spare them the antagonism of their English competitors. The Italians' financial collapse in the mid-fourteenth century put an end to the Englishmen's grievances.

There were common complaints against Italians and Jews. They appeared to enjoy royal favours; they were usurers. And, in the case of the Jews, they practised religious beliefs which many English found unacceptable. Most crucial of all, however, they were the objects of rumour and mythology which converted their customs and habits into forces of evil, and even murder. The forces of mythology proved more potent than reality, unleashing on the heads of medieval English Jewry destructive forces from which Jewish society was not able to recover. But mostly, however, the

Jews and Italians were disliked because of their success and importance. In retrospect, we can measure the contribution they made to the English state by the antipathy directed towards them by their contemporary opponents. But they were, notwithstanding their economic importance, a very small minority.

The Jews did not effectively return to England until the seventeenth century when, once more, they were the objects of commercial antipathy, religious dislike and social distaste. By the time of the Restoration they were firmly ensconced once more in London, exercising their traditional commercial and banking skills, to the envy and dislike of many.

Antipathy to outsiders, for whatever reason, was not reserved solely for 'exotic' peoples or religions. There were, for instance, regular injunctions against the people from the remoter corners of Britain. But that did not prevent them being lured towards the more attractive economic prospects of life in England. Poor people from Ireland, Scotland and Wales regularly found their way to England.

The Welsh were specifically excluded by an Act of 1400 but once Wales was absorbed, in law if not in social reality, into England in the mid-sixteenth century, migration became easier for the Welsh. Scots were similarly disliked and attempts made to keep them north of the border. But this proved impossible, more especially in those northern towns and cities which lay across the march south into England. The accession of a Scottish king in 1603, however, provided a formal easing of relations, although in fact the 'Scottishness' of the new royalty and its court developed into one of the smouldering English complaints against the early Stuarts. James I's dream of unity between the two nations was not realized until the annexation of Scotland by Cromwell's conquering army in 1650–51. The political context was crucial because the Scottish view of England was determined by English aggression and violence in Scotland itself, more especially by the rapacious Highland clearances of the eighteenth century. These added to the sense of bitterness and economic despair which uprooted generations of Scots from their bleak homelands and sent them south – or later westwards – in search of a livelihood. The Scots who settled in England from the seventeenth century onwards rarely had reason to feel gratitude towards their adopted home. Formal relations between the two countries were uneasily settled by the Act of Union of 1707.

It was natural that many Scots, like other migrant groups, should find themselves drawn south to London. Indeed, the very growth of the capital in the sixteenth, seventeenth and eighteenth centuries was largely through the agency of immigration, from countryside as well as from more distant parts. Without immigration, London's population would, in the pre-modern world, have collapsed, through the ravages of the city's heavy deathrates. Of course the Scots, like the Irish, became an emigrating people; forced to leave an inhospitable northern habitat for any region that offered prospects of material improvement. By the late eighteenth century, the researches of a London doctor showed that one in fifteen of his patients in Westminster had been born in Scotland. And there were twice as many men as women. It was not, however, just the poor who fled south. Lowlanders in particular headed for England, not merely because of the accidents of geography, but because their superior education gave them a marketable commodity much prized among employers in London and, later in the eighteenth century, among the burgeoning textile trades in the north-west of England. The ambitious, bright and energetic Scots, many of whom left their considerable mark on eighteenth-century England were, if anything, more resented than the poor. Success as much as poverty could generate hostility and resentment among the English hosts, and this resentment was accentuated by the remarkable successes of a host of well-remembered Scots – engineers, entrepreneurs and manufacturers – who rose to wealth and prominence during the English industrial revolution.

Large numbers of emigrating Scots had, traditionally, returned to their homeland later in life. But the flow of people south and westwards continued through the nineteenth century, encouraged by indigenous poverty or, for the educated, by lack of real local opportunities. Scots and Scottish settlements elsewhere specifically lured other fellow countrymen. In London, for instance, there developed Scottish enclaves with their own distinctive organizations and clubs. At certain peak periods, the physical movement of Scots and others was extraordinarily high. In the 1840s, for instance, no

fewer than 8,000 settled in London alone. But in those same years
the number of Irish settling in London was 46,000, an indication of
that wretched emigration which, though long a feature of Ireland's
troubled history, became the most crippling and distinctive factor
in nineteenth-century Irish experience.

England's relations with Ireland were troubled and painful,
especially from the sixteenth century onwards. Ireland was increasingly viewed and treated as a colony, and was 'bullied and bled by
a frequently absentee Protestant landlord class'. The largest English
armies in peacetime were to be found in Ireland, whose native
Catholic population was discriminated against in a number of
ways. And so too were Irish industries. All this was made worse, as
the eighteenth century advanced, by the inexorable rise in population. The Irish had been settling in England for centuries; many
more had arrived simply to do seasonal (harvest) work to pay their
Irish rents on return. It is true that much of this migration, especially in the eighteenth and nineteenth centuries, derived from
straightforward hunger and poverty. But it is also true that Ireland,
rather like Scotland, was economically much less developed than
England. The Irish had moved to England for the better opportunities. And again like the Scots, the Irish established their
own distinctive communities which attracted and helped fellow
countrymen often to the extent of advertising and circulating relevant information back in Ireland.

In London there had been a thriving Irish community since the
seventeenth century and although they were renowned as labourers,
Irishmen were able in time to occupy a range of artisanal and
entrepreneurial skills. They ranged from the desperate and the
beggars, through to the armies of labourers who clustered around
any building or major engineering project and their strength was
substantially responsible for reshaping the industrial face of England, building the canals, the railways, the tunnels – and of course
constructing the towns themselves. And many of the characteristics
of the Irish communities in nineteenth-century England seem to
have been there, if on a less striking scale, for at least two centuries.
Proclamations against Irish vagrants, riots against Irish farm
workers, regular complaints that Irish labour undercut English
wages – these and myriad other issues created regular friction

between Irish and English. After anti-Irish riots in London in 1736 mobs

arose in Southwark, Lambeth and Tyburn Road and took upon them to interrogate people whether they were for the English or the Irish . . .

In the words of the most notable historian of eighteenth-century London, Dorothy George, the Irish were 'a police problem, a sanitary problem, a poor law problem and an industrial problem'. It could, of course, be replied that in fact the Irish did not so much create these problems but inherit and accentuate them. And when we try to explain their troubles in the context of Ireland itself, it becomes clearer that English policy was much more responsible for the problems of Irish poverty than contemporaries, or even later commentators, are prepared to admit.

It is undoubtedly true that crime clung to the London Irish like the telltale signs of their daily squalor. But they were not alone in this. Unable to survive within the law, poor people – of whom the Irish were the most spectacular, numerous and obvious – were obliged to live outside the law. Crime figures for the eighteenth-century Irish in London, working-class men in the nineteenth century or even blacks in the U.S.A. in the late twentieth century reflect not upon their 'natural' criminal proclivities but upon the socially determining aspects of crimes against property among the unpropertied and the dejected. Nonetheless, the convergence of poverty and crime upon the Irish in England was a recurring complaint among English commentators. Francis Place, that prime chronicler of working-class life in early nineteenth-century London, remarked, 'the poorest and most dissolute people in Spitalfields are several grades above the mere Irish'.

Irish drinking, their funeral wakes, violence, the Irish tendency to gang up on their nearest English opponents, these and a multitude of social habits came to be the standard English view of Irish communities in England. And by the late eighteenth century they were perceptions which could focus on the growing Irish communities not only in London but also in the burgeoning cities of Liverpool and Manchester. By the beginning of the nineteenth century, as population growth, poverty and the development of Irish communities in England grew apace, the common trickle of

immigrants became a flood. In the 1840s the Irish fled their homelands in unimagined numbers; they also died, miserably, on a scale
not seen in Europe for centuries. Alone of western European countries, the population of Ireland actually fell in the nineteenth century, a time elsewhere of unprecedented population growth.
London, Manchester, Liverpool and Glasgow (and of course cities
in the U.S.A.) received tens of thousands of Irish. In 1841, 126,321
Irish people lived in Scotland. By 1847, 300,000 Irish had landed in
Liverpool alone, though it is also true that many merely passed
through, fanning out into industrial Lancashire, on to London or
merely changing ships to cross the Atlantic. By 1851 half a million
Irish had settled in England and Wales. It was quite simply the
most massive influx of people English society had ever experienced.
And even though contemporary port officials and census officers
recorded the enormity of this troubled movement of people, they
significantly underregistered its precise size.

Irish settlement in the 1840s cannot be understood outside the
context of the famine. This is, however, just one acute and fearful
illustration of the general proposition that migration to England
was essential for survival, a necessity not so much because of the
particular attractions England offered but because of the problems
experienced in the indigenous region. It provides a constant reminder that any study of England's immigrant and minority groups
must consider the local as much as English forces. When the Irish
came to England in the nineteenth century (just as Jamaicans in the
twentieth), their decision to quit their homelands was as positive as
their choice of settlement in England. This movement of peoples
tells us as much about Ireland or Jamaica as about England; we
should also remember that conditions 'on the peripheries', in the
colonies or in Ireland, were often shaped by the English and their
policies. But this is not to say that the English were intimately
responsible for the development of every facet of society in all their
colonies, possessions or dependencies; for example, the English did
not *cause* the famine of the 1840s. Nonetheless the movement of
peoples from around the world to England was in large part a
result of the relationship forged over the centuries between the
forceful and, at one time, ascendant, imperial power, and the
dependent, weaker and often subjugated region.

Ireland, however, was an unusual case, for it was effectively a colony long before the age of English colonialism. Also, the relative proximity to England had, since the seventeenth century, made it relatively easy for the Irish to travel to English cities. As communications improved in the late eighteenth and especially nineteenth centuries, the practicalities of population movement became less daunting (and cheaper). But distance alone does not explain the massive movement of peoples from the nineteenth century onwards, for tens of thousands of Irish in the early nineteenth century chose to endure the rigours of an Atlantic crossing to escape their homeland for America. By the mid-twentieth century, modern communications were to introduce a new dimension to population movement; distance became no object.

The Irish in mid-nineteenth-century England were exceptional. They were the largest immigrant group in a society which, outside London, had largely been sheltered from foreign 'incursions'. In the capital itself, however, 'exotic' groups were regular features of late eighteenth-century society. A Jewish community had, for instance, once more consolidated its precarious mid-seventeenth-century foothold, and it increased periodically in the eighteenth century as European pogroms drove fleeing Jews to the relative safety of England. But whether from Eastern Europe or North Africa, these new arrivals were, by and large, poor, and they placed an unwelcome strain on the resources of established English Jewry. Once again (just like the Irish) Jews were denounced for their poverty and their criminal tendencies, and efforts were made, through the good offices of the local synagogue, in the hope that 'some restraint could be laid in this importation consistent with the wisdom and policy of good government' (1771). Established English Jews, anxious not to jeopardize their own position, cooperated in keeping out poor European Jews. But still they came. By 1734 there were some 6,000; 5,000 twenty years later. By 1800 it was calculated that there were between 15,000 and 20,000 Jews in London and upwards of 6,000 in provincial towns. Inevitably perhaps they were distrusted and denounced. Hated when poor, the Jews were also condemned when rich. Attempts were made to devise charitable and educational schemes to alleviate Jewish poverty and to create new economic openings, but little could be done to diffuse a wide-

spread antisemitism which periodically erupted in the eighteenth
and early nineteenth centuries. Murder by a Jew provided the
occasion for mob attacks and public insult on other Jews; Jewish
crime was quoted as proof of the natural criminal tendencies of the
Jewish race. 'All the children of Israel' in England 'live by cheating
and nocturnal rapine; and if they do not themselves steal, they aid
the thief in concealing and disposing of stolen goods.' When Dick-
ens created Fagin, he employed an easy and popularly recognized
caricature, an artistic stereotype well known and shared by the
English public.

In the last years of the seventeenth century large numbers of
immigrant French Huguenots fled to London following the revoca-
tion of the Edict of Nantes in 1685. The actual number is difficult
to assess, but it has been calculated that upwards of 50,000 arrived,
thus swelling the ranks of English Protestantism against the
dwindling support for Catholicism. Over the next century and a
half the Irish were to tip the scales the other way, their tens of
thousands making mid-nineteenth-century Catholicism a more
genuinely popular religion than at any time since the Reformation.
By 1718 there were no fewer than thirty-five Huguenot churches in
London alone. The Huguenots brought their famous silk-weaving
skills, grafting the industry on to an even older tradition in Spitalfields. Many Huguenots also became private tutors to families who
valued Protestantism and French in the education of their children.
Less well remembered is the Huguenot tradition of gardening which
was passed on to the English. Thus all these skills became part of
English society in the course of the early eighteenth century. The
Huguenots did not, however, settle easily in the industrial climate
of the period. Silk weaving was a competitive trade, facets of which
could easily be undertaken by women, children and other semi-
skilled migrants. Thus there was early tension between various
groups of weavers: Huguenots particularly disliked Irish immigrant
weavers. There were riots in 1719 and 1736 and Huguenot complaints against Irish weavers were to be heard a century later. One
Huguenot complained in 1838: 'There are many Irish weavers in
Spitalfields ... [who] come here and work among us at a lower
rate than they are willing to do at home, and injure both themselves
and us.' The creation of economic rivalry came to be a criticism

which could be levelled at immigrants, but in this case it was levelled by the descendants of established immigrants against the new.

Foreign settlers and immigrants were more obvious because more numerous and concentrated in London, but there were pockets of immigrants all over urban England. Southern and eastern coastal towns were especially notable for their immigrants, just as Liverpool and Glasgow were to become in the nineteenth century. Sandwich, it was claimed, had been almost transformed into a Flemish town; Colchester had a large Dutch population; Norwich too had longstanding groups of European settlers and workers. Some of Ipswich's most strikingly successful late eighteenth-century families were of French Huguenot descent.

By the late eighteenth century, when England entered that new economic phase we commonly describe as 'the industrial revolution' the economic contribution of foreign settlers to English well-being and development had been remarkable, though largely unsung. They had, as we have seen, brought their muscle-power and their labour into a variety of demanding roles; the Irish were to continue that tradition into the twentieth century. Immigrants had established and enhanced a host of skills and abilities. European, as opposed to Irish, settlers had considerably augmented the ranks and the values of English Protestantism. Equally important perhaps for long-term economic development, European Protestants had established a host of important businesses and family concerns. In the process there developed that infra-structure of economic organization and finance, significantly known as 'Dutch finance', which was to prove vital in the economic transformation of England. Enterprising, ambitious and well-educated Dutchmen and Scots (like the Jews fleeing Europe for the U.S.A. in the 1930s) implanted in their new home social and economic qualities which were of abiding and transforming importance. Clearly, it would be silly to claim that foreign settlers laid the basis for the industrial revolution. But it is important to stress the degree to which non-English people were instrumental in creating a social and economic climate in England which was conducive and encouraging to the subsequent development of a new industrial order.

By the mid-eighteenth century England began to gather to its bosom large numbers of non-English people. While in many respects this gathering was merely a culmination of events, of forces long at play, it was also evidence of the social and economic changes unleashed by the 'age of revolution' which were directly responsible for the increase in immigration to England. The rise of the first major British empire, the development of a modernizing and urban society with all the attendant improvements in physical communications and the increase (and movement) in the western population, all cumulatively created a growth in the number of outsiders settling in England. It was the beginning of a new and recognizably modern phase in the history of the English population.

2
The Empire and Race

By 1763, when the Peace of Paris ended hostilities with France, Britain was the unquestioned ruler of the largest empire the world had ever seen. Not since the days of classical Rome had a European nation wielded such extensive power over so vast a stretch of the earth's surface. The whole of North America was, nominally at least, British, offering that irresistible lure of settlement and westward expansion which was to characterize its history thereafter. The resources of the Caribbean, tapped by the efforts of generations of black slaves, had provided riches which had been enjoyed for more than a century: that string of luxuriant islands which formed an arc from the tip of Florida to the north-east coast of South America contained some of Britain's most prized and valuable possessions. And so too did the Indian sub-continent, now released from French control and, apparently, securely under British rule; while on the coast of West Africa, Britain maintained a string of important naval and trading posts, especially vital for the defence and preservation of the triangular slave trade. All this was in addition to a myriad informal trading links with the wider world which generated such trade and wealth to the imperial metropolis. It was no accident that when British towns began to grow at an unusual rate in the course of the eighteenth century, the sea-ports were among the most sizable and significant.

It is true that a great deal of growth in the ports was generated by Britain's *internal* trade. But most crucial of all, from the seventeenth century onwards, was the massive development of British overseas trade. Ships from ports all around the British Isles could, increasingly, be found plying their trade in the most exotic and distant foreign waters. Such ports as Newcastle, Sunderland, London, Bristol, Exeter, Great Yarmouth, Liverpool, Whitehaven and Hull, even Whitby and Scarborough, were joined by a host of smaller (and, by contemporary standards, unlikely sounding) ports whose vessels turned increasingly to international trade. It now seems unlikely, but it is nonetheless true, that vessels from Whitehaven regularly crossed the Atlantic: 'I trading constantly every year to Virginia, and God be thanked have had a very good success . . .' were the thankful comments of one Whitehaven merchant in 1707.

The economic and social networks forged in this outstanding period for British maritime and commercial trade from the seventeenth century onwards brought British traders, merchants and settlers abroad face to face with the more 'exotic' foreign peoples. The English had traditionally regarded foreigners (be they Irish, Scots, French or Jews) with a curiosity and disdain rooted in insularity and encouraged by stereotypical views of outsiders. The English were, it was commonly alleged, obsessed with themselves and therefore unable to appreciate others. A Venetian ambassador remarked in the sixteenth century,

> The English are great lovers of themselves and of everything belonging to them; they think that there are no other men than themselves; and whenever they see a handsome foreigner, they say 'he looks like an Englishman' and that 'it is a pity that he should not be an Englishman' . . .

With economic transformation, advancing military and political power and the urge to conquer, trade, travel and settle distant parts of the globe, the British found themselves faced by ever more curious peoples. The world began to yield to the British and to other expansive Europeans, not merely its riches and prospects, but its peoples – in all their colours, social diversities, shapes and religions.

Europeans had long known of the more exotic peoples from distant parts of the world. Biblical sources, classical texts, overland trading routes and popular oral traditions had bequeathed to successive generations images – real and legendary – of the bizarre and strange sights of human nature to be found lurking beyond the pale of European society. Few offered a more startling contrast to contemporary values, of beauty, social virtue and godliness, than the black Africans, familiar through various sources but, from the sixteenth century onwards, brought into an even closer economic relationship with adventurous and marauding European privateers. It was inevitable that returning merchant-adventurers would bring back to Europe the human curios they had encountered around the world.

Africans had been in Britain for centuries but it was the development of maritime links with West Africa which saw the growth of a sizable black population in Britain. In 1555 John Lok returned to England with 'certain black slaves, where of some were tall and strong men, and could well agree with our meates and drinkes'. As the trade in slaves developed – initially in Iberian colonies in the New World – British slavery interests grew in size and complexity. By the time the early British colonies had gained a foothold in the Caribbean and North American mainland, the 'triangular trade' had developed linking the commercial, banking, insurance, manufacturing and shipping interests of major British ports to West Africa and thence to the slave colonies of the New World. Slaves created wealth in the Caribbean, particularly after the establishment of the sugar economy. Writing from Barbados in 1645, George Downing remarked, 'I believe they have brought this year no lesse than a thousand Negroes, and the more they buie, the better able they are to buy, for in a yeare and a halfe they will earn (with God's blessing) as much as they cost . . .'

As the slave empires prospered, ever more blacks – often enslaved – found their way to England. Some came direct from Africa; in 1651 the Guinea Company ordered its factor to 'buy for us 15 or 20 lusty young Negroes of about 15 years of age [and] bring them with you to London'. Many more, however, came via the New World, the flotsam and jetsam of imperial trade and conquest. Many were enslaved; many were resold or bartered in England, often through the columns of London newspapers. And, despite a great deal of confusion, English law on balance confirmed the legality of black slavery in England. By the mid-eighteenth century, there was a sizable black population in London, its members engaged in various occupations, though mainly used as domestics. By 1764 *The Gentleman's Magazine* thought there were 20,000 in London alone. Another publication boldly asserted, 'every man who has ever stepped beyond the place of his birth has seen them'.

Most blacks were poor. Some became quite prominent and respected, others developed a certain notoriety. The more famous even had their portraits painted – for instance, Equiano, Francis Barber and Sancho. Richmond and Molineaux were successful boxers, Saartjie Baartmann – 'the Hottentot Venus' – became infamous for displaying her bizarre naked body at London's early-nineteenth-century fairs. Billy Waters, the one-legged fiddler, was a notable personality in the streets and low taverns of the East End; he was 'King of the Beggars' and a common sight in Cruickshank's cartoons of early-nineteenth-century England. But for every black whose name and life is now remembered, there were thousands whose wretched lives remained quite anonymous. Occasionally, however, the most ordinary black managed to appear in contemporary accounts, usually when he was to be sold, or had run away from his owner.

> Run away the first Instant from Sir Phineas Pet at the Navy Office, a Negro about 16 years of age, pretty tall, he speaks English, but slow in speech, with a livery of a dark coloured cloth, lined with Blue, and so edged in the seams, the Buttons, Pewter, wearing a Cloth Cap, his Coat somewhat too short for him, he is called by the name of Othello ... whoever gives notice of the said Negro ... shall be very well rewarded.

Since the majority of blacks in late eighteenth-century England were male it was inevitable that a large number of them would form liaisons with – or even marry – poor white women. This provoked in many commentators such expressions of outrage about miscegenation which had been an intellectual issue for centuries. Again and again specific relations between black men and white women were denounced. 'Jack Black' of Ystumllya in Wales was one such. 'It is difficult to fathom the attraction which this dark boy had for the young ladies of the district,' commented his biographer. As early as 1710 one man spoke of the 'little race of mulattoes' to be found in England. But it was left to the racist scribes of the late eighteenth century, writing in support of planters and slave traders, to denounce miscegenation in the most rabid terms. One feared that soon the whole nation would 'resemble the Portuguese and the Moriscos in complexion of skin and baseness of mind. This is a venomous and dangerous ulcer, that threatens to disperse its malignancy far and wide, until every family catches infection from it.' Of course fear and distrust of racial mixing was also a reflection of contemporary views about race, a topic which became of great interest later when Victorian scientists began the serious analysis of racial characteristics.

From the early contact with black Africa, Europeans had shown enormous curiosity about the differences between blacks and whites. In the years of slavery and the slave trade (in the British case, up to 1838), all sorts of conclusions were drawn to justify the enslavement of the African. By trying to illustrate the inferiority or inhumanity of the black African, proponents of slavery made the point that bondage was an improvement on African freedoms and that, without the restraints of slavery, Africans and their descendants could not be expected to work. It is important to stress that the English interest in race which reached its apogee in the nineteenth century was first effectively aroused and focused in the years of black slavery. And while it is true that much of the debate in eighteenth-century England tended to focus on reports of African or West Indian slave society, English people could test whatever rumours they heard, or arguments they read, by scrutinizing black society around them. There was no excuse for not knowing about black humanity, and this was especially true of the wealthy, amongst whom blacks were commonly employed as domestics.

In London in particular blacks were a common sight in the late eighteenth century – on the streets as sweepers and beggars; in private homes as servants; in pubs and at the periodic fairs as entertainers. A number of them enjoyed even more exalted positions: Sancho, for example, was a shopkeeper in Westminster. Many were devout Christians and frequent worshippers. Indeed, it was customary for white employers to baptize and convert their black servants. And since it was commonly held that blacks were especially musical, many were employed as musicians. In addition to the many blacks who resided in England in the late eighteenth century, and largely in London, there was a regular stream of black visitors spending time in Britain for education or training. African children attended schools in London, Bristol, Liverpool and Lancaster; there was a constant flow of black sailors in and out of British ports.

It is, naturally, difficult to assess the treatment – the hostility or friendship – towards such a diverse people over so long a period. The English responded towards blacks in a number of different ways. Until the ending of slavery it was impossible to escape the shadow of bondage: in many cases English blacks were abruptly (and sometimes quite illegally) shipped back to the slave colonies. Most, as far as we can detect, were poor. It was symptomatic that in 1834 a proposal in *The Times* suggested that almshouses should be built for the black poor in London – to celebrate the ending of slavery. But as long as slavery persisted, it was clearly impossible for many not to regard the black as a *thing*. As late as 1789, a commentator on West Indian laws informed Parliament,

> The leading idea in the Negro System of jurisprudence is that ... the Negroes were *Property*, and a species of Property that needed a rigorous and vigilant *Regulation*.

Thus the treatment of blacks in late eighteenth- and early nineteenth-century England ranged from brutal slavery (though never as widespread or as savage as in the New World) through to benign friendship and intimacy. After all there were large numbers of English people married to or living with blacks. A certain Thomas Hardy, a prominent London radical of the 1790s, had a black named Equiano as his house guest in Piccadilly. Some, however, were brutalized and degraded; families were broken up and spouses dispatched out of the country; others were shamelessly beaten or similarly treated to arbitrary and unwarranted inhumanities.

We can compare the recorded facts we have about the treatment of blacks with a number of personal accounts of the time. Fortunately we have, in the writings of a number of contemporary blacks, numerous accounts of the treatment meted out to them. Sancho's letters are particularly revealing. In 1766 he described himself as 'one of those whom the vulgar and illiberal call "Negars" ...'; again and again his letter spoke of, or hinted at, popular hostility towards blacks. Coming home from an evening out with his family, Sancho wrote, they 'were gazed at, etc., etc., – but not much abused'. On another occasion, 'they stopped us in the town, and most generously insulted us'. He spoke of 'the national antipathy and prejudice towards their woolly headed brethren'. Sancho complained that, in English eyes, 'from Othello to Sancho the big – we are foolish – or mulish – all – all without a single exception'.

Understandably, blacks in London organized themselves into formal and informal social and political groups which sought to free local black slaves and provide them with help and security. Large numbers met communally for social activity: some 200 gathered at a ball in 1772, admission five shillings. However helpful and important were the efforts of white friends and sympathizers (and those efforts became crucial in the legal and political struggle against slavery and the slave trade), English blacks looked to themselves for the more mundane and daily forms of assistance and organization. It was understandable that caution should be the watchword in the relationship between blacks and the white host society. One did not need a detailed knowledge of British imperial history to realize who was responsible for the widespread and continuing plight of blacks in England, or of black slaves throughout the American colonies. Moreover, white assistance could sometimes prove less than attractive or successful. The recruitment of English blacks to settle in Sierra Leone in 1787 proved catastrophic for that small unhappy band who, unlike the majority of London's black, were tempted to quit England for West Africa.

The apogee of black society in England before the twentieth century was reached in the last quarter of the eighteenth century. By then, black slaves had become too valuable in the Caribbean to be shipped to England. Furthermore, the campaign against the slave trade, successful in 1807, firstly enhanced the value of slaves in the islands and then, after 1807, made it illegal to export as well as to import slaves. Thereafter, black slaves were rarely brought to England and the predominantly male population declined sharply, at the same time progressively mixing with and marrying local white women.

It would be wrong, however, to suggest that black society died out in nineteenth-century England. It seems perfectly clear that the number of blacks living in England fell, and that at a time when the population as a whole registered amazing increases. Nonetheless the main and determining force behind black settlement up to the 1830s – the British slave trade and slavery – had exhausted itself.

So too had Britain's earlier preoccupation with the West Indies. No longer the prized imperial possessions, the Caribbean islands underwent a rapid and major decline. With the slaves freed, sugar, the main product of the region, continued its decline in esteem and utility; it could, in any case, be bought more cheaply elsewhere. The British had, by the second quarter of the nineteenth century, effectively severed their connections with their slaving past. They had lost the American colonies in 1776; the West Indies were now free but destitute. And the metropolis, through the Royal Navy and the Foreign Office, embarked on a policy of eradicating or preventing slavery wherever it was encountered. The leading advocates of the slave trade in the eighteenth century thus became the prime abolitionists in the nineteenth. Then and subsequently, Britain's opponents saw in this *volte face* evidence not of altruism and upright morality but of simple self-interest and cynicism. The British no longer needed black slaves for, through the complex processes of free trade, there developed an even mightier *informal* empire which could tap the resources of the world, the labour of an expansive British population, and create global markets for British goods – all without recourse to slavery of a formal kind. The industrial revolution and the transformation of Britain were, after all, made possible not by restrictions, tied labour and detailed controls and regulations (all of them features of the old slave empires), but of freedom and *laisser-faire*. Yet, while Britain spurned its old slaving instincts and interests, many others clung to black slavery, notably of course the U.S.A. until 1863. It was inevitable that American abolitionists should turn to Britain for help and support in their efforts and in the process a number of American blacks made regular visits to Britain.

Many American blacks fled to England and, however unusual an impression they created in nineteenth-century towns, they preferred the attendant curiosity to the hostility – or slavery – in their own country. Other blacks came to England on being released from impounded slave ships, and the flow of black sailors in and out of British ports continued throughout the nineteenth century. Such a traffic of people became more popular when the development of new steamship lines and the transformation of the West African and West Indian economies (through cocoa and bananas) created firmer economic ties between Britain and those black societies. But this was to take place late in the nineteenth century; by mid-century there were still only black faces in the crowd. William Cuffay was a black Chartist tailor transported to Tasmania for his radical politics; Ira Aldridge, a black actor who made extensive acting tours throughout mid-nineteenth-century England and whose children continued his theatrical talents into the late century. Another black was Samuel Coleridge-Taylor, born in Holborn in 1875, who lived much of his life in Croydon and was a prominent composer and conductor. Much rarer still were black women. One, Mary Seacole, who died in London in 1881, had made a name for herself nursing British troops in the Crimean War. Virtually unknown in Britain, she is fittingly remembered in the University of the West Indies in a building dedicated to her name. We also know of numbers of blacks, generally of West Indian origin, who spent part of their army careers in England, normally training for West Indian regiments. Suggestions that men of 'mixed race', Eurasians from India, should be recruited to British regiments were bitterly resisted. The Adjutant-General wrote, in 1886,

to establish any rule to allow 'men of colour' to enlist in our British Regts would sooner or later lead to the enlistment of full blown black men. The arguments as to the dangers of introducing a cowardly element into our ranks are ... sufficiently strong without seeking for others.

He later repeated the point, 'If ever we begin to fill our ranks with alien races, our downfall must soon follow . . .'

Such comments – commonplace in mid- and late Victorian society – need to be placed in the context of changing British racial attitudes. The racism generated by slavery – the vital view that blacks were things, inhuman, chattels – had been gradually but effectively pushed aside between 1787 and 1838 by the abolitionists' insistence on black equality. Their fundamental tenet 'Am I not a man and a brother', emblazoned on the famous Wedgwood plaque, was a bold assertion of human equality which utterly overturned the older commitment to inequality and inhumanity, so vital to the slave-trading interests. In the years when the English black community began to decline, the well organized abolitionist movement was able to rally unprecedented support for the campaign to end slavery. In the 1820s and 1830s tens of thousands of people, of all social classes and from both sexes, registered their opposition to slavery. Indeed it was widely believed that the popularity of the anti-slavery movement and the overwhelming support for the idea of black equality was one of the key factors in bringing slavery to an end. Even the slave lobby was forced to admit that their cause had been overwhelmed by public opinion. However, the British were once more to prove fickle in their opinions. Firstly, the institution of slavery in England and the colonies had in general gone unchallenged for more than a century. Then from the late eighteenth century a contrary mood swept over the British people. Yet, within a few years of black freedom in 1838, the public mood changed once more.

By the mid-nineteenth century, there had been a revival of widespread public opposition to black humanity; a deep disappointment in the former slaves in the Caribbean, a disenchantment with the old support for black freedom. By the 1840s when Britain was beset by its own unique difficulties – the Irish famine and immigration into England, the terrible industrial upheavals of the 'hungry 40s' and the upsurge of a troublesome radicalism – many became disillusioned with the altruism which had been invested in the black cause. Why worry about former slaves, 5,000 miles away, when there were so many problems at home? Thus there emerged a revived form of racism which was to characterize Victorian responses to non-white people throughout the rest of the nineteenth century.

Early Victorians became increasingly interested in race, partly because of their own explorations and conquests all over the world. But race also became one of the key classifications (along with social class) used by doctors, scientists and anthropologists in their categorization of mankind, at home and abroad. The world was increasingly seen in terms of racial ranks and orders, with the white man at the top. 'Race implies difference and difference implies superiority, and superiority leads to predominance,' said Disraeli in the Commons in 1849. In this drift towards the use of racial categories, contemporary science played a crucial role. When, for instance, the Ethnological Society was established in 1843, its purpose was to inquire into 'the distinguishing characteristics,

physical and moral, of the variations of mankind . . .'. Marx was
unusual in turning to *class* as the key explanatory division for
mankind. Much more commonplace was the use of race. The Scottish anatomist Robert Knox asserted,

That race is in human affairs everything is simply a fact, the most
remarkable, the most comprehensive, which philosophy has ever an-
nounced. Race is everything: literature, science, art – in a word civilization
– depends on it.

As the preoccupation developed with race, there emerged a
related disillusionment with those black races formerly held in
bondage. The magazine *John Bull*, remarking on former slaves in
the West Indies, asserted,

There is no question, from what we have witnessed in the West Indies
but that the negro is disinclined to labour, and has not the disposition
towards self-improvement manifested by the white man.

The facts of empire (the slow conquest of other races and peoples
by white societies), distrust of the abilities and intentions of subject
peoples and the rapid development of widely propagated concepts
of racial superiority, cumulatively served to convince generations
of Victorians of their divinely inspired – and justified – role in
dominating and manipulating the non-white races. The American
Civil War, which many thought to be fought for slavery, created
widespread doubts about whether it was really worth going to
such trouble for black people. In *Blackwood's Magazine* in 1866 it
was asked, '. . . is the negro worth all the trouble, anxiety, blood-
shed and misery which his wrongs and his rights have produced?'
Asking the question, 'Did anyone ever hear of a negro mathema-
tician, of a negro engineer, or a negro architect or a negro painter,
or a negro political economist, or a negro poet, or even of a negro
musician . . .?' this author thought some improvement could be
expected by racial mixing. But

left to himself and without white control and guidance he (the black)
forgets the lessons he has learnt, and slides rapidly back to his original
barbarism.

Again and again, commentators of all disciplines turned for an explanation of history and social behaviour to race. Historians agreed with anatomists; history was used in conjunction with anatomical experiments to 'prove' white superiority and black inferiority.

The comparative anatomist agrees with the historian in placing them on a lower level than the European. And the phrenologist agrees with the comparative anatomist.

In 1861, Frederick William Farrar, popular novelist and headmaster of Marlborough, argued that 'the savage races'

are without a past and without a future, doomed as races infinitely nobler have been before them, to a rapid, and entire and perhaps for the highest destinies of mankind, an enviable extinction.

So powerful did the commitment to the concept of race as an explanatory tool become that by the 1860s it was even being used to analyse and explain *domestic* society. The upper and middle reaches of British society were thought to hold sway, to have dominance over the poor and the working classes, because of their *racial* superiority. This was most forcefully argued in relation to the Irish in England who were described by many Victorians in racial terms. Some doctors, obsessed with the shape of the head and the skull as an indicator of racial type and of intelligence, felt that the 'non-European skull' was no different from those 'of the uneducated and lowest classes of day-labourers in this country and in Ireland'.

What needs to be stressed, however, is the degree to which the growth of racial attitudes took place in a racial vacuum. Victorian racism developed and reached its apogee not when there were sizable non-white communities in England but, on the contrary, when non-whites had become comparatively rare. The English, when talking or writing about the black, were normally dealing with an abstraction, even a stereotype. Those stereotypes undoubtedly had their roots in reality, however geographically or historically distant: the West Indian slave, the 'musical black' or the U.S. cotton slave. But it had little substance in domestic experience.

The flowering of mid-nineteenth-century racism, more particularly scientific racism, was to prove of great value from the 1880s onwards when the 'grab for Africa' heralded a new phase in

British and European imperialism. It was possible, in the years leading up to the Boer War and beyond, to explain and justify imperial conquest and dominance in terms of white superiority and black inferiority. Empire once again (as in the seventeenth and eighteenth centuries) was to feed upon and then expand prevailing racial myths and attitudes.

What helped to make mid-Victorian racial sentiment so potent a force were the severe political blows inflicted by major rebellions of subject peoples against British rule. The Jamaican uprising of 1865 seriously jolted the flagging confidence of many friends of the former slaves. Hostile commentators fell back upon the well-worn themes of African savagery:

> The original nature of the African betokened itself in acts of horrible mutilation . . . the rabble of this rebellion were in all likelihood drunken and worthless savages scarcely responsible for their misdeeds.

Governor Eyre, whose bloody reprisals far outweighed the initial black violence, took a less charitable view and shot or executed 439 blacks. There followed in Britain a bitter argument about the events of 1865. More significant for our purposes was the recrudescence of widespread racist views which relegated the black to the level of inferior and savage, unworthy of the white man's care and consideration. But of all the political incidents which soured white attitudes to non-whites, the Indian Mutiny proved most decisive.

The Indian uprising of 1857 came close to overthrowing the tenuous British hold over India. There were, after all, only 45,522 European troops in that massive empire. The fighting, which lasted for fourteen months, was savage and quickly took on a racial quality. It became widely accepted by Hindus and Muslims that the British intended to convert everyone to Christianity, and indeed there were many British who wished to do just that. It became part of that drive to change subject peoples, part of that 'moral and intellectual advancement of the people' that they should be obliged to cast off the 'superstitions' and customs of their indigenous religions and turn to the civilizing habits of Christianity. In the mid-twentieth century, this view was to be repeated time and again when urging immigrants in England to conform to English customs.

Of course there were numerous other objections to British policies in India – to the educational, economic and land reforms – all of which exploded into violence in the mutiny.

The effects and aftermath in India were far-reaching. In Britain, news of the mutiny, normally exaggerated and glorified, served to compound the growing disillusionment with non-white peoples. Significantly, the word 'nigger' came back into common English usage and was frequently repeated, despite official efforts to stop it, in newspapers and private correspondence. 'Every nigger we meet we either string up or shoot', wrote one man. An author in these same years wrote openly of 'the nigger – I mean the Oriental gentleman . . .'. The concept of 'the damned nigger' was a commonplace in mid-Victorian discussions about India, but it is significant that it referred not merely to blacks but to Indians of all kinds. It had become a generic term of racial abuse, categorizing all sorts of non-white peoples and was, as is obvious, to become the most abusive epithet used by successive generations of white people throughout the world. When, in later years, growing numbers of non-white people travelled to or settled in Britain, they entered a society where widespread racial attitudes had developed, through a complex process of imperial aggrandizement and changing scientific and social discussion, which instantly relegated non-whites to an inferior status and rank. Furthermore, such views about race were widely shared and were clearly not restricted to those educated circles most closely involved in the theory and practice of race and empire. Racial attitudes were, for instance, widely disseminated through children's literature and in formal school instruction (which was compulsory by the last quarter of the century). The lessons of history, more especially the recent lessons of imperial conquests, served merely to confirm the view that the English were, by divine appointment, the natural rulers and masters of less advanced peoples. And it was a view which, although it did not go unchallenged, was repeated again and again by politicians.

I believe in this race, the greatest governing race the world has ever seen; in this Anglo-Saxon race, so proud reaching, self-confident and determined, this race, which neither climate nor change can degenerate, which will infallibly be the predominant force of future history and universal civilization.

How hollow and absurd this was to sound within less than a century. Indeed, it was an inflated view which received a number of early and severe blows, firstly in the setbacks of the Boer War and, more profoundly, in the horrors of the First World War.

The racial attitudes of the British cannot be divorced from the complex history of their imperial adventures. This is not to argue that the British empire created racial thinking, but rather that the development of racial thinking and imperial advancement were mutually reinforcing and inter-dependent. And as empire became ever more important – ever bigger, global and, apparently, vital to Britain's economic and strategic role in the world – it was natural that attitudes should accommodate themselves to that empire. Indeed, the simple facts of empire seemed to confirm the common view that the British were destined to rule and conquer their subject peoples. What could be better evidence that the British *were* the dominant and ascendant people than a mere glance at a map which, by 1900, had turned imperial red?

The course of empire after 1815 was fundamentally shaped by industrialization. When the late Victorians prided themselves on their global domination they looked not merely to their own formal empire, but also to the extraordinary transformations at home which had, within only two generations, made Britain an un-paralleled industrial giant. Economic pre-eminence and imperial sway went together, each a reflection and proof of Britain's un-questioned superiority, and each reinforcing the other. The empire of the mid-eighteenth century had a clear and indisputable economic basis – in India (governed, symbolically, by a company), in the Caribbean and in North America. But the economic basis of Britain itself was transformed between the 1780s and 1880s. Britain's superior technology and productive capacity and her financial and commercial infra-structure enabled her to reach most parts of the globe for raw materials, manpower or markets. And white emigra-tion to the white colonies was creating an economic and political power-base of a different kind but which, in the short term, seemed once more to confirm the natural pre-eminence of white people.

Native peoples were crudely and violently pushed aside: Maoris in New Zealand, Aborigines in Australia, Africans in South Africa, Indians in North America. In league with the European metropolis, the white colonies launched into that remarkable economic and demographic advance which continues to this day. The 'white races' increased in numbers from 22 per cent of the earth's population in 1800 to 35 per cent in 1930. Economically the dominance became even more pronounced. Of course, Britain was not alone in this imperial and economic advancement, but, until the late nineteenth century, she unquestionably led the field. By 1900, however, Germany and the U.S.A. had overtaken Britain.

Industrialization meant in many respects that Britain and other industrial nations did not always need direct formal empire. So powerful – at times irresistible – was the power of economics that less powerful nations and peoples simply succumbed to market forces, without the need for direct imperial aggression. But, for our purposes, the effects were similar. More and more countries were drawn into direct dependence on, or economic relationship with, Britain, and communications greatly increased between Britain and the furthest corners of the world. The British and their industries began to consume the goods and foodstuffs of the most exotic parts of the world. Tea came from China and India, coffee from Brazil, tobacco from Cuba, cocoa from West Africa, diamonds and gold from South Africa, beef from the Argentine and the mid-west of America, wheat from the vast Canadian prairies, lamb from the Antipodes, timber from the great forests of Africa, South America and Canada. The list is almost endless, and is so obvious because so familiar to any modern reader. British merchants, manufacturers and workmen, British sailors, soldiers and civilian administrators came into contact with almost every conceivable type of humanity. And rarely was the relationship any other than one of British dominance and control.

It is true that there was an intellectual and political tradition which despised the trappings of empire and which rejected the intellectual arguments seeking to justify imperial dominance by racial arguments. There has been, since the late eighteenth century, an egalitarian tradition which spurned all new intellectual justifications for racial superiority and which was located not so much in the passing events of empire – of this triumph and that conquest, or in the most recent advances in sciences or social thinking – but in a fundamental commitment to human equality. This had been first spelled out in the 1790s by Tom Paine in *The Rights of Man* but it also had a religious as well as a secular dimension; a belief that all mankind was the same and equal creation of the same deity. Yet such a view, which changed over time, was unquestionably a minority sensibility. More commonplace, indeed at times an overwhelming view, was the *assumption* of the white man's superiority. True, some white men were superior to others (the Irish were, inevitably, at the bottom of the white men's heap, little better in many Englishmen's eyes than the black African) but, from the mid-nineteenth century it was hard to escape the widespread British commitment to white 'racial' superiority.

This sense of unparalleled and unquestioned superiority was shaped not by direct, face-to-face contact with non-white peoples within Britain. It was a product (yet both cause and effect) of imperial expansion and unique global economic pre-eminence. But, when the British *did* come face to face with non-white peoples, at home or abroad, the racialism of empire served them well in allocating their visitors, settlers or merely the passing stranger to a subservient, inferior and often despised position within the complex hierarchy of British urban society.

3
The Special Case: Ireland

We have already touched on aspects of Irish settlement in England. Indeed it is impossible to observe nineteenth- and twentieth-century English history without considering the Irish dimension, which, from the vantage point of the 1970s and 1980s, hardly needs stressing. For our purposes, however, there are two related matters which need further investigation: firstly the nature (extent, history and impact) of Irish immigration into mainland Britain; and, secondly, the development of attitudes specifically directed towards the Irish.

As we have seen, the Irish had been leaving their homeland for centuries before the catastrophe of the mid-nineteenth-century famine. But it was the eighteenth century which saw the origins of the significant modern exodus of the Irish. And yet despite regular emigration, and despite economic distress (worsened by the Act of Union of 1800), the increase in the Irish population (it doubled between 1780 and 1840) threatened Irish stability and well-being. Many took the only real alternative and emigrated. By 1770, 9,000 Irish were leaving for America each year. For obvious geographical reasons, migration to England and Scotland became regular and easy, to be characterized as much by temporary migrations as by permanent settlement. Nonetheless there were, as we have seen, large numbers of Irish settlements in English towns, more especially in London. With the coming of the steam packets sailing between Irish, English and Scottish ports, the costs of transportation fell dramatically (at one point in 1824 it fell to 3d. for deck passengers) and consequently the numbers of Irish immigrants increased.

It was, however, the famine which drove tens of thousands eastwards and westwards on the waves of a turbulent upheaval. But even before then, the English had begun to count the Irish in their midst, doing so formally for the first time at the 1841 census. It was calculated in that year that there were 400,000 Irish in England, Scotland and Wales. Of course when those figures were broken down into smaller regions or towns, the proportions were even more striking. Six per cent of the population of Lancashire for instance was Irish-born. The 1840s, however, compounded these figures at an extraordinary rate and for the same reason that Ireland itself was, in many respects, denuded of population. The 1851 census showed an increase of 314,610 Irish people in England and Wales in the previous decade; but this was unquestionably an *under*-estimate. Even 400,000 would scarcely allow for the fearful mortality levels in Irish settlements. Equally significant is the fact that the Irish had in the course of the 1840s settled not merely in their traditional towns and ghettoes, but now begun to fan out to remoter areas – to Devon and Cornwall, for example. But it was, naturally enough, the expansive *urban* areas which continued to provide a new home, or a temporary residence, for armies of Irish.

In addition to London – with a recorded 108,548 Irish-born in 1841 – the Irish headed for Manchester, Bradford, Halifax, Birmingham, Leeds, Bolton and Preston. Of course all these towns were at the forefront of contemporary economic transformations, and offered the prospects, if not always the reality, of work and improvement for the immigrant Irish. The levels of immigration of the 1840s could not be sustained; the following decade showed a decline in numbers of Irish in some of the major towns. But it is also true that the Irish discriminated between towns, opting, understandably, for those towns thought to be more economically buoyant than others. Throughout the second half of the century, Irish immigration continued, but at nothing like the pace or volume of that traumatic second quarter of the century. By 1891 only 1·6 per cent of the population of England and Wales had been born in Ireland, some 458,315. In Scotland, where the percentage had been consistently higher, it was 4·8 per cent (194,807).

By the end of the century, the Irish could be found throughout the country, having recently settled in cities previously unaccustomed to Irish settlement. This was particularly noticeable in garrison towns – York and Colchester, for example – for the Irish had become a striking minority in the British armed services; some 14 per cent in 1891. Indeed it had been one of the ironies of British control over Ireland that large numbers of the occupying soldiers were Irishmen. But these calculations about the Irish in nineteenth-century England have certain obvious flaws. By counting only the Irish-*born*, the census returns fail to include the numbers of people born in the mainland to Irish parents. Equally, the figures do not include those people who came to England in transit, normally en route to the U.S.A. Indeed emigration to the U.S.A. – cheap if nonetheless bleak and comfortless – remained at 60,000 until 1914. Similarly, the figures are also complicated by the migratory Irish, in England only for harvests and other seasonal work, following the centuries-old tradition of their forbears.

There were, as we have seen, a string of recurring complaints levelled at Irish immigrants across the centuries. It was, perhaps, understandable that these, and new complaints, increased in volume and stridency as Irish immigrants swept across England, especially in the early nineteenth century. One major objection (one which was to be directed at regular intervals in the late twentieth century towards Indians, West Indians and others) was that the Irish were country folk unable, unwilling or unaccustomed to living in an urban environment. It is certainly true that the majority were country people unaccustomed to city life. In fact this had been true for centuries of whole sections of London's population; rural immigrants lured to the capital year after year and inevitably becoming the object of ridicule and jest. Like countless others, the Irish became through migration an urban people, though this was more especially true of those who travelled to the U.S.A.; between 1874 and 1921 84 per cent of Irish emigrants went to America, and only 8 per cent to Britain.

Naturally enough, those with more money could choose to travel further afield; but the poorer were normally obliged to move shorter distances from home. But as the nineteenth century advanced this distinction became less marked, firstly because labour in Ireland was able to earn more (thanks to the labour shortage after 1846), and secondly because the Irish already settled in America sent money home for other relatives to migrate.

The largest Irish community in Britain was in London, bigger still when second- and third-generation descendants are added to the census returns of 'Irish-born'. Moreover, the Irish community in London in the second half of the nineteenth century was far and away the largest 'foreign' group in the capital. Not until late-century Jewish migration from Russia and Eastern Europe did another alien community begin to challenge the Irish, and inevitably if unwillingly compete for their traditional difficulties, hardships, and for the antipathy of their English hosts. The Irish, however, continued to settle in England in large numbers, sometimes because of the greater economic opportunities, sometimes because of the constraints of political pressures.

The campaign for Irish independence, Irish home rule, had been a volatile issue for successive British governments more or less continuously since the late eighteenth century. But the Easter Rising of 1916, the consequent 'troubles' and the eventual establishment of the Irish Free State in 1923, stimulated a new wave of Irish emigration. After 1920, however, it was no longer an easy matter for the Irish (or anyone else for that matter) to settle in the U.S.A., for the Americans, faced by massive immigration after the 1914–18 war, began to control immigration through stricter quotas. In 1924 the Irish Free State was granted a quota of only 28,567, reduced to 17,853 in 1929 and finally, in 1930, it was hedged in by financial guarantees and the requirement of sponsors. Mainland Britain therefore became the natural destination for emigrating Irish. By 1931 there were 381,089 Irish-born in England and Wales and a regular flow continued to 1939. The Second World War was to change dramatically not only the relationship between Britain and Ireland, but, perhaps even more fundamentally, Britain was to become an unprecedentedly mixed home for the most varied groups of people these islands had ever experienced.

For many centuries, the English had developed distinct attitudes towards the Irish, attitudes which were at the same time racist in certain respects and yet quite separate from the contemporary attitudes towards other racial groups or subject peoples. It is easy in retrospect to see the historical and social forces, which, over the centuries, helped to create such attitudes. Even today there seems no escaping from the standard, offensive image of the Irishman as he has been portrayed for centuries, someone who has been reduced in English eyes to the level of caricature; the ignorant and brutish labourer, too fond of his drink, not over-endowed with wit or intelligence and as keen to fight as he is to drink. There was, it is true, a contrary tradition; of the popular Irish view of themselves, purveyed in abundance through street literature in eighteenth- and nineteenth-century England, which portrayed only virtue where the English saw vice and which offered a variation of the 'good-natured Paddy' to offset the English version.

Like so many racial or national stereotypes the idea of 'Paddy' – amiable or malignant – had certain value for both Irish and English. Much the same was true among Caribbean and southern slaves where 'Quashie' and 'Sambo' created images in the mind of local whites; such names were, through necessity, sometimes adopted by the slaves themselves, for it was useful for slaves to appear exactly as their owners saw them.

Historians continue to argue about whether the English attitudes traditionally displayed towards the Irish were racial, or merely national. One problem here is that contemporaries were themselves confused about concepts of race; about what they meant by race, its historical development and its significance for the world around them. But it is fair to point out that similar confusion is commonplace today. It was for instance certainly accepted among mid-nineteenth-century observers that the mixing of certain races, Saxons and Celts for example, had been beneficial, whereas the mixing of white with non-white races was uniformly bad. Nonetheless, many regularly commented on the Irish 'race', as the Earl of Kimberley did in 1869: '. . . the true source of Irish unhappiness is the character of the Irish race: it must take many generations to alter that character for the better'.

If, from the eighteenth century onwards, English commentators on Irish immigrants did not specifically resort to racial categories, they placed the Irish at the far end of the chain of being. This was partly because in English urban society the Irish invariably had the worst of everything: they were unquestionably the poorest, the worst-paid, most badly-housed and most alien of all urban groups. Merely to describe their social rank and suffering was to speak of the lowest orders of urban people, all without imputing to them the vices and shortcomings of their 'nation' or their 'race'. At this level it is possible to compare the English relationship to the Irish with that of Americans and their black population. But the suggestion that the Irish were the English blacks is both deceptive and only partly true. Whatever other objections are directed against it, the most pertinent and important is that the English had blacks of their own, at home and in the colonies, who were, without doubt, widely regarded as the lowest order of humanity and even, at crucial times, denied humanity at all.

The truth is that the Irish in England commonly attracted antipathy from a range of quarters, and those criticisms might reflect diverse (indeed sometimes conflicting) philosophies and attitudes. There were many English who clearly dismissed them as an inferior race; an immigrant *untermensch* which threatened to gnaw at the vitals of English society. Others disliked them for their 'Irishness', for displaying all the vices of a troublesome nation which constantly bridled at English control. Some despised them for the complexity of social and economic problems which, apparently, they imported into England (and Scotland), while many bitterly objected to their religion. Indeed at certain critical stages of Irish immigration, notably in the 1840s, it appeared likely that Catholicism, swept along by Irish immigration, might actually displace the floundering Church of England as the most popular religion in the country. Ultimately, whatever objections there were to the Irish settlement in England often converged into a single noxious stream of abuse which denounced them for all these reasons and more.

Whether dealing with the nineteenth-century Irish or the West Indians in the mid-twentieth century, it would be misleading to discuss their histories and the English response to them without placing them in their relevant political contexts. The relationship between English society and its immigrants and settlers was forged primarily within a broad political framework. It was the varied forms of British political control or domination over different parts of the world which were, in large measure, directly responsible for the movement of peoples to the imperial heartland. In the case of Ireland it was, as we have already suggested, primarily geography and economics which lured (or propelled) so many Irish across the Irish Sea or the Atlantic. But the relations between Irish and English were shaped by politics in their wider sense. Many Irish took to England and America the bitterness of frustrated Irish political expectations or, worse still, painful memories of the violence and counter-violence which were so much a part of Irish history. For their part generations of English resented the legacy and continuing experience of Irish violence towards their English governors, and particularly when violence, or threats of violence, spilled out on to mainland and urban Britain.

From the revolutionary decade of the 1790s when Ireland, like the rest of Western Europe, was caught up in revolutionary turmoil, through to the present day, few generations have not at some stage experienced bitterness and grief caused by violence between Irish and English. The 'rebellion' of 1798 and the ghastly blood-letting of its suppression; the horror of the famine; the insurrection of 1848; the Fenians, committed to overthrowing British rule, with the attendant violence on the British mainland in the 1860s: it was this intellectual and political legacy which fed directly into the movement which, in 1918, became the I.R.A. Punctuated by acts of individual and collective violence on both sides of the Irish Sea, the struggle for, and resistance to, Irish home rule culminated in the 1916 Easter uprising and the eventual foundation of the Irish Free State, though the existence of a separate Ulster was to remain a continuing problem between the two countries. This is not the place to linger on the details of Irish political history, but it is crucial to recall that it was this political relationship, and the continuing friction it caused, which shaped the experiences and responses of one side in relation to the other.

It was a common argument against the claims of Irish independence that the Irish were, at worst, incapable, at best, unworthy of home rule. To justify their opposition English observers had only to resort to caricature to come up with any racial or national image of the Irish which suited their purpose. No matter the variation of the caricature: the important point is that, as with the black in Britain, the legacy of mythology became instrumental in shaping substantial political issues.

One dimension of the Irish presence in England rested more securely than others in observable and undisputed reality – the power and ascendancy of Roman Catholicism. Since the Reformation, the Catholic church had been relegated to a subservient role, though the early days of its persecution had effectively passed with the triumph of the Protestant ascendancy, more especially during the years of the seventeenth-century revolution. Nonetheless, eighteenth-century Catholics faced a series of punishing social and legal disabilities which, together with widespread and open suspicion and antagonism, served to make them an oppressed and blighted minority. And as Parliament tightened its grip during the eighteenth century, it became apparent that there would never be a political revival of Catholicism – least of all a Catholic monarch. In many areas, Catholicism survived thanks only to the persistence and strength of prominent Catholic families, although it was given a new boost after 1789 when the émigré French fleeing from the Revolution implanted their faith in England. It was however the Irish who, once more, made Catholicism a major religion in England and Scotland. In the words of a Jesuit writing of Scotland, though his point was equally valid for England,

God sent the Irish people to swell to large proportions the members of this Church, and to sing the song of the Lord in a strange land.

It is true that the drift of some Irish migrants away from their native Catholicism in England was a major concern to the Catholic hierarchy throughout the second half of the nineteenth century. Nonetheless, the Irish overwhelmingly clung to their distinguishing faith; its priests, churches, organizations and *esprit* providing them with invaluable institutional, spiritual and political assistance in the troubled times which characterized their migrations and settlement in an alien land. What alarmed so many English contemporaries was not merely that the Irish were increasing in numbers, but that the English were becoming less and less religious. More especially in the towns and cities religion seemed to be declining among the lower orders; where it survived – and thrived – it tended to take the form of the newer non-conformist sects (notably Methodism) and, of course, Catholicism among the Irish. The power of the Anglican church, the spiritual pillar of the state, was demonstrably in decline. Yet set against that decline was the alien religion harboured by the Irish. Of all the groups which apparently remained impervious to the overall 'secularization' of nineteenth-century urban life, the Irish and their descendants stood out. For this and for a host of other reasons they were distrusted and feared.

The Anglican hierarchy remained fearful of Catholic progress throughout much of the nineteenth century, and such fears were fanned by even more outrageous sentiments disseminated through the medium of peripatetic lecturers exploiting anti-Catholic and anti-Irish issues. With its Irish base and its Italian allegiances, it was widely alleged (even by Gladstone) that this revived Catholicism could not owe its proper loyalty to England. And yet the policies towards mid- and late-nineteenth-century Catholicism served merely to isolate it from English life. Middle- and upper-class Catholics were ostracized, debarred from a range of social and economic activities and even, at times, excluded from their wider families. At the other social extreme, the Irish communities were, by definition, largely beyond the pale of English urban life. Far from threatening to take over English religion and social life, Catholicism was, because of its Irishness and because of the ostracism exercised towards it, primarily a sub-culture existing outside the mainstream of English social and religious experience. Nonetheless, there was a huge distrust of Irish Catholicism and it was a sentiment shared by wide sectors of the non-Irish public which viewed it as a subversive force, with alien sympathies and loyalties. It was regarded by many as an institutional and theological Trojan horse in an insecure society.

Historians continue to argue about the pros and cons of Irish immigration in the nineteenth century. Did it, as so many Victorians alleged, worsen the already bad conditions of urban England while simultaneously forcing down low wages for the working people? Some historians have been in no doubt that the Irish presence was harmful, 'a net liability' in the words of one of them. Another has remarked that those English cities which avoided Irish immigration in the 1840s avoided the worst of social problems. Yet it is unreasonable to assume that we can come to a clear and undisputed conclusion by drawing up an economic balance sheet of immigration. Wage levels, housing conditions and the like, while having an undoubtedly statistical basis, can not easily be used to answer the wider questions raised by Irish immigration. Furthermore, it would be pointless to consider Irish immigration *outside* the context of Britain as a whole. It is true that the Irish increased certain English and Scottish urban problems, but their flight from Ireland eased a number of pressing issues in their homeland. And, as we have seen, the English were instrumental in shaping, and sometimes in creating, some of the major social and economic problems of Ireland itself. If Ireland was plagued by apparently intractable issues – of land-holding, alien land-ownership, a clash of religions and, after 1800, the virtual impossibility of Irish industries to compete against English rivals – it seemed both understandable and not unfair that the mainland should partly offset these difficulties by providing a home for Irish people uprooted from their homes.

The Irish undoubtedly had good qualities to offer English society. Muscle power alone was not in short supply, and rural England continued to provide the major source of labour for expansive urban industries. But it is important to recall that the Irish were famous for and accustomed to intensive bouts of *casual* labour, a type of labour which, despite the unquestioned advance of industrialization requiring a more disciplined and ordered labour force, remained in great demand throughout the century and beyond. Commentators who have regarded the Irish propensity for casual labour as a mixed blessing in an industrialized society have generally overlooked the remarkable and continuing demands for huge amounts of casual work. Although Irish temperament and experience were suited to all kinds of work, in all weather, even here it is tempting to offer and extend the traditional stereotype of the labouring Irishman fit for nothing but the most casual form of labour. Nonetheless it was precisely that kind of labour which attracted generations of Irishmen and which they undertook so effectively.

The building trade provided a notable home for Irish labour. Building the new English towns was itself a major and expanding English industry as the nineteenth century advanced and as ever more people turned to the towns. By 1901 more than 80 per cent of the population were town dwellers. Those arteries of a modernizing society, the canals and, later, the railways, were also largely the work of legions of Irishmen. Indeed, the Irish 'navvy' digging and shovelling his way across the length and breadth of the English countryside, and cutting huge swathes through the towns, became a popular (and abiding) image of contemporary life. Cartoonists had a field-day with the Irish navvy whose image had its literary counterpart in the handbills, street ballads and the like which formed the basis for that rich popular culture of nineteenth-century urban England. And yet, though the building of canals and railways was a new phenomenon, it was nonetheless casual work and in the long tradition of Irish seasonal and migratory roles within English society, going back to the pre-modern harvesters. However many modern historians are apt to feel that the arithmetic of Irish immigration produces a negative answer for domestic English society, it is hard to imagine these major labouring enterprises being undertaken without the strength and experience of successive generations of Irishmen.

Thus, it is important to stress the degree to which the Irish *complemented* the labouring communities of England which already existed. No matter how badly they were exploited, or how ill-paid, the Irish continued to be needed even in a society which seemed already to have its own ready-made industrial proletariat. Nor, as far as we can tell, did the presence of this casual labour have those 'unhappy effects' on working-class mores suggested by others. It has also been argued that the history of English–Irish relations was generally peaceful and uneventful. Violence against the Irish was uncommon, except in Lancashire where pronounced Protestant–Orange and Ulster communities created what amounted to a microcosm of the homeland. But what is surely important is both the commonly held myths and reality of Irish individual and communal violence. The infrequency of anti-Irish violence in England may, ultimately, tell us more about Irish *strengths* than about the relative absence of English fears and dislikes. Certainly it would be quite wrong to feel that the tranquil relationship between English and Irish in the nineteenth century was necessarily an indication of benign English attitudes towards the Irish. It may just as easily have been through fear and apprehension which, if that were true, is likely to have compounded the distrust and antipathy evidenced by the English in so many other respects.

One difficulty in assessing attitudes is that we are faced by printed or written historical evidence which originates overwhelmingly from the propertied sections of society. Middle- and upper-class attitudes have been much recorded; not so working-class responses. More recently however, social historians have been able, by tapping the previously neglected fields of popular culture – of songs, music-hall ditties and the like – to re-create lost and previously unimagined sensations. By and large this popular cultural tradition confirms the more broadly defined images of the Irish in England. In songs and rhymes, in street ballads and in the popular culture of the pub, the Irishman's image among his English peers was very similar to that shared (and purveyed) by the middle and upper classes: it was the familiar caricature of the violent, drunken, wage-cutting beast of burden.

One notable factor eased relations between immigrants and hosts: successive generations simply merged into the anonymous background of English and Scottish urban life. This is not to say that the descendants of Irish immigrants lost their cultural or religious roots, but that their distinguishing characteristics were muted and, in some cases, even evaporated. Offspring born and bred outside Ireland did not have an Irish accent. Often, to the chagrin of the Catholic church, they even lost their faith or, just as bad, married into another faith. But we should also remember that in many respects the Irish on the mainland bettered themselves. As the nineteenth century advanced material well-being increased throughout society (notwithstanding the fact that so too did urban poverty). More and more people were materially better cared for, better housed, dressed and fed by, say, 1900 than they had been in 1850. This is not to claim that the material benefits of industrial society were shared equally between the social classes. Nonetheless it is clear that the standard of living undoubtedly rose, and it was the expectation of a better life which was instrumental in luring many immigrants in the first place. And as more of them began to enjoy the limited improvements which industrial change yielded to working people, they – and more especially their descendants – blended more easily with other sections of English urban plebian life. They had their own religion and their politics, but they were otherwise generally indistinguishable.

At the turn of the century the large majority of Irish in England were 'wage earners, increasingly established and benefiting from the generally improving conditions in the country at large'. They were, in effect, an old 'problem' which the English had learned to cope with and which, with time, seemed less obviously troublesome at every level (barring perhaps the political relations between England and Ireland). Throughout the subsequent history of Irish immigration into Britain (there were 1 million Irish-born in mainland Britain in 1961) the Irish were never again to be regarded as the problem they had been in the early and mid-nineteenth century. By the end of this period the special place the Irish had traditionally occupied in the demonology of their English opponents was being usurped by new and more glaringly obvious and distinguishable arrivals: Eastern European and Russian Jews.

4

Newcomers, 1880–1914

During the last quarter of the nineteenth century the Irish community on the mainland decreased in size. The census indicates that the Irish population stood at 566,540 in 1871; by 1901 it was 426,565. Equally significant for the wider history of immigration and settlement was the fact that during that period more obvious and, in British eyes, more troublesome groups, had made an impact in British cities. Many were new (the Chinese, for instance), others had connections with Britain which stretched back for centuries (the blacks most notably) while the largest and most controversial could claim a settlement in England beginning with the Normans. The Jews who settled in Britain from 1881 onwards were unlike most of their forebears both in national origin and social class. Overwhelmingly the Jews who descended on Britain in their thousands were Eastern European and were poor, working-class or rural folk, unlike earlier generations of Jews who had tended largely to be Sephardi and Ashkenazi.

Once more we need to understand the engine which drove the Jews to emigrate. Whereas the Irish had traditionally been uprooted and propelled abroad by economic distress, the late nineteenth-century Jews were fleeing from persecution. Following the assassination of Czar Nicholas II in March 1881, a wave of terror engulfed the Jewish settlements. In many respects this was rather commonplace, for major political and social disasters in Russia were often blamed, sometimes with official support, on the Jews. And on top of that, the stringent limitations on Jewish economic and social life prevented them from enjoying the full benefits of the upturn in the Russian economy from the 1860s onwards. This was also accompanied by the periodic persecutions characteristic of czarist Russia. The Jewish communities were massive and expanding: there were more than 5 million Jews in Russia in 1897. But it was the more outrageous repression following the assassination of the Czar which finally uprooted growing numbers, scattering them westwards in a desperate scramble for security and a new life.

The U.S.A. was the natural and favourite target for the fleeing Jews but, like the Irish before them, many of them had to pass through Britain en route to America, for transportation tended to be much cheaper from Britain. The migrations to the U.S.A. were enormous; those to England, by comparison, were relatively small but it is worth stressing that, by the turn of the century, only the U.S.A. housed more Eastern Europeans than England. In 1901 this was some 82,844, a figure which only formed 65 per cent of the total increase in foreigners since 1891. Jews were not alone in fleeing west, for there were other non-Jewish Germans, Poles and Russians fleeing from various persecutions and disabilities. The numbers actually settling in England fluctuated of course. Between 1881 and 1883, some 5–6,000 settled each year; from 1884 to 1886 it had fallen to 2–3,000. But new Russian laws of 1890 uprooted still more; 7,000 settled in England in 1891, 3,000 the year after, while for the rest of that decade the annual figure was about 2,500. After 1899 the migration of Jews became more desperate and large-scale, pushed along by famines, violence, warfare and finally, in 1905, the revolution, all culminating in pogroms, which now took on an added, savage dimension. Immigration thus trebled between 1899 and 1902; by 1905–6 it had grown even more. But in 1905 the Aliens Act was introduced, controlling the inflow of settlers and, incidentally, laying the basis for future legal control over immigration.

Two features above all others characterized the settlement of Eastern Europeans in England. Firstly, the word 'Jew' became, somewhat uncorrectly, synonymous with the word 'immigrant'. Secondly, the very great majority settled in London, the bulk in the East End, a fact which in large part explains the growing political and social concern about that area of London. Indeed the East End emerged in these years as perhaps *the* problem area of English urban life; a threatening and unknown slice of the metropolis which housed alien peoples with alien habits. Fifty years before, contemporaries had made similar alarmed noises about the threats posed by the new industrial cities of the north. Now however, the undoubted social problems embedded in the East End seemed to be heightened and compounded by the sheer 'foreignness' of armies of its inhabitants. Seventy per cent of all Poles and Russians who came to England disembarked in the capital; and most of them settled in the East End, especially in Stepney which was home to 40 per cent of all the aliens in London.

There was, in the same period, parallel growth in provincial Jewish communities and while this growth was important for the subsequent development of non-metropolitan Jewish life, it was initially relatively small. Manchester and Leeds both attracted immigrant Jews in the late century, to add to the existing nucleus. By the end of the century both communities were perhaps only 12,000 strong. Other smaller communities grew in Glasgow, Liverpool, Birmingham, Newcastle, Sunderland, Portsmouth and Hull, but London, especially the East End, with its existing Jewish connections and its apparent abundance of cheap accommodation and plentiful though ill-paid casual and unskilled labour, lured the overwhelming majority. And as new waves settled, they had the familiar languages, customs and habits of earlier settlers to provide them with a sense of place, an indication of familiarity in an alien world. Efforts by 'native' Jews to disperse the new arrivals, if only to deflect the mounting animosity against Jews in general, were largely unsuccessful. There emerged a distinct community, with all the benefits which ready-made communities can offer to new arrivals.

Just as commonwealth immigration provoked argument during the 1960s, so Jewish settlement between 1881 and 1905 generated a growing chorus of political concern. It was, however, a debate normally informed by ignorance of the demographic data; it revealed scant regard for the available evidence and seemed to rely greatly on imagination. The figures for alien settlement bandied about in the political debate often bore no relation whatsoever to reality. The census returns, themselves not without imperfections, were ignored if they did not suit the political case; the evidence was often dismissed because so many critics could not bring themselves to believe that Jews or Jewish organizations could or would file accurate returns. The Aliens Lists (issued by the Board of Trade) were in some respects more troublesome. Drawn up monthly, they were a product of the 1836 Registration of Aliens Act which ordered all masters of arriving vessels to provide a list of aliens to customs officials on arrival. The system was so imperfect and used so sparingly that its evidence was almost worthless. But the fresh arrivals in the 1880s and a Select Committee on immigration led to a tightening up of the system in the 1890s. Even without political bias – to say nothing of malice – the figures readily lent themselves to distortion and deceit. Inflated figures, often of the most grotesque order, peppered debates in Parliament and the press. And in the process what was in fact a manageable, finite and restricted affair (notwithstanding its manifold social and economic ramifications) became a major, intractable and divisive political issue. The press ran increasingly alarmist stories about 'the foreign flood' and similarly emotive issues. When the statistics seemed to deny the extent of immigration, it was always possible to sidestep them. 'Gentlemen [said one London politician], I don't care for statistics. God has given me a pair of eyes in my head . . .' It was only a matter of time and argument before restrictions of some kind would find their way into the statute book.

The arguments about Eastern European and Jewish settlements concentrated on some obvious and, in the long term traditional, themes: work, wages, housing, poverty – and, of course, anti-semitism. It was widely and unquestioningly argued that foreign settlers undercut wages, competed unfairly and engaged in unfair trading practices. It was even claimed that they threatened to displace the English from their homes, as the M.P. for Stepney argued:

There is hardly an Englishman in this room who does not live under the constant danger of being driven from his home, packed out into the streets, not by the natural increase of our own population, but by the off-scum of Europe.

Even if we look only at the numbers involved, it is abundantly clear that these, and similar, alarmist claims, could scarcely be true. Between 1891 and 1901, the increase in Jews was almost 59,000; in the next five years it grew by 67,000. Thereafter, because of the Aliens Act, it fell away quite markedly. By 1916 fewer than 30,000 had settled in the past eleven years. In the middle of the First World War the total Jewish population stood at a little over a quarter of a million. The number of Jewish settlers, in a little over a quarter of a century, was 155,811. When we compare this with the Irish figures (the numbers of Irish-born living in England in 1891, 1901 and 1911 were 458,315, 426,565 and 375,325 respectively) it is clear that the Jews came nowhere near the level of Irish immigration. They had, however, come to dominate the political arguments about immigration and settlement. Nonetheless, in the years up to the First World War (which naturally curtailed immigration from Eastern Europe) the immigrants from Russia and Eastern Europe formed 30 per cent of all foreigners living in England and Wales. And 40 per cent of the Russians and Poles had, by 1901, settled in Stepney. Only in thirteen other towns was Jewish settlement in these years a statistically significant factor.

It would be wrong to deny that large numbers of these settlers endured (though rarely created) some of the most abject of urban conditions. For many, the persecutions of Eastern Europe had been replaced by urban poverty in England. It is true that established Jewish communities sought to ease the burdens of the immigrants and, despite political concern, there is very little evidence that poor Jews were a burden on the poor rates. Indeed, in 1901 although 15·2 per 1,000 of the population were in the workhouse, the figure for European immigrants was a mere 1·7 per 1,000. However abject their conditions, the immigrant poor did not tax the English public purse with their poverty. The workshop rather than the workhouse became the natural habitat for the Eastern Europeans in London.

The sweatshop trades of the late century were buoyant; they produced an abundance of material and personal consumer goods, but they also gained an unenviable reputation for the exploitation of their workforce. Long hours, very low wages and intolerable working conditions were the hallmarks of the sweatshops, as they had been throughout the century. What made the problems more acute in the late nineteenth century were the changes in the economy which gave a major filip to such workshops and their produce (notably clothing), and the available labour market, especially among immigrants. Large numbers of Eastern European, especially Jewish, immigrants were familiar with the trades of the workshops. And in any case there were legions of willing hands desperate to work for the pittance offered in the sweatshops. The workshops soon became dominated by the immigrants (as indeed they did in the U.S.A. at much the same time and for much the same reason). Between 1901 and 1911 some 40 per cent of Polish and Russian men and 50 per cent of their womenfolk worked in the clothing trades; another 12 per cent worked in the shoe trade, while 10 per cent were cabinet makers. It was widely agreed by all parties that the presence of immigrant labourers depressed wages, but it was likely that the clothing trade in the East End of London would have collapsed but for the low-paid army of immigrants.

The major immigration of Eastern Europeans and Russians was effectively curtailed by the 1905 Aliens Act. The residue of antipathy and ill-feeling – more often than not there for mythical reasons – was less easily dispersed. There were a myriad other complaints from all social classes. Working people living close to the immigrants disliked most of their social habits; their domestic overcrowding, their alleged lack of hygiene ('they chuck the fish heads over the yards, and the fish guts stink, and it is altogether disgraceful and disgusting'). Immigrants were thought to be dirty, though as one observer of the East End noted, 'the prejudiced Englishman is apt to call "dirty" whatever is foreign'.

And, of course, the immigrants were distrusted for their clannishness, while the Jews were the objects of a traditional dislike because of their religion. Moreover, whenever they were commercially successful, as many soon were, they were commonly accused of deceit or criminality.

At the heart of such antipathy was embedded a xenophobia and an antisemitism which, though highlighted after 1880, had traditional and ancient roots in Britain. As foreigners, the immigrants were, like the Irish, widely suspect in those episodes of national political crisis which brought forth excesses of jingoism, notably the Boer War and the outbreak of the First World War. It was enough for a shop or a business to have a foreign name for it to be attacked by marauding bands of zealots anxious to prove their love of country.

Between 1906 and 1914, the Aliens Act proved highly effective in the task for which it was designed: keeping immigrants out. It did not of course curb the wild and widespread allegations about the excesses of the aliens. In the words of one prominent judge, his cases consisted of 'the Russian burglar, the Polish thief, the Italian stabber, and the German swindler'. In 1914, in that initial wave of jingoism, a Restriction Act was passed allowing the authorities to repatriate or intern foreign nationals. It was passed in a Parliamentary mood of persecution, to the disgust of only a small minority of M.P.s. The principles of that Act, ordering the registration of aliens, were continued after the war by Orders in Council and formed the basis for alien control until the 1970s. The whole problem of antisemitism and of Jewish immigration was to be revived, in a more familiar form, in the 1930s when the Nazis threatened firstly German Jews and, later, Jews from the whole of Europe.

Jews and other Eastern Europeans were only the most obvious and controversial immigrants in the late nineteenth century. Certain new arrivals were, if anything, even more exotic, but much less numerous. Few were more exotic than the Chinese. In the nineteenth and twentieth centuries, Chinese immigrants were to have a major impact on distant parts of the world. Indeed there are few major cities in the western world which do not have their own Chinese quarters or communities. Within the British empire Chinese labour was to play a crucial role in late nineteenth-century economic developments, as untold thousands of Chinese quit their homelands for the labouring life on the Canadian railroads, 'coolie' labour in South Africa and indentured labour in the British West Indies. Even had the Chinese not settled in mainland Britain, the British were directly responsible for encouraging the development of substantial Chinese communities around the world.

Chinese styles and forms had been a marked feature of English fashionable society since the eighteenth century. Indeed one English aristocrat – a traditional employer of black servants – was persuaded, because of the widespread employment of black servants in the eighteenth century, to employ Chinese servants instead. And of course the legacy of *chinoiserie* can still be found in a number of architectural survivals and furnishings within stately homes. Nowhere is this better captured than in that strange hybrid of India and China, the Brighton Pavilion. It is of course the word 'china' which to this day describes the tableware first brought to Europe by the Portuguese from China centuries ago.

At a less exalted level, Chinese sailors were a regular sight in late eighteenth-century British ports, their faces appearing in a number of contemporary pictures and cartoons, especially of London's 'low life'. But, as far as we can judge, these were few in number, although this began to change from the mid-nineteenth century. Shipping lines with trading routes to China, especially from Liverpool, were primarily responsible for bringing more and more Chinese into English ports. But this seems not to have been on a noticeable scale until the mid-century when the economic and demographic forces within China itself began to propel people abroad. Viewed from China the most attractive of all destinations was the Pacific coast of North America; by 1877 it was calculated that San Francisco housed 35,000 Chinese, and at the time there were also 17,000 in New South Wales, Australia. As with the Irish in an earlier period, the Chinese abroad made efforts to attract other relatives and friends to join them, thus compounding the forces behind migration. And, again like the Irish, the Chinese were commonly and universally accused of working for low wages, lower, indeed, than any of the European settlers. Of course, it was this factor which initially made the Chinese 'coolies' such ideal human material for those enterprises which were labour intensive – in the Caribbean, North America, Australia or South Africa. It was no accident that the Chinese – along with Indians – were recruited to fill the gap left by black workers on the Caribbean sugar estates. Coolies were prepared to work for wages, and under conditions which even the former black slaves refused. But this, once more, reminds us that in many mass migrations, conditions at home – hunger, poverty, disease, for example – were responsible for uprooting millions of people, rather than the seductions of their new-found homes. Desperation was often the driving force behind emigration. Indeed it is symptomatic that Beatrice Webb described working women in the East End in the late nineteenth century as 'the Chinamen of this class: they accept work at any wages'. In the years leading up to the First World War, spokesmen for the British radical and working movements bitterly resisted the prospects of Chinese immigration for the simple reason that it threatened the wage levels of local workers. One French commentator remarked that, in time 'the Chinese will end by fixing themselves among us like the Jews . . .'

When the demographic evidence is examined, it is clear that such alarms were greatly, often outrageously, exaggerated. It is important to stress that British responses to the 'threat' or prospects of Chinese immigration were shaped in large part by the experience of empire and overseas trade which filtered through to a wider British public through the media of political debate and popular (and often zenophobic) journalism. Chinese seamen formed the largest single occupational group of Chinese in Britain according to the 1911 census; only 480 strong, although the total number serving on British ships amounted to 4,595. When it is recalled that the number of 'lascars' in the same work *increased* by 21,583 in the twenty years before 1911, it can be appreciated how insignificant the Chinese presence really was. This did little to prevent the continuous union and political sniping at the Chinese. They were, quite simply, cheap labour. But whereas British labour disliked them for that reason, British capital (and capital throughout the world) found them very attractive.

It is true that there was a contrary feeling, a humane (normally radical) response which sought to *protect* the Chinese from the worst forms of exploitation. This became a major political issue when fierce arguments about coolie labour in South Africa played such an important part in the 1906 General Election. But it also seems clear that there was, among the electorate at large, an abundance of antipathy and distrust towards the Chinese, even though they were many thousands of miles away. There was a feeling that further coolie settlement in South Africa would endanger the future of white immigration to that country. But in the process, the deepest of racialist slurs became commonplace in the vocabulary (and iconography) of British politics. Images of the wage-cutting Chinaman were reinforced by cartoons which appeared on the hustings.

In reality, the Chinaman bore no relation to his caricature; numerically, the Chinese were insignificant and yet they had, along with the Jews, come to the forefront of British political and social debate. Furthermore, the widespread impressions about Chinese life were made worse by the reinforcing imagery of an older stereotypical judgement. That the Chinese had sexual relations with white women and used opium had long been popular complaints. Opium taking and opium dens were thought to be a peculiarly

Chinese phenomenon. In fact, opium had been readily and easily available throughout Britain until it was brought under control in 1867. Indeed, a recent observer of the history of the drug has remarked that opium was, in many respects, the aspirin of the nineteenth century. The effective outlawing of opium – or rather its tight restriction to strictly professional medical usage – made the Chinese use of opium all the more unusual. And yet the Europeans were instrumental in securing the manufacture and retailing of opium in their piratical trading and military operations in mid-nineteenth-century China. Equally ironically, in China itself resentment of the sexual abuses of the invading Europeans led to the belief that 'Christianity was a religion of debauchery, and that missionaries practised magical means of enslaving women'. In Britain, officials in cities with Chinese settlers returned again and again to the 'problem' of sexual relations. In London and Liverpool before 1914, the local authorities and police continually investigated allegations of sexual relations between Chinese and under-age girls.

As we have already seen, the sensitive issue of sex had long been a matter for prurient curiosity and censure, especially between black and white. The analogies between the problems of eighteenth-century blacks and early twentieth-century Chinese are very similar. In an alien world and without their own womenfolk, men from black and Chinese communities turned to poor white women for sexual or more permanent relationships. When such relationships did develop, abuse was directed as much at the 'offending' white woman as at the immigrant male. But it was commonly assumed that such women fell into obvious categories: prostitutes or young girls 'taken advantage of' by scheming foreigners. It was clearly hard for those people fond of declaiming on the topic to imagine that the women might, in fact, have made their own choice in the matter, for whatever reason. It was a complaint which was revived with even greater force before 1914, when more and more blacks began to settle their own communities in England.

There were, inevitably perhaps, other complaints commonly flung at the Chinese in Britain. They were notorious for their gambling, and we know a great deal about this because of the history of prosecution surrounding gambling. But since the Chinese gambled among themselves it was hardly likely to pose a threat to wider British society. Similarly, the allegations that the Chinese were inclined to certain forms of violence again ignored the fact that any such violence tended to take place amongst the Chinese. Records confirm that Chinese communities were essentially law abiding and peaceable. Indeed, the most recent historian of the Chinese in Britain has confirmed that the only substantial and enduring criticism of the Chinese before 1914 was about their position in the labour market. Even then, it seems clear that the objection to Chinese labour derived largely from the 1906 General Election campaign against coolie labour in South Africa. Whatever antagonism thrived in Britain did so primarily as a reflected imperial issue. Of course, the key factor was one of size; unlike in the U.S.A. or Australia, the number of Chinese in Britain was very small indeed – hundreds where others had thousands. However antagonistic or racist the criticism of the Chinese, it could not be denied that the ranks of the Chinese were thin and strictly concentrated in London and Liverpool.

Much less exotic than the Chinese – if only because familiar for centuries – were the new black arrivals who settled in England from the late nineteenth century. We have already explored the pre-modern history of black settlement in Britain, a history which was given a new impetus, from the late nineteenth century, by the expanding shipping lines to West Africa and the Caribbean. Africans had been regular, if not very numerous, visitors throughout the nineteenth century as students, residents, runaway slaves or sailors. By the 1870s, however, blacks had become comparatively scarce.

In the last quarter of the century things began to change, more especially because of the remarkable and rapid growth of the British empire in black Africa. British missionaries established themselves in new regions while their British organizations often took in and educated increasing numbers of black Africans. Moreover, as the newly established or reorganized British universities began to offer useful undergraduate courses, more and more African and West Indian students took up their studies in many of Britain's major cities. Wherever they studied there was strong evidence of antipathy and discrimination against them, but this was more strikingly the case with their Indian contemporaries. One direct result of this hostility, and of the Africans' determination to resist it, was the establishment in 1913 of an African students' association, a tradition which of course survives to this day.

Much more numerous than black students however were black sailors, many of whom put down their roots in British maritime communities. From these roots were to flower the first effective modern black communities in Britain. The most important community was in Cardiff, home of the 'tramp' steam trade, the long-distance maritime trade which offered sailors longer voyages but less permanent employment. Black sailors landing in Cardiff after such voyages stayed and quickly established a distinctive black community close to the Cardiff docks. Blacks were simply the most obvious of a growing number of foreign sailors securing employment on the new shipping routes. Between 1890 and 1903, for instance, the number of foreign sailors increased from 27,000 to 40,000, at a time when the numbers of British sailors had declined by 10,000, though this was a trend which was sharply reversed in the decade before the First World War. It is significant that, in the 1911 national seamen's strike, the employment of foreign sailors was a bitter issue in the sailors' litany of complaints against the shipowners.

Of course in the years before 1914 British sailors could reel off a string of major grievances. But however bad their lot, especially when discharged in port and seeking fresh employment, few had to endure the extra disadvantages suffered by the foreign sailors. By 1914 there were clear and geographically defined black quarters in Cardiff, Liverpool and South Shields. Such communities – small-scale as they now seem – were to the outsider exotic, mysterious and not a little troublesome. Social customs, recreations, cooking – and the inevitable associations with white women – all compounded the British sense of curiosity about these emergent black communities. They also attracted the scrutiny of local politicians and local policemen. Writing of the Tiger Bay district of Cardiff, one turn-of-the-century author wrote,

Chinks and Dagoes, Lascars and Levantines slippered about the faintly evil by-ways that ran off Bute Street . . . children of the strangest colours, fruit of frightful misalliances, staggered half-naked about the streets . . . It was a dirty, rotten and romantic district, an offence and an inspiration, and I loved it.

Despite the number of black communities that had sprung up in many British seaports as a result of the available employment, many blacks found themselves without work for long periods and were forced to go on the road in search of alternative employment. Many inevitably had to resort to charitable relief provided by church organizations or local authorities. It is important to remember that the basic experiences of many of these men who laid the foundations of modern black communities were, from the very beginning, of dire economic conditions when at work, interrupted by extensive bouts of unemployment, with a regular taste of local charities. Throughout, and at every level (at sea, in British ports, in daily intercourse and social life), these men were faced by regular and unavoidable racial antagonism of a kind which was worse – harsher, more pervasive and more far-reaching – than that suffered by other settlers, notably the Jews. Of course the numbers involved were clearly very small; much smaller for instance than the many thousands of East Europeans settling in Britain at the same time. And even the East Europeans were completely overshadowed by those regular infusions of tens of thousands of Irish who continued to flock to Britain up to 1914.

Indeed it seems clear that the political and economic hostility towards the Jews, Chinese or blacks was not precisely related to their numerical size. Only the Jews settled in appreciable numbers, though not in the numbers alleged by their enemies. The Irish alone continued to settle in numbers which might make an appreciable impact on overall population trends, and in the Irish case that was a pattern of great longevity. Of course the Irish were much less obviously different than Russian Jews, Chinese or Jamaican sailors, although it is perfectly true that they had, for centuries, been denounced for those distinguishing 'anti-social' characteristics now imputed to the newer settlers. There were also scatterings of other settlers to be found throughout late nineteenth- and early twentieth-century Britain. There were, for instance, large numbers of

Germans living in Britain, many of them refugees from the various political upheavals in Germany. But there were also communities of successful German businessmen. When war broke out, some 40,000 Germans were interned for security reasons. In terms of immigrant settlement the largest group, as revealed by the censuses in the years before 1914, had been born in the white colonies, Australia, New Zealand, Canada and South Africa. Furthermore, there was a traditionally large group of American aliens living in Britain: 18,496 in 1881 and 16,860 in 1911. But it is hard to glean from the evidence the antipathy and outrage displayed by their British hosts towards less numerous (though more visible) settlers. It is likely that the numbers of Chinese and blacks formed barely one tenth of the American-born residents in Britain. And the same was true for settlers from Germany, France, Italy, Holland, Switzerland, Belgium and Austria, all of whom immigrated in their thousands according to censuses between 1880 and 1911.

One factor worth remembering is that, by the beginning of the twentieth century, the state machinery was more complex and sophisticated than ever before. One aspect of that sophistication was the ability to monitor, tabulate and, in large measure, to control population movement and change. The demographic data compiled by the state bureaucracy was progressively more accurate and comprehensive than in previous eras. Thus it was possible, by the early twentieth century, to be better informed about population than ever before. Yet what is equally striking is the degree to which the available evidence was often overlooked or ignored in the excitement of political argument, or in the need to steal a march in the fight for circulation among the popular newspapers. The issues of immigration and alien settlement readily lent themselves to distortion and manipulation, a process which normally involved losing sight of the substantive points. This was not new, for it was but a more recent manifestation of a longstanding pattern. Nor was it to end then; it was to remain one of the more durable features of the British experience of immigration. Of course there were about-turns in the various British responses to alien settlement, often in a very short space of time. One such dramatic change took place in 1914 when, with the outbreak of war, new national groups became the object of deep and violent animus, while others, long treated despicably, became invaluable working allies. Germans and Austrians became the enemy for the next four years; blacks were part of the imperial labour force or military strength needed to fight the strength-sapping war.

5

Wartime and Hard Times, 1914–39

In 1914 the British presided over the most remarkable of empires – bigger, more varied and more self-confident, indeed, than the British empire of the eighteenth century. It was, in many respects, the size, location, strength and viability of the British empire which so provoked Germany from the 1890s onwards. And when war erupted in August 1914 it was clearly a war between a number of great empires: Austria–Hungary and Turkey on the one side, Russia and Britain on the other. But it was also clear that the war would have ramifications far beyond the European geographical limits of empire. Whoever lost the war stood a very good chance of losing their empire, and this is precisely what happened to the Turks and the Austrians. The First World War brutally occupied Europe itself, but there was also fighting all over the world – in the Pacific, in Africa, in the Middle East, as well as at sea. But it was undoubtedly true, and obvious to all, that the future of empire hinged on the war in Europe.

Imperialists appreciated that the war offered room for further imperial expansion, for victory would produce vast tracts of enemy-held territory as the spoils of war. Moreover, the war itself revealed how important the empire was to Britain as a source of manpower and raw materials. By 1918 some 2½ million colonials had fought for Britain and many others had worked for the war effort as non-combatants. The ghastly casualty figures are evidence of the colonial military efforts; alongside 59,330 Australians were to be counted 56,639 Canadians, 16,711 New Zealanders, 7,121 South Africans, and 62,056 Indians plus about 2,000 blacks. British politicians *assumed* that the empire would rally to their side, and they were not to be disappointed, for the peoples of the far-flung British possessions did indeed rally to the flag. In retrospect the support of some of those peoples, more especially the subject non-whites, seems ever more inexplicable. It is hard to imagine the appeal of a European war for Indians from the sub-continent or for West Indian blacks whose grandparents had been slaves. Nonetheless, for whatever reasons or motives, colonial subjects from home and abroad joined the armed forces in their millions. In 1914, Prime Minister Asquith received a telegram, 'Do not worry England, Barbados is behind you'. After initial hesitation, the recruitment of a black West Indian regiment began; eventually more than 15,000 men were to join it from most of the British Caribbean islands.

The West Indians fought in most of the theatres of the war, in Europe, the Middle East and even in the Cameroons. They lost a substantial proportion of their numbers and took home their own fair share of the battle honours. But beneath this apparently simple account lay deeper and more unpleasant stories. The War Office positively resisted the integration of black and white regiments; commissions for men of 'mixed blood' were bitterly resisted. Efforts were made to keep black troops out of combat, confining them where possible to labouring duties. It was in fact yet another variant on a well-worn theme that even in the desperate times of warfare the blacks were to be used primarily as the beasts of burden for their imperial masters. Naturally enough, both during and after the war, black West Indians were based in British camps, often in areas where blacks had been virtually unknown before. Understandably a number of the West Indian troops settled in Britain when hostilities ended, preferring to sample whatever Britain had to offer rather than return to the economically depressed West Indies.

The 1914–18 war required much more than massive enlistment of troops from all over the empire, for it was a 'total' war which demanded extraordinary amounts of labouring manpower and untold volumes of raw materials simply to keep the armies in the field. And just as British women found themselves elevated to a previously unknown and unrecognized level of economic importance (taking over many of the jobs of their menfolk), so too was the empire tapped for its abundant reserves of labour. Black labour thus found itself in demand by an imperial nation which had until now done its best to keep it at arm's length. Large numbers of West Indians joined the expanding merchant marine, easily securing fairly lucrative work where before there had not only been few prospects but strong union resistance. Numbers of black sailors quit their vessels and took better-paid work in wartime industries, but there were plenty of other Africans and West Indians ready to step into their seafaring jobs. It was a seller's market and there was work in abundance for whoever volunteered to travel to Britain or those who, if here via a mercantile trade, were willing to seek work in the industrial cities. Thus, numbers of black workers found their way into the munitions and chemical industries. Often, particularly in the seaports, they joined the existing black communities. Elsewhere, they became the founding fathers of new black settlements.

Cardiff more than any other city became an immigrant area as ever more blacks settled, partly because of the distinctive nature of the local shipping trade, but also because its existing black community formed an obvious attraction for arriving blacks. In the process, the nature of local black society itself changed, and more attention was given to black living conditions. But the picture for black society was to change completely with the coming of peace in 1918. The full employment and high wages of the war years gave way to contraction, depression and wage cuts. In some industries, it is true, there was a brief post-war boom, but shipping was not one of them. Demobilization of sailors, and the release of others from coastal work, flooded a mercantile labour market at the very time shipping tonnage began to contract sharply. Shipping companies and their ships' masters had an open policy of employing British rather than black sailors. Not surprisingly, the ranks of the black unemployed swelled rapidly. And to compound their problems, they became the objects of deep resentment on the part of large numbers of returning British sailors and soldiers. It was a dangerous and volatile social mix which threatened local peace and tranquility.

The hot month of June 1919 provided the setting for a series of serious and far-reaching urban riots between black and white. A scuffle between blacks and whites in Cardiff on the night of 10 June attracted a large crowd; shots were fired and large mobs of whites began to attack blacks and their properties. Buildings were gutted and a number of casualties (one of them fatal) ended up in the Cardiff hospitals. There followed days and nights of similar incidents; of white mobs attacking black homes, and blacks defending themselves as best they could, sometimes with firearms. Police, fire brigade and armed units rescued beleaguered blacks; some were held in custody for their own safety. The pattern was consistent: white mobs attacked blacks, often to a descant of racial abuse. Moreover, the violence spread to other cities such as Newport, Liverpool and London. In Liverpool a mob of 2,000 attacked black lodging houses; black families sought protection in the local police station. In Canning Town, London, local butchers, meat cleavers in hands, joined in the attacks on the local blacks, who retaliated with guns. The magistrate in this last case remarked, 'These inhabitants of Jamaica . . . were British subjects and entitled to equal treatment by the law. During the war the coloured races of the Empire had done splendid service, and it was a very shabby thing for those who had loafed about the docks to turn round on them.'

The motives behind the attacks and general abuse of the blacks followed a similar pattern in all the riots. Racial abuse was commonly flung at the heads of local blacks. Blacks were criticized for taking work from local whites (despite the obvious levels of black unemployment), and there were also parallels of sexual jealousy. Complaints about black and white sexual or emotional relations were commonplace, just as they had been in the eighteenth century. Even *The Times* joined in the debate, writing of Liverpool blacks,

Many have married Liverpool women and while it is admitted that some have made good husbands the intermarriage of black and white men and women, not to mention other relationships, has created much feeling.

The story was the same in Cardiff where white women with black boyfriends or husbands were rooted out and abused. Again, to quote *The Times*, local 'sober-minded citizens'

deplore the familiar association between white women and negroes, which is a provocative cause.

The Times in fact shared the common prejudice towards the black: 'His chief failing is his fondness for white women.' The obvious answer remains: where else was he to turn? For as in the late eighteenth century, British black society was predominantly male and could only turn to local women for friendship or sexual relations. But in the twentieth as in the eighteenth century, such relations were singled out for abuse, even among people who had no particular local experience or any particular interest in the matter. Indeed, it could be that this antagonism was a common phenomenon in western societies. Where affectionate or sexual relations between local women and other outsiders might pass without remark, when the outsider was black it evoked a series of deeply hostile reactions.

The events of 1919, which paralleled a series of major riots in American cities, were important in a number of ways. For those blacks who experienced the terrifying attacks of local mobs, the riots left a permanent scar, a fearful memory which erased whatever praise and credit had come their way in return for their wartime efforts. From the British viewpoint, the riots of 1919 helped confirm the image of blacks as a particular 'problem'. One solution, devised by national and local authorities, was to encourage repatriation; it was almost a repeat of 1787. Indeed, when black immigration once more became a major issue in the 1960s and 1970s, repatriation was again the response of the host society. By 1921, some 627 blacks had accepted repatriation to their homeland.

However many actually quit Britain, they did not cancel out the numbers of new arrivals in the major cities and ports. Throughout, their lot was overwhelmingly abject, not least because most were obliged to register as aliens despite the fact that, legally, the great majority were British. But once registered as aliens they were liable to deportation, and it was for this reason, together with the open discrimination operated by British trade unions (with the support of the Labour Party), which prompted the establishment of 'The League of Coloured People' in 1931. The founder of the League was Dr Harold Moody, a Jamaican doctor determined to secure equal rights and opportunities for all blacks in Britain. Not content merely to provide a political framework for black rights, the League became a major force in black social life, organizing holidays and celebrations for black children from all over London. But its main task was the defence of black interests. Extraordinary as it now seems, when much of the Health Service depends heavily on black labour, hospitals in the 1930s would not employ black nurses. This began to change under pressure from the League, but as late as 1938 there were eighteen hospitals which simply refused to accept or train black nurses. Such blatant discrimination was the common lot of blacks in the 1920s and 1930s. Refused work by shipping companies, excluded by unions, rebuffed by hospitals, blacks were also subject to the arbitrary whims of local police forces. By registering *all* local blacks as aliens (including those actually born in Britain) local police forces had the perfect reason for harassing and even deporting any blacks they thought troublesome.

There was, in the inter-war years, a new generation of blacks; born in Britain, of black working men, they faced that unique combination of disadvantages – of being both black and working class at a time of economic distress. Large numbers of these black children were born into public assistance, only to find nothing but unemployment for themselves on leaving school. It was well known, said one black spokesman, 'that at present no coloured boy or girl can procure a job in an office no matter how qualified he or she might be'. Such difficulties were only partly due to the shortage of jobs; often they derived simply from discrimination.

Many of the children and young adults who faced these compound difficulties were the children of mixed marriages. Once more, it provided political ammunition for those who thoroughly disapproved of miscegenation and who saw in its result a disruptive people unsuited for British life. The Chief Constable of Cardiff, reporting to his Watch Committee about 'the association of coloured seamen with white women and the consequent growth of a half-caste population, alien in sentiment and habits to the native white inhabitants', suggested

the desirability of bringing into existence legislation similar to that found necessary in South Africa to check this demoralizing development.

There was a traditional dislike of miscegenation, stretching back for many centuries, which encompassed a range of biological and genetic myths. But it was also reinforced by social values which sought to keep blacks and whites in their own distinct social, as well as biological, camps. Even in the Caribbean, where racial mixing had long been commonplace, the offspring of such relations had been allocated a distinct social and economic role, both in slave days and after. Moreover, by the eve of the Second World War, these old, well worn and widely rehearsed arguments about miscegenation were commonplace in Britain.

Britain between the wars was home to more than mere transient immigrants or embryonic immigrant communities. There were, for example, many thousands who fled from the Russian revolution in 1917, although Britain did not receive anything like the numbers settling in France or the U.S.A. In the 1920s and 1930s, there developed in London important groupings of colonial nationals who sought to press the case for the independence of their different homelands. In the process, and through the medium of widespread and varied newspapers and publications, there evolved a sense of black nationalism and pan-Africanism which was to have major repercussions, especially after the Second World War.

There had been early efforts at black publications as early as the 1890s, but the process did not take firm root until the years immediately before and after the First World War. There were, it is true, personality and political clashes between the various Africans and West Indians in London who formed the nucleus of this early pan-African movement, but the message of their various publications was unambiguous: to promote the interests, rights and freedom of black people throughout the world. These newspapers were quick to point out the commonplace indignities and discriminations suffered by black troops in Britain during the First World War. Furthermore, this black literature achieved an unusually wide, global distribution, even penetrating the far-flung regions of British possessions – places where, of course, their message could have a damaging effect on British control.

There was also established, in the mid 1920s, an organization and related publication for West Africans, more and more of whom came to study and work in London. A number of these organizations were to prove seminal, and they were remarkably durable, spanning the years between the 1920s and the more full-blown campaigns for African independence in the 1940s–1950s. A number of prominent black nationalists and future heads of independent black African states came to political awareness and maturity in the black political organizations in Britain in the inter-war years.

And their political creed and ideology were developed through the columns of black newspapers and journals published in Britain (as well as other European countries) in the same years. Some of those newspapers were, in the eyes of imperial authority, subversive in the extreme; some indeed openly advocated a Marxist interpretation of politics which doubly offended their imperial masters.

Of all these black journals the most impressive, and possibly the most influential, was *The Keys* published from 1933 and the organ of The League of Coloured People, formed in London by Dr Harold Moody. Moody's organization and *The Keys* were remarkably influential among the black residents and students in the London of the 1930s. The journal attracted the varied talents of a number of black and white authors, and provided a focus for news of black life in Africa and the Caribbean. Furthermore, Moody's League came to play an increasingly important role in the formulation of colonial policy. Of more immediate and direct consequence, however, was the activity of the League on behalf of those legions of black sailors who, as we have seen, suffered open discrimination from ship-owners and unions during the serious contraction of shipping brought on by the Depression. The League took up their case, and more especially the outrageous categorization of black British citizens as aliens by local police forces, notably in Cardiff. Thanks to astute lobbying of M.P.s, unions and the Home Office, the League was able to persuade the Home Secretary to rescind the unjust registrations.

Other organizations and journals were more concerned with wider black problems, more especially the emergent demands for black freedom in Africa and the Caribbean. Often they provided a political and literary base for some extraordinary talents, and at certain key points they merged with those British left-wing groups and individuals themselves anxious to promote an anti-imperial policy. The course of black nationalism in Britain in the 1930s was often helped by fortuitous events: the Italian invasion of Ethiopia provided a glaring example of the worst form of imperial dominance in black Africa. New arrivals from Africa or the West Indies often brought a new talent and energy to the cause. But wherever discontent erupted in black societies, for instance during the major labour disputes in the West Indies in 1938, the black London press offered a salutary source of information and an alternative view to the one invariably peddled in the British press in favour of British colonial policy.

During the 1930s there had developed a remarkable cluster of black political and literary talent, feeding the needs and interests not merely of the relatively small British black population, but spreading its message, varied and sometimes conflicting as it was, in black colonial societies of Africa and the Americas. While the local black population remained small, the influence of its spokesmen and activists was out of all proportion to their numbers. Indeed their long-term influence can be assessed by the debt which so many blacks today openly admit to their political mentors of the 1930s. Of course, the fundamental demand of London's black nationalists – for black freedom everywhere from white discrimination – was, by definition, an international issue; it was not one which was uniquely relevant to blacks living in Britain. Moreover, the demands for black nationalism were clearly part of a long-term programme. Even the most optimistic could hope to see the realization of their ambitions later rather than sooner. Indeed, their cause looked doomed to a long, drawn out and tedious future, a protracted political struggle against an unflinching and resistant imperial power. Few could have realized that the catastrophe of the Second World War would, in a very short space of time, prove to be the major solvent of British (and other European nations') imperial dominance. The Second World War, like its forbear a generation before, was to loosen and finally destroy the imperial bonds which had subjugated so many colonial peoples to the arbitrary will of a distant imperial power.

The turmoil into which Europe was plunged by the rise of expansive and aggressive Fascism, particularly Nazism, was felt initially by the political (and religious) opponents of those regimes. None were to be more traumatized than German and, later, European Jews who bore the brunt of Nazi violence. The earlier waves of Jewish immigrants had, as we have seen, been arrested before 1914. Jews continued to arrive in much smaller numbers but the persecutions of the early 1930s once more sent a new generation of European Jews fleeing westwards for safety. Naturally, it is difficult to calculate the numbers with any great accuracy. One survey concluded that 60,000 Jews settled in the U.K. between 1933 and 1939 but the figures might be even higher. Between 1933 and 1939 some 80,000 refugees arrived from Central Europe, and a further 70,000 during the war itself, followed by 60,000 displaced people after 1945; and of this total number, it is calculated that some 80 per cent were Jewish.

The Jews settling before 1939 were, by and large, quite different from the poor Jews who arrived before 1914. They were largely middle class and often prosperous people who had once been very much a part of German society, and many were established professional people. Such qualities enabled them to gain easier acceptance in Britain; although many of these immigrants had lost their possessions to the Nazis, they were neither as destitute nor as alien as the poorer Russian and Polish Jews of earlier in the century. They were, in fact, the very sort of respectable people who would, and generally did, quickly establish themselves and make their own independent way in the world. Thus there was little of that fundamental dislike of their poverty, of their dependence upon philanthropy, which so characterized an earlier British response to Jewish settlement.

There was, furthermore, quite a different attitude and climate from the mid 1930s onwards. It is perfectly true that antisemitism was a pronounced and undeniable feature of British life among, for example, the upper classes who sympathized overtly with Oswald Mosley's British Fascists and especially in that fashionable coterie which clung to Nazi diplomats in London. It was also a shamefully pronounced feature in the upper reaches of political and diplomatic life, nowhere more clearly so – with major and dire consequences during the war itself – than in the Foreign Office. There were many Britons who did not welcome Europe's Jews, however bestial the regime from which they had fled. In some respects, this hostility to Jewish settlement was sharpened by the thorny question of Palestine – a British mandate since the First World War – which seemed an obvious (and, to Zionists, the natural) home for fleeing Jews. But the British found themselves on the horns of a familiar imperial dilemma, of trying to reconcile conflicting claims among subject peoples; Jews and Arabs alike claimed the land, and this dilemma remained with the British until 1948 and the formation of the state of Israel. Before (and during) the war the delicate issue of Jewish immigration into Palestine served to accentuate antagonism towards Jews in general, but especially towards Jewish settlement in Britain.

Jews in Britain faced overt displays of antisemitism, notably at the height of popularity of Mosley's British Union of Fascists. British Fascism was very much a product of the economic turmoil of the early 1930s, but its direction and nature was the creation of the Labour Party renegade, Sir Oswald Mosley, who was himself deeply influenced by Mussolini. Only later did Mosley adopt the antisemitism of Nazism. Appealing to young men from the middle classes, Mosley established his headquarters in Chelsea and by the mid 1930s his party was thought to have a membership of some 20,000. Their public meetings, in town halls and in the open air, attracted large crowds and were orchestrated carefully with lavish displays of militarism by Mosley's followers. Like its German equivalent, British Fascism was host to a thinly disguised and vaguely controlled fund of violent animosity. At certain 'flashpoints' the Fascists broke rank to attack and brutally assault their opponents. Despite attempts to ignore this violence – notably by *The Times* – the truth eventually began to dawn. This was especially true when the Fascists made provocative marches into Jewish communities in the hope of attracting and combating physical opposition. Then, as in the recent revival of British Fascism, the police often seemed more concerned about protecting the Fascists than their victims. From the mid 1930s, however, the increasing excesses of the Nazis began to discredit their British supporters, but the decline of Mosley's power can also be dated from the 1936 Public Order Act, specifically designed to prevent the worst forms of militaristic displays by Fascists in Britain. When war broke out in 1939, Mosley and other leading Fascists were imprisoned, but of the 1,769 British subjects interned, only 763 were from Mosley's Union.

It is hard to calculate the damage done by Mosley and his men. Numerically they never posed a serious threat. But their antics, and the often overt connivance of the authorities and even of the press, badly scarred their intended victims. It was alarming for those Jews – and of course other political refugees – who had fled the brutalities in Germany or Austria to see a reflection, however pale, of the horrors they had left behind. The simple truth was nonetheless that fleeing Jews had few options but to settle in Britain. Between 1933 and 1939 something like a quarter of a million German – and later 140,000 Austrian – Jews fled their homelands, about one third of all the Jews in those countries. They fled to all corners of the world, from Shanghai to South America, scattered like leaves before a storm. Those who stayed or who lived in other mainland European countries were to face the unimaginable horrors of 1939–45. But even before the outbreak of war, governments throughout Europe had begun to complain about the problems of Jewish immigrants and settlers. However, only Palestine accepted more refugee Jews than Britain. And in the British case, the difficulties of settlement were eased by the efforts of existing Jewish communities to bear the financial brunt of the settlements. But even then, there were British Jews who, like their forbears, feared that further Jewish settlement would aggravate the existing animosity towards Jews, a fear made worse by the activities of Mosley's Fascists.

There were echoes of more traditional objections to immigration. Trade unions, bothered by the consequences of the Depression and severely shaken by their defeat in 1926, feared that immigration would further threaten the livelihood of their members. Even professional organizations disliked Jewish settlement, more especially because so many German Jews were skilled professional men. Naturally enough, the popular press was ever ready to issue cautionary alarms about the dangers of immigration. In the words of the *Daily Express*, 'it would be to overload the basket'. Many of these concerns were reflections of genuine determination to safeguard sectional or trade interests. But it is easy to see how they could, quite easily, be transformed into a qualitatively different antagonism. Indeed, as the prospect of war became more likely, the question of Jewish refugees became a security matter, if only because they were German citizens. Bizarre as it may now seem, in 1938 M.I.5 reported to the Cabinet that

the Germans were anxious to inundate this country with Jews, with a view to creating a Jewish problem in the U.K.

This was an extraordinary reading of events; more revealing of the mentality of the security services than of the issues they were handling. And the perception of the Jews, as Germans and as a threat, was to be fully realized in the war years when thousands of aliens were rounded up and interned. The irony was that many thousands of people who had sought security and freedom in Britain found themselves behind barbed wire; those people, notably the blacks, who had been so disliked and subjected to such a host of indignities in the inter-war years, were to be greeted with a new-found welcome and amity. Black workers were henceforth important, Germans (even if Jews) the object of suspicion. The British were able quickly and unblushingly to change their mind and express utterly contrary responses. Of course, the exigencies of war undoubtedly demanded a number of previously inconceivable *voltes faces* (not least the offer of a united Ireland). To the victims of this change of heart – German Jews or British blacks – it was a change which, at best, invited the most cynical of responses.

In numerical terms, the settlement of aliens in Britain before 1939 did not threaten to alter the demographic balance, even if we include the continuing settlement of Irish. There was, after all, the countervailing factor of emigration *from* Britain to be considered. In the fifty years to 1931, for instance, an annual 56,000 emigrants quit Britain for the U.S.A. or Commonwealth countries – countries where healthy young men could easily find work, especially on the land. Indeed it was widely appreciated that the future of the Dominions could not be guaranteed *without* regular supplies of immigrant labour. The Depression, however, halted migrations to the U.S.A. and some Commonwealth countries, but Britons continued to quit their homes for life abroad, between 1931 and 1939 about 60,000 annually. But of course the debate about foreign settlement in Britain was not concerned with this outward flow. Indeed, the arguments (unlike those in the early years of the century) were rarely about numbers. Nonetheless it was, at least, a story infused with strands of prejudice – more especially a crude antisemitism which was to reveal itself, with more appalling consequences, as the war progressed.

6

The People's War, 1939–45

Many of the consequences of the Second World War are obvious and well known, if only because they survive to this day. But there were other complex changes which, though scarcely noticeable at the time, were to produce global transformations of the most fundamental kind. Long before war itself broke out in September 1939 more and more people had reconciled themselves to its inevitability, although few could have envisaged the enormous impact of the subsequent conflict. Even before the fighting in Europe erupted, it had become evident that the disputes between Nazi Germany and other Western European countries were markedly ideological, as well as the more obvious clash over boundaries. As the European war progressed, the ideological content of the struggle became clearer: a fight by the allies not merely against Nazi tyranny, but a fight for self-determination and liberty for subject peoples. It took no great imagination to see that the rhetoric which demanded the restitution of human and political rights throughout occupied Europe had equal force in imperial regions. What right had the British to demand freedom and self-government for, say, the Poles, and yet feel able to deny it to millions of Africans, Indians and many others? Notwithstanding the initial Russian support for the Nazis, once Russia belatedly sided with the allies in 1941, the ideological dimension of the war became even clearer. And this was compounded by the entry of the U.S.A. and the Japanese attacks on a string of colonial possessions in the Far East. There were, in many respects, a number of contradictions developing within the war. Were the British fighting to preserve their Asian empire while arguing a contrary theme in Europe? Were the Americans to help the British maintain that empire, and yet assist in the liberation of Europe? These and a host of major questions lurked behind the long-term strategies and the short-term exigencies of survival and battle.

Whatever the long-term results of the war, the British immediately appealed to the empire and dominions for the manpower,
foodstuffs and raw materials badly needed first to stave off defeat
and later to launch the counter-offensive. And as the German
armies fanned out rapidly across Europe, armies, governments and
simple refugees fled to the British Isles, safe across the English
Channel from the rapacious attack of the German army. Refugees
from all over Europe found themselves seeking a home in Britain,
or preparing for the eventual liberation of their homelands. Their
numbers, and exotic qualities, were augmented by the waves of
colonial and dominion troops which soon began to swell the armed
forces and the war industries.

Between 1939 and 1945 Britain experienced the most remarkable and large-scale migration of peoples in its history. It
was as if Britain had been rapidly converted into a giant transit
camp, and all this was in addition to the movement of millions
of British people, particularly the young, who were relocated to
safer zones. The result was that Britain in wartime became a
fascinating mix of nationalities and races. Contemporaries were
aware of the swift, physical sense of the mixing of nations and
peoples.

French sailors with their red pompoms and striped shirts, Dutch police
in black uniforms and grey-silver braid, the dragoon like mortar boards of
Polish officers, the smart grey of nursing units from Canada, the cerise
berets and sky-blue trimmings of the new parachute regiments, the scarlet
linings of our own nurses' cloaks, the vivid electric blue of Dominion air
forces, sandy bush hats and lion-coloured turbans, the prevalent Royal Air
Force blue, a few greenish-tinted Russian uniforms and the suave black
and gold of the Chinese navy.

And all this was in addition to the hundreds of thousands of U.S.
troops, many of them black, who descended on Britain from 1942.
By the late spring of 1944, in preparation for the D-Day landings,
the very great majority of foreign troops in Britain were American.
They left their own distinctive and indelible mark on a society
which lacked the glamour, the colour, the material well-being –
and the money – which invariably clung to the U.S. troops. In a
society beset by austerity, the Americans cut a style quite unlike

anything the British had ever experienced. Their material goods
were envied, but their purchasing power, and their appeal to British
women (who were starved both of their menfolk and material
glamour), often caused resentment. There was a great deal of resentment against the undoubted sexual appeal of American troops,
and it found its way into contemporary popular culture. According
to a wartime joke, utility knickers were useless; 'One Yank and
they're off' was the cry. It was common to denounce American
troops for a series of faults, more especially for being 'overpaid,
over-sexed and over here'. These, and other such quips, however
vulgar, were reflective of a smouldering envy among people quite
unaccustomed to the openness, the behaviour and the consumer
power of our U.S. allies.

The story of the massive settlements of foreign people in Britain
– settlements which were, eventually, to change certain aspects of
post-war society – had begun even before the outbreak of war
itself. As we have already seen, refugees, notably Jewish, had been
arriving in large numbers since 1933. Even the outbreak of war did
not prevent this flight. Indeed, as the Nazis conquered vast tracts
of Europe they were prepared, in the first two years of the war, to
allow some local Jews to leave, at a price. But the numbers involved
were a mere fraction of all the Jews menaced by the Nazis. Nonetheless the problem, in the early stages, was as much the refusal of
other governments to take in more Jews. The U.S.A., for instance,
despite its large Jewish population, took in only 37,000 in 1940. The
British, who apparently had plenty of room in their colonies, considered diverting Jewish refugees to far-flung reaches of the world;
they considered Guiana, Ethiopia, the Philippines and Australia.
Even the Americans thought along similar lines, considering the
prospects of dispatching Jews to Angola, Alaska and the Dominican
Republic. But the doors into the U.K. and the U.S.A. were virtually
closed. Only 10,000 Jews managed to squeeze into the U.K. between
1939 and 1945. It would be disingenuous not to point to Nazi
persecution for the prime cause of the miserable sufferings of
European Jewry, but it would also be less than honest to overlook
the part played by other governments. Long before the massive
killings began, the doors had been slammed in the face of desperate
Jews. In the words of the most recent historian of this vile story, 'as

the escape routes were sealed so too was the fate of the majority of the Jews imprisoned in Nazi Europe'.

Those lucky enough to have escaped tò Britain before 1939 suddenly found their position transformed by the declaration of war in September. Now they were enemy aliens. The Foreign Office worried that there might be a difficulty 'in distinguishing the sheep from the goats'. Tribunals established to vet all such aliens had interned 528 and placed restrictions on 8,356 by January 1940. The process was too lax, too sympathetic for the liking of growing numbers of critics, especially those newspapers who had made their positions so clear in the anti-Jewish campaigns forty years earlier. With the end of the 'phoney war' and the German conquest of the Low Countries and France in early 1940, public feeling swiftly changed. Alarmist newspapers and the more extreme M.P.s began to utter thoughts. 'You cannot trust any Boche at any time,' was the comment of one M.P. 'Would it not be far better [asked another] to intern the lot and then pick out the good ones?' The crisis of 1940, the formation of Churchill's government and the gathering mood of defiant desperation led to a rapid change in policy towards aliens. Within weeks, 30,000 people had been interned, many of them in the Isle of Man. In a hysterical climate, politicians, newspapers and the security services nosed around for the much-feared 'fifth column', and found it somewhere in the ranks of the refugees who had fled from German persecutions.

The bizarre, and even absurd, incidents surrounding intern-ment give some indication of the quixotic qualities which remained its highlight. Italian restaurateurs, resident in the U.K. for a life-time and who had fought with the British in the first war, now found themselves interned. C.I.D. men walked into Hampstead Public Library and ordered all Germans and Austrians to follow them. Many other incidents would have been laughable if not so tragic and absurd. Anti-Nazi activists, secure in Britain, were imprisoned. So too were many others. In the words of Bernard Wasserstein, 'German socialist politicians, former inmates of concentration camps, an official of the Dutch government, and a Norwegian general were all arrested.' One man interned had lived in Britain since the age of three. It is important to recall the very real fears of invasion and of internal treachery, but it is equally hard not to suggest that the authorities were over-reacting in their urge to 'collar the lot'. Furthermore, public opinion un-questionably supported the widespread internments; critics of the policy were initially few and unheeded. Many internees were shipped overseas where they could do less 'harm', though there were scandalous tales of maltreatment and robbery by their captors en route. One sorry result of this shipping overseas was the drown-ing of internees in a torpedoed boat in the Atlantic. This, and mounting criticism from many quarters, led to a political and public change of heart.

By 1941 more and more internees were being released, but while they were treated better, there was a resistance to allowing further refugees into the country. It is true that none who managed to arrive here was turned back – but it is equally true that many, many more, anxious to leave occupied Europe for Britain, were discouraged or refused. Jews from Luxembourg and Vichy France, for instance, who asked to be admitted to Britain or British colonies were simply refused. Most were later deported to Poland, to share the ghastly fate of Poland's Jews. Nor was this a matter simply of numbers, for in 1940 the British government had seriously con-sidered allowing in upwards of 300,000 Dutch and Belgians. But the same open and generous policy was never countenanced for Europe's Jews. This was not simply a matter of antisemitism in official bureaucratic circles – though it was there in abundance – so much as 'the limited horizons of bureaucratic thinking'. Whatever the reason, its consequences were to be catastrophic for many thousands of Jews who, faced by closed doors to Britain, were soon to find themselves herded into the sealed trains which took legions of innocent people to their deaths in Eastern Europe. While the British congratulated themselves on their distinctive liberties – the national hymn concluding with the bizarre line 'Britons never never shall be slaves' – they had few compunctions in refusing to bestow their liberties on others, choosing instead to seal the fate of thousands. However difficult the times, however pressed the government and people of Britain in 1940–41, it is hard to look back on the policy towards Europe's Jews without a sense of mor-tification. And to make it worse, few people today know the truth of those events. It is undoubtedly true that the nation was, collectively, fighting for its life, but it would not have added to Britain's dangers to provide a home for Nazi victims.

Before the easing of the severest restrictions on internees there had been a host of scandalous incidents; violence against the persons and properties of Italians, Germans and Austrians. But naturally enough the ranks of the internees contained an unusual number of talented people – doctors, scientists and the like – all of whom were vitally necessary to the war effort. Other internees put their abilities to good use in a more informal way: the Amadeus Quartet was formed in an internment camp, as was an informal 'university'. These and a host of other ventures provided some indication of the remarkable resources of talent and skill waiting to be tapped by a more appreciative and realistic policy towards internees.

If refugees were rebuffed and kept away, Britain was undoubtedly in need of major supplies of skills and manpower. Of the tens of thousands of foreign troops to arrive, the first were the defeated Poles, many of whom stayed after the war. The Polish armed forces had been devastated in 1939, their fleeing ranks of survivors scattering throughout Europe and the Middle East. Of these only 17,000 arrived in Britain. But from this nucleus there was reconstructed an important and valiant Polish army which was to distinguish itself in the later invasion of Europe. But even the qualities of the Poles paled in comparison with the American troops who formed the very great majority of allied troops in Britain by 1944. Few who recall the dramatic impact of the arrival of U.S. troops failed to be impressed by their individual and collective appearance. 'How different they looked from our own jumble-sale champions, beautifully clothed in smoothed khaki, as fine in cut and quality as a British officer's . . .' Americans drank dry the local pubs, poured whisky into their beer, courted, wooed or seduced local women, bestowing on a deprived people a material largesse unknown even in peacetime. There was among many Americans an unhappy tendency to treat Britain more as occupied territory than as an ally, but without them – and the apparently endless hardware disgorged by U.S. industries – the war could not have been won. Germany was to be ground between the raw strength and tenacity of the Russians on one side and the supreme power and confidence of the Americans on the other. And for the best part of three years, before the invasion of Europe in the summer of 1944, Britain played host to this extraordinary gathering of foreign, largely American, personnel.

Britain was a wartime host to more than mere fighting men. The governments of Poland, Norway, Holland, Belgium, Luxembourg and the Free French were based in Britain; so too were various royal families, and the remnants of whatever armed forces and shipping the defeated Europeans were able to snatch from the maw of the German armies. However varied this foreign presence, it was above all the Americans who caught the eye – if only for simple numerical reasons. Not surprisingly, they elicited mixed feelings. There was a pronounced anti-American sentiment, especially (and significantly) among British men; a survey of 1943 showed that only a third of respondents spoke favourably of American troops. Politically, both the left and right had their own reasons for disliking the Americans. Yet, however strong this dislike, the sheer pressure of American influence proved to be irresistible.

One striking legacy of the overwhelming American presence was a confirmation of the Americanization of popular culture, long in progress but now compounded and made more immediate by many of the styles, tastes and cultural forms which had, until 1939, been mere shadows or images. From the 1920s American music and dance had begun gradually to displace 'indigenous' popular musicality, a process accentuated by the impact of talking pictures and the proliferation of wireless sets. American jazz and swing, American singers and bands, even American clothing styles and American films became the basic cultural diet of millions of Britons. This was a process which was accelerated after 1942 when U.S. troops imported these cultural tastes into the heart of Britain – even into the remotest rural areas where they established new bases. They had their own radio stations, their own newspapers and films, even their own distinctive foodstuffs and drinks, much of which inevitably filtered through to the locals. In a society starved of both commonplace enjoyments and even of the basic needs of life, all things American seemed irresistibly seductive to many. Of course it is also true that there was a contrary British tradition which eschewed all manifestations of American culture as attributes of common vulgarity. Less demanding folk, however, were often over-whelmed by it. (As a child in Oldham the author was exposed to the full power and persuasiveness of U.S. culture in the form of the American floating soap which bobbed around in the zinc bath. A society which could make its soap float was clearly one to be envied.)

The Americans also brought distinct problems, none more troublesome than the racial discrimination which was common in all branches of the U.S. armed forces. Black servicemen were provided with their own separate social facilities on U.S. bases, while their career prospects were severely limited within all of the services. Indeed the discrimination within the U.S. forces was merely a reflection of the discrimination rife in U.S. society at the same time. In Britain, black troops were even expected to pursue separate and distinct social lives and not to mix with the white troops. Not surprisingly this led to a series of clashes on and off the bases. It was natural that British voluntary services would follow the U.S. lead and make separate social provision (canteens, for instance) for black and white U.S. troops. It was only a matter of time before the discrimination exercised within the U.S. forces found its way into wider British society. Indeed by late 1942 the Labour M.P. Tom Driberg raised the issue in the Commons, ques-tioning Churchill about 'the introduction in some parts of Britain of discrimination against negro troops'. Officially, the wartime government was opposed to it, but preferred to do nothing to inhibit it, not surprising perhaps since segregation was widespread and officially recognized within the U.S. forces.

Whatever officialdom might say, blacks were unquestionably exposed to a series of racist insults in the latter part of the war. One American commanding officer took to providing his black troops with a covering note in the hope of easing their diffi-culties.

Pte .... is a soldier in the United States army and it is necessary that he sometimes has a meal, which he has on occasions, found difficult to obtain. I would be grateful if you would look after him.

Nor did people care to differentiate between black U.S. and West

Indian personnel. Just as in 1914, the West Indies, along with other
colonies, responded promptly and in strength to the war effort.
Troops, labourers and skilled men from the Caribbean joined the
armed services or war industries. In fact by the end of hostilities
some 8,000 West Indians had joined the services, 1,000 of them in
R.A.F. flight crews. In fact the Central Office of Information
produced a pamphlet, *West Indies Towards Victory*, with lavish
illustrations and biographical details of some of the West Indians
in the armed forces and industrial occupations. There were also
small numbers of West Indian women who volunteered for military
or civilian work in wartime Britain. For many of the West Indians,
the prospects of life in Britain, however bleak and austere, were
preferable to the chronic economic problems and the unemployment of the Caribbean. As recently as 1938, the region had been
wracked by serious labour troubles in a number of islands. Nonetheless, a year later, the imperial power was able to benefit from
the undoubted groundswell of patriotic feeling for the British
cause.

The 'colour bar' in the armed services was lifted for the duration
of the war, and governors in the islands were instructed as how
best to recruit industrial and military manpower. Above all else,
the British needed certain types of skilled men for military training.
Throughout, however, the Colonial Office displayed that profound
racist view of black abilities and efforts which acted as a brake on
the initial efforts to recruit West Indian workers. Once West Indians
had got past that hurdle they faced a host of practical and racial
obstacles in Britain. Provided with basic and often inadequate
facilities, they were plunged into the cold austerity of northern
industrial cities, confronted by alien social conditions and often
discriminated against at work. The attractions of Britain were very
limited indeed, especially when the war, and the establishment of
military bases in the West Indies, began to create employment in
the Caribbean itself.

There were, then, contradictory forces at work helping to shape
the direction and nature of West Indian settlement in wartime
Britain. The need for labour in Britain, more especially skilled
labour, was tempered by the commonplace racism within civil
service and administration cadres that regularly placed obstacles in

the way of black settlement in Britain. And anyone in doubt of this central and seminal fact has only to consult the abundance of documentation in the Public Record Office. Notwithstanding such problems, blacks poured into wartime Britain. Some 900 came from Honduras for forestry work in Scotland, hundreds of Jamaican technicians worked in munitions and chemicals, while many more worked in the merchant marine. Seven hundred Indians were even brought to Britain for industrial training. Quite simply the manpower of the empire, like its raw materials, was deployed as thoroughly as was thought prudent and practical to fight the all-consuming war.

West Indians who spent these years in Britain often comment that whatever discrimination they suffered was accentuated after the arrival of black U.S. troops, and the U.S. institutionalization and promotion of discrimination after 1942. Nonetheless, it was common enough even earlier than this. When in 1939 the nation's children were evacuated to safer areas, away from the major conurbations, black children faced serious problems of rejection. As the war developed blacks faced growing discrimination at social events. Black nursing staff were turned away from ENSA entertainments. When they complained, twenty were arrested at the orders of a senior officer: 'Arrest the black monkeys for disobedience of order.' West Indians in the R.A.F. complained of being unable to gain admission to local canteens. One uniformed West Indian turned away from a dance retorted by refusing to attend his Home Guard duties. In the subsequent legal arguments, the man's initial fine was reduced to a farthing. The words of the Recorder were pertinent:

People come over here to risk their lives on behalf of what they proudly call the Mother Country, and he considered it impertinence for any country to accept the aid of coloured people from any part of the world and then to say 'our laws do not enable us to deal with you in terms of complete equality'.

The problem remained how best to guarantee and implement such high-principled claims in a society which, at so many levels, exhibited contrary sentiments.

The difficulties facing blacks in wartime Britain were clear and undeniable, though the social reality could normally be obscured by reference to official attitudes. Yet even such official denunciations of discrimination were at odds with what we now know to have been the widespread antipathy and racism within official circles. To tackle some of the more practical problems facing black workers the West Indian cricketer, Learie Constantine, then resident in Lancashire, was appointed as a welfare officer. Ironically he became the centre of a *cause célèbre* in 1943–4 when, following the refusal of the Imperial Hotel in London to allow him in because of his colour, he successfully prosecuted a case for compensation. In their defence the hotel claimed that the presence of '200 or 300 American and Colonial officers and other ranks . . .' might lead to a strained atmosphere. They had in Constantine not merely a prominent sportsman, but a man of extraordinary presence and probity. It was an incident which might have caused justifiable anger; instead, Constantine conducted himself with a dignity and gravitas which impressed the Court. Summing up, the judge remarked,

Mr Constantine bore himself with modesty and dignity and dealt with the question with intelligence and truth. He was not concerned to be vindictive or malicious, but was obviously affected by the indignity and humiliation which had been put on him, and caused him distress and inconvenience which he justifiably resented.

One particular issue of the black presence in wartime Britain caused notable concern and friction. But, again, it was a well-worn theme which had existed for centuries in black–white relations, namely sexual liaisons. For whatever reason, the jealousy and passions aroused by the sexual or affectionate relations between blacks (mainly servicemen) and local British women created fierce opposition in many quarters. Of course this had been a common fact in Britain (and elsewhere of course) since the seventeenth century and earlier. Notwithstanding this overt antipathy, there were legions of women who formed permanent, or transient, relations with black troops, often following them from town to town or base to base. In one famous incident near Bristol, a crowd of young women, anxious to see their black boyfriends and singing the popular song 'Don't Fence Me In', broke down the base fencing and enjoyed

their company for some hours before order was restored by rein-
forcements of military police.

It should now be clear that the experience of blacks in wartime
Britain was remarkably varied. In terms of contribution to the war
effort, there could be no denying the major impact of blacks. In
many respects, the Second World War, like the First, served to
illustrate the contradictions within the empire. Colonial possessions
which were pressing for change – for reform, economic improvement and even independence in the late 1930s – rallied to the
distant war in a quite remarkable way. Men whose forbears had
been slaves were now to be found in their hundreds flying bombing
missions over Germany, on behalf of the nation which denied
them their own full democratic rights in their distant homelands.
Despite the many contradictions in the relationship between blacks
and whites, blacks also encountered a host of private acts of kind-
ness, friendship and generosity: taxi-drivers who refused to take
fares from black servicemen; homes voluntarily opened to passing
West Indians. Perhaps most ironic of all, white air crews often
wanted black personnel on their flights for it was widely thought
that they brought luck.

Peace brought its own distinct problems, many of them exacerbated by the unrealistic expectations inevitably generated by
the rhetoric of wartime. Clearly, Britain no longer had the need for
its extraordinary military and wartime industrial manpower, and
there followed as rapid a dismantling as could easily be managed.
West Indian contract workers were shipped back home; the bulk
of R.A.F. groundcrew were similarly discharged at home. Flight
crews, however, were demobbed in Britain and many of them were
encouraged to stay and pursue university studies with special
government grants. The black intellectual coterie which had made
such an impact in the late 1930s was poised for a new venture in
1945. The war had of course helped their cause, if only because it
exposed so many West Indians and Africans to social experiences
and the wider world which would, under the proper conditions,
break down the old colonial system. West Africans returned to
London in large numbers to pursue their studies; by 1947 there
were some 2,000 there. They, in conjunction with revived black
publications, formed a new basis for the rapid development of

post-war African nationalism. Thus, British Africa began the painful process of releasing itself from formal imperial control – in the austere conditions of post-war Britain. But after 1945 it had the added bonus of a sympathetic (i.e. anti-imperial) administration in the form of Attlee's Labour government. While the Africans sought to secure their own freedom, many of those West Indians who had spent the war years in Britain looked forward to a future not in the Caribbean, but in the country they had made their home in wartime.

Many people had no choice about their post-war homes. The turmoil of 1945 threw up millions of refugees uprooted by the cruellest and most traumatic of wartime conditions. Millions of people, many of them penniless, possessionless and without families, were to be found in camps scattered throughout Europe. And as the famous 'Iron Curtain' – the name devised by Churchill in 1946 – clamped shut, dividing east from west, millions of Eastern Europeans resolved not to return to their homes in East Germany, Hungary, Poland, Russia or the Baltic states. By May 1945 Europe faced an unprecedented and quite staggering refugee problem: more than 40 million people had become refugees; seven million had no country to turn to. Large numbers were to find their way to Britain. Indeed, one major consequence of the war was that Britain began to receive the settlements of alien people and colonial citizens on a scale and at a pace which had never previously been experienced. It was of course impossible to realize it at the time, but the war was ultimately responsible for many of the demographic changes which took place in Britain in the post-war years.

7

The Post-war World 1945–62

In the summer of 1945 mainland Europe was a veritable refugee camp, with millions of people encamped across the ravaged continent awaiting repatriation to their homelands. The practical difficulties were awesome for, in addition to the weight of numbers involved, conditions in Europe made it complicated and difficult to move people around. Roads, railways, cities and ports were all in ruins and the equipment needed for transport was generally inadequate. On top of that, food and fuel were in short supply. It was an unimaginable problem, but the good weather of the summer of 1945 and the temporary honeymoon between the western allies and the Russians eased some of the difficulties. But this began to change. As the winter set in, accentuating the difficulties, relations between east and west also began to freeze. It was in these fearful conditions that a new expression entered the English language. D.P.s (displaced persons) quickly became part of the vernacular, often used abusively to describe so many of Europe's wretched victims of war.

Some 1½ million Eastern Europeans and Russians refused repatriation; they and a varied collection of other uprooted Europeans were to be found scattered throughout Europe, all in need of short-term care and long-term settlement. The most traumatized were the Jews, the small numbers of whom had managed to survive the murder camps. Not surprisingly, few could bear the thought of picking up the broken threads of their lives in countries which had so willingly offered them as sacrificial victims to Nazi ideology. Something like 750,000 European Jews sought to break from the scenes of their misery and to begin life afresh in another land. The problem, however, was which country would accept them.

Britain was immediately and closely involved, and the Anglo-American committee established to find a home for Europe's sur-

viving Jews concluded in April 1946 that only Palestine offered a
reasonable home for the numbers concerned. As a British mandate,
the problem of Jewish immigration into Palestine thus became a
major and sensitive political and diplomatic issue for the British.
Indeed, the British refusal of admission to wartime Jewish refugees,
and the attendant military activity and loss of life, had already
soured relations between Britain and Jewish communities in Palestine and elsewhere. Of course the British also felt obliged towards
the Arab citizens of Palestine and the consequent conflict of interests, accentuated by the rise of effective Zionist organizations in
North America and Europe, created that unhappy sequence of
events which prefaced the foundation of the state of Israel in 1948.
When the British quit Palestine, they left behind few friends among
either Jews or Arabs. This is not the place to document the founding
of the state of Israel, but the events leading up to it reveal a number
of points relevant to this argument.

Firstly, the flight of surviving Jews from Europe was a direct
cause of the war. It was one specific and traumatic illustration of a
wider phenomenon which was to have a direct impact on Britain,
namely that the war, in its wider setting, loosened the ties of untold
legions of people to their birthplaces and homelands. Secondly, the
British policy towards refugee Jews was shaped in large measure
by the complex problems of exercising the Palestine mandate. And
thirdly, the British response both to European Jews and to their
possible settlement in Palestine was permeated, in official bureaucratic and political circles, by a pronounced antisemitism which
had characterized British dealings with European Jews since the
1880s. As the violence in Palestine worsened, the submerged British
antisemitic traditions became ever more obvious. When Jewish
resistance fighters killed British soldiers, it became possible and
even respectable to utter the most outrageous of antisemitic re-
marks – in Parliament, in the press or in public. In September 1944
the head of a Foreign Office section had remarked, 'In my opinion
a disproportionate amount of the time of this office is wasted in
dealing with these wailing Jews.' Such sentiments, widespread and
widely expressed in the upper reaches of British government,
formed the basis for the flowering of post-war antisemitism. And
after the unhappy experiences of governing Palestine, the British

were to experience a furthering of such antisemitism which, in its turn, was bequeathed to a later generation.

Between 1946 and 1951 more than one third of a million European Jews migrated to Palestine/Israel. While more than 120,000 went to the U.S.A. and Canada in these same years, only 1,000 settled in Britain. It is perfectly obvious that, in simple numerical terms, Britain was *not* faced by a 'problem' of Jewish immigration comparable, say, with the last quarter of the nineteenth century. And yet antisemitism was still rife. This was not surprising if only because antisemitism had been an age-old phenomenon in Britain. But it also illustrates a more significant phenomenon. The political and public sentiments expressed about Jews in the 1940s were influenced and shaped to a marked degree by a distant, rather than a domestic, sequence of events. Just as in the eighteenth century slavery and the slave trade had moulded responses to the blacks, now Palestine shaped reactions to the Jews. For an imperial power – and Britain remained the world's pre-eminent imperial power throughout these years – the perception of subject, alien or immigrant peoples was often filtered through the distorting lenses of imperial dominance or control.

There were, however, problems of alien settlement of a more immediate and domestic nature. Of the 1½ million Poles scattered throughout Western Europe, many thousands now found themselves refugees in Britain. Their prospects of returning home were soon curtailed by the control of the Soviet Union over much of Eastern Europe and the establishment of a puppet communist regime in Poland itself. Among Poles in exile in Britain there was a bitter and frustrated response; sometimes even debarred from returning home, most were obliged to wait cautiously for a change of heart and regime. (It is scarcely worth repeating an obvious point, but the survivors still await this change.) Britain was thus to become a reluctant home for thousands of Poles, anxious to return to their own country, but who found their route blocked by an impassive regime and its Russian allies. Instead of going home, thousands of Poles and other Eastern Europeans put down new roots in Britain; in the textile towns of Lancashire, the mining communities in South Wales and even in the remoter communities of rural England and Scotland. In time, of course, many moved away from their original jobs and homes and were eventually to be found in most parts of Britain, enjoying varying degrees of economic prosperity. Initially, however, they were offered the alternatives of work in those occupations desperately in need of labour, notably in mining and farming. Indeed the British devised recruiting schemes to attract Poles and others to settle in Britain and to fill the labour vacuum which developed in the early years of peace. European refugees were plucked from the camps and put to work in hospitals and factories, a scheme described by the Minister of Labour as 'partly an act of charity and partly to suit ourselves'. By 1950 more than 100,000 workers – Lithuanians, Ukrainians, Poles, Latvians and Yugoslavs – had been imported to add to those stranded in Britain in 1945. By the mid 1950s, however, upwards of one half of the recruited labour had moved on, to the U.S.A. or to other Commonwealth countries.

The largest group of Europeans in Britain was the Poles – some 157,300 by 1949 – many of whom resettled in Britain after the war. With a powerful national identity and a strong church, the Poles re-created in Britain many of the institutions and rituals common to life in their homeland. And this was specifically encouraged by the British government, through the Polish Resettlement Act, which even allowed the foundation of Polish hospitals, schools and a variety of other social and welfare organizations. There was thus created that social infra-structure which sought to preserve not merely the language but also the various attributes of Polish society, but in exile. The Poles and the other Eastern European workers in the late 1940s were in fact the only group since the 1905 Aliens Act to be recruited and settled from Europe, notwithstanding the restrictions under which they had to live and work. This came about as much through economic need on the part of the British as anything else, though this is not to deny the genuine obligation felt both by the wartime and the post-war Labour government towards the Poles, in return for the Poles' distinctive wartime effort and in acknowledgement of their special difficulties. It is also worth pointing out that it was the attack on Poland which ultimately forced the British and French to declare war on Germany.

The Irish, unlike the Poles, had become so much a part of the mainland population that it seems scarcely worth repeating the facts of their migration. At the outbreak of the war, Irish neutrality had prompted British restrictions on further Irish immigration. The British, however, were even more dependent on the willingness of the Irish to work on the mainland in wartime industries, to say nothing of the substantial number of Irish volunteers in the British armed forces. During the war almost 65,000 Irish (9,000 of them women) travelled to Britain under formal governmental schemes, although 50 per cent of them later returned to Ireland. With peace, the immigration restrictions were lifted, although the British government, faced by a chronic labour shortage in certain key industries, continued its recruiting schemes in Ireland. But as the economy slowly returned to normal, industries began successfully to recruit their own specialized or unskilled labour forces.

Although the war years had seen moderation and control in the flow of Irish into Britain, numbers picked up in the late 1940s. Between 1946 and 1951, an estimated 100,000 entered from Ireland. By 1959 this had risen to an estimated 352,600, although researchers have pointed out the flaws in the available statistics and the system used for establishing them. Nonetheless, if we put the figures in perspective and contrast Irish settlement in the 1940s with the migrations of exactly a century before, we can begin to appreciate both the size of the nineteenth-century migrations and the reduced migration of the 1940s. This is not to deny the importance or significance of the Irish presence by the mid-twentieth century. There were, after all, 1 million Irish people living in Britain in the 1950s. By 1951 the census recorded more Irish-born living in Britain than at any previous period. The characteristics of that Irish presence remained remarkably familiar however. Most of them were to be found in the major industrial urban areas of London, the Midlands, the North and Scotland. Indeed more than half of all the Irish people in mid-twentieth-century Britain were to be found in only six conurbations. Not only that, but within any particular town or city the Irish were to be found concentrated in specific locales. This is not surprising, however, for like many other migrants (no matter how vast the distance from their homelands) the Irish settled close to relatives, friends, neighbours, or merely friends of friends. The Irish naturally gravitated towards people they knew, to those who could provide something familiar and recognizable in an alien world. There was nothing distinctively Irish about this; it was true of Lancastrian country folk settling in the new factory towns of the nineteenth century; it was true of migrants into eighteenth-century London, be they foreign-born blacks or rural people. And it was to be true of newer Commonwealth immigrants into Britain in the 1950s.

It needs to be stressed – for it has long-term consequences in the debate about post-war immigration – that Irish settlers in the decade up to 1951 were not merely the traditional immigrants in search of work. Britain did indeed provide employment opportunities, but the important point to remember is that the British, through various government or sponsored agencies, actively recruited foreign labour. Labour was at a premium throughout the war as the nation re-equipped itself for a major war effort, and then in peacetime in the initial painful readjustment to normalcy. Workers were employed from Poland, Eastern Europe and Ireland, and even further afield. It was these latter arrivals who were not merely to affect the demographic face of mainland Britain, but to create debates about immigration and settlement which were quite new and distinctive.

Many West Indians were so attracted to Britain that many of them stayed after wartime service. Others had no option but to return home, for demobilization took place in their home territories. However unhappy the wartime experience, it nonetheless provided an alternative way of life for many thousands of West Indians. In fact, black West Indians had for a long time been a migrating people. Since the building of the Panama Canal in the 1880s, West Indians – notably Jamaicans – had quit their homeland in their thousands simply to find work. Many others travelled north to Cuba and to the U.S.A. but this latter escape route was effectively sealed by new immigration controls in 1924. Of course the basic reasons for these migrations were economic and demographic. Jamaica's in particular was an expanding population, growing at a rate which could not easily be contained by the economy. So poor were opportunities and conditions at home that it proved very hard for many West Indians returning from wartime service to readjust to the limitations afforded by their homelands; and future prospects were bleak. Britain, for all its inhospitable qualities and its cold and dreary winters, could at least offer the prospects of work.

Legally it was easy to migrate back to Britain. With a legal right of entry not to be ended until the 1962 Immigrants Act, West Indians simply needed money for the journey. Initially, the migrations to Britain were irregular, partly because there were few regular shipping services. Soon, however, these services began to expand to satisfy growing demand. Within Jamaica, a new network of travel agencies sprang up throughout the island, with their headquarters in Kingston, the capital. Extensive advertising and the offer of credit facilities to pay for the travel soon attracted customers who would otherwise have been unable even to contemplate emigration. Thus, the great bulk of emigration was privately organized and privately financed. There were, however, some striking exceptions to this rule.

Barbados, an island no larger than the Isle of Wight, had had since slave days a densely populated society with little scope for economic or demographic expansion. As migration to Britain developed in the late 1940s, the Barbadian authorities (still, of course, not independent of British colonial control) provided loans and assistance for local migrants to travel to Britain. In other cases, British organizations actually recruited West Indian labour in the islands. London Transport, a number of British hotels and restaurants, regional hospital boards and the British Transport Commission all made prominent recruiting drives in the Caribbean to satisfy their own particular labour shortages. London Transport sent recruiting teams, first to Ireland, and in 1956 to Barbados, a visit which led to the creation of an elaborate recruiting scheme in that island, all encouraged and assisted by the Barbadian government.

However oppressive conditions in the Caribbean islands, the crucial determining factor in West Indian immigration into Britain was the British shortage of labour. It was widely known throughout the West Indies that work was there for the taking. It was less well known, however, that West Indians might expect to be demoted to a level below their skills or experience; they were normally used at a lower, and therefore cheaper, level of attainment and importance than they would have a right to expect in their homeland. Nonetheless, the crucial point is that when Britain needed labour up to the late 1950s, West Indians were available to satisfy that demand.

By late 1958, London Transport employed almost 4,000 black workers, about one quarter of whom had been recruited directly from the Caribbean. A welfare officer was even appointed to safeguard their interests on arrival in Britain. In the initial years of post-war migrations from the West Indies, most of the migrants were men. Women and children tended to come at a later stage when their male spouse or father had established a new home and a secure job. Throughout the 1950s then, the proportion of women and children among West Indian immigrants began to increase, to offset the male dominance of the early years of settlement (though it was on nothing like the scale of subsequent Indian and Pakistani male-dominated immigration).

The West Indians were not the only people to settle in post-war Britain in significant numbers. In the 1930s there had been small but noticeable pockets of Indian seamen living in some of the major seaports. Others were recruited during the war, much like the West Indians, to work in wartime industries. In Birmingham, for example, which had an Indian population of 100 in 1939 (including twenty doctors and students) the Indian population had grown tenfold, to stand at 1,000 in 1945, the bulk being former sailors who had resettled in local industries. By 1953 the Indo-Pakistani population of Birmingham had doubled again and was 2,000 strong. But it was only after that year that emigration from the sub-continent began to make an impact on British cities. And as more and more settled, the British government began to put pressure on the Indian and Pakistani governments to exercise tighter control over the allocation of passports, which was, with finance, the key to resettlement in Britain. Even before the Commonwealth Immigrants Act of 1962 the restrictions in the issuing of local passports had ensured that the uneducated and unskilled were no longer able to travel to Britain, unless they were dependants of settlers already here.

Calculating the numbers from the sub-continent has proved difficult for students of immigration. There is no doubt that the economic attractions which lured West Indians served also to attract ever more Indians and Pakistanis to Britain. And throughout the 1950s the numbers grew apace, both in relation to economic prospects and as the early arrivals provided British contacts, a source of money, or a new family base. Immigration once more revealed its self-generating qualities; of being able to create a natural, and understandable, gravitational pull for new migrants. The precise number of immigrants remains unclear. By 1955 there were perhaps fewer than 11,000 Indian and Pakistanis; by 1958–9 this had grown to between 50,000 and 55,000. By early 1960, it was calculated that there were between 70–100,000, although the imprecision of these estimates ought to caution us against being dogmatic about the phenomenon. Nonetheless, it is clear that Indian and Pakistani settlement had grown significantly throughout the 1950s. While the official figure stood at 50,000 in 1960, Indian and Pakistani officials were generally agreed that the real figure was much higher. It is hardly surprising that the topic of immigration would invite unusually varied political comments. In fact the response to this immigration was not unlike the response to Jewish immigration at the turn of the century; the very uncertainty about the numbers involved invited a cavalier approach to immigration statistics from those who stood to gain political capital from the debate.

The politics of immigration will be dealt with elsewhere, but the heightened debate about immigration from 1960 onwards served to accelerate the rate and the numbers of immigrants landing in Britain. Although the mid-1950s boom in job vacancies had effectively dried up by 1960, two factors above all else served to increase immigration. Firstly a substantial number of those who had settled in the 1950s had left their families in the homeland. It was therefore natural and just that dependants should, when the time was right, join their menfolk. This created problems in that the authorities had to decide which dependants they would allow into the country. Societies with different patterns of betrothal, marriage and family relationships created difficulties for British Home Office officials, and for the law itself, with a consequent friction between immigrants and the host society. This was especially so among Indians and Pakistanis, where the proportion of women among the early settlers in the 1950s was low. Among Sikhs in Southall in the late 1950s, for instance, it was as low as 4 per cent. And it was even

lower among Pakistanis in Bradford in the early 1960s. Not surprisingly the young men who formed the very great majority of
these communities wished to be re-united with their families as
soon as was economically convenient. As limitation and control of
immigrants began to be discussed with seriousness, it was only
natural that men should seek to bring relations to Britain before
any new law made that task more difficult, if not impossible.

The evidence from the census returns of 1951 and 1961 enables us
to plot with some accuracy the nature and degree of immigration
into Britain during the 1950s. Whereas in 1951 there had been in
Britain an estimated 30,800 Indians, 5,000 Pakistanis and 15,300
West Indians, a decade later the figures stood at 81,400, 24,900 and
171,800 respectively. The numbers of immigrants from the Far East
had shown a similar growth, from 12,000 to 29,600, and from West
Africa from 5,600 to 19,800. The total 'coloured' population had
increased from 74,500 to 336,600. But the largest immigrant group
was still the Irish. Moreover, the population of immigrants
remained small, though this is not to deny that in those communities to which they naturally gravitated and settled they had
begun to register an important demographic impact. While it is
true that more than half of what constituted the coloured population had come from the West Indies, it needs also to be stressed
that it was smaller by far than the total number of *aliens* living in
Britain of whom there were 415,700 in England and Wales in 1961.

The census figures, spaced as they are by decades, can prove
deceptive; they fail to measure the short-term changes in patterns
of migration and settlement. A closer look at other figures reveals
some equally telling evidence. In eighteen months between 1961
and 1962, immigration into Britain was greater than in the previous
five years, a factor to be explained solely by the threat of imminent
controls. Reaching its peak in 1961, immigration was, from 1 July
1962, subject to new and increasingly stringent regulations. Thereafter, the settlement of people into Britain became a reflection of
governmental policy rather than of economic and social attractions
of life in Britain. Until the early 1960s the force of economics – the
real or imagined economic benefits of life in Britain – attracted
immigrants from the Caribbean and India and Pakistan. Thereafter,
however, the forces were utterly transformed. The debate about

immigration in 1960–62, more especially the more forceful arguments in favour of control (and even repatriation), served to compound the very forces they wished to restrict or stop. The debate
about and around the Commonwealth Immigrants Act served
dramatically to increase the rate of arrivals.

The events of 1960 and after were, then, extraordinary, a distortion of patterns of migration which had evolved and been encouraged since 1945. Of course it would be wrong to imagine that
this process of immigration was uniquely 'coloured'; it was not.
Between 1945 and the late 1950s, for example, more than one third
of a million European nationals migrated to the United Kingdom,
overwhelmingly for work opportunities. Moreover, it is agreed on
all sides that despite this – and Irish and 'coloured' immigration in
these same years – one of the key difficulties facing the British
economy was the shortage of labour. This was all to change not
merely with the advent of stringent regulations but with that
downturn in the economy from which the nation has not yet recovered. Britain did not face such economic problems alone. There
was a shortage of labour throughout Western Europe as these
varied societies sought to reconstruct economies shattered by the
war. Often, however, they employed labour schemes which were,
from their inception, not only transient but also provided for the
return of the immigrant workers to their homelands. The 'guest'
worker helped to rebuild the economies of Germany and Holland
and, unlike the Commonwealth immigrants to Britain, they
occupied a different social and legal position. This is not to claim
that no other European country shared the pattern of immigration
to be found in Britain. Other post-imperial countries experienced
similar patterns with all their attendant difficulties, notably the
French with their North African possessions and the Dutch with
their Javanese colonies.

Given that immigrants came for work, the location of immigrant
settlement is more easily understood. By the early 1960s almost
three quarters of all immigrants from the New Commonwealth
were housed in the major conurbations: London, the West Midlands, South-East Lancashire, Merseyside, Tyneside and West
Yorkshire. London contained almost one half of the nation's total
immigrant population. Moreover, the new arrivals – those admitted

after the restrictions of 1962 – followed the paths of the earlier settlers. By the mid 1960s, the patterns of settlement remained substantially unchanged. Since new arrivals headed for the established communities naturally the concentration of immigrants in certain communities began to increase. It was from these demographic and urban outlines that the more recent history of the immigrants in Britain was forged.

The 1962 Act was clearly a watershed in the history of immigration into Britain and it also provides a revealing insight into the nature of the host society. This Act was by no means the first attempt to restrict the flow of foreign-born people into Britain, but it heralded the complex and tortuous political and legal reinterpretations and redefinitions of British citizenship which continue to this day. 1962 clearly does not mark the end of the migration of people to Britain, but it unquestionably marked a new relationship between host and immigrant (and, of course, potential immigrant). In the following two decades, successive governments of quite contrary political persuasion have never reverted to the relatively unrestricted entry to Britain of before 1962. Indeed, as we shall see, fresh legislation was periodically introduced to make settlement in Britain progressively more difficult and restrictive. There was at the same time an effort (partly through legislation) to safeguard the rights and prospects of those immigrants (and their offspring) who had settled in Britain. Many critics found the duality of restricted entry coupled with liberal 'race-relations' legislation and policy both contradictory and unseemly.

It is important, however, to remind ourselves of the degree to which the complex problems faced by a post-imperial power, trying to cope with substantial immigrant communities and their British-born descendants, were substantially a historical force. It is easy to argue that the difficulties of black–white relations since the 1960s are new ones. The purpose of this book so far has been to suggest that these issues cannot be fully understood, still less solved, unless we remember that they have been, in large part, historically determined. Whether Irish, Indian or Jamaican, the people who took the passage to Britain to seek a new life for themselves and their families were following a course plotted by complex historical forces at work throughout much of the twentieth century. The

Irish story is, of course, even older. But in all these cases immigrants had been drawn to Britain by social and economic conditions which were primarily of British making. In common with other imperial powers, the British relationship with their colonies had been fundamentally exploitative, however benign or beneficial some of the attitudes and consequences might have been. In search of prosperity – of goods, materials, areas for expansion or simply manpower – imperial powers had subjected millions of people to direct or indirect control. When that control began to disintegrate, as it did so rapidly in the British case after 1945, many of the subject peoples justifiably looked to Britain for more than the former control and guidance. The British had, especially in wartime, introduced their imperial subjects to the material virtues of the mother country, just as they had exposed or nudged them towards the virtues of the English language, culture, education and political system. When, in the post-war years, the bonds of empire were rapidly loosened, the material attractions of Britain proved irresistibly enticing to growing numbers of people around the world who had already experienced them, or even merely heard of them. Indeed, there is a strong case for claiming that in the post-imperial world, the legacy of empire was to be borne not merely in the form of colonial independence and reconstruction, but also in the troubled relationship which emerged between metropolis and immigrant peoples from the colonies. This was not peculiar to Britain, but was a phenomenon common, for example, among all former colonial powers in Western Europe, notably Belgium, France, Holland and Portugal. In the British case, however, it was to be one of the most important social changes in the post-war years.

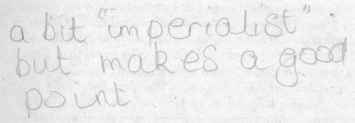
a bit "imperialist" but makes a good point

PART TWO

RECENT TIMES

8
Closing the Door: Immigration and Race since 1962

Immigration had been a feature of British life for centuries but, as we have seen, the immigrations of the 1950s were of a different nature. Numerically, immigration in this period was less significant than, for instance, the arrival of the Irish in the nineteenth century. When in the 1950s people talked of immigration they usually meant 'coloured' immigration; what increasingly worried them was the colour of many of the immigrants and the nature of the alien cultural values and beliefs transplanted into British cities. Furthermore, people worried about the numbers of immigrants. Estimates of the number of settlers had been available since 1945, but these were largely imprecise. By the late 1950s, however, Home Office statistics clearly registered the extraordinary increases in immigration, especially from India and Pakistan.

The political argument, culminating in the 1962 Commonwealth Immigrants Act, took place at a number of levels. But at the heart of that debate lay the questions of numbers, and of the alleged transforming power of those numbers on British society as a whole. Although the demand for immigration controls was voiced most influentially within Parliament, outside pressure groups and the local press were the first to express unease about the impact of immigration on their communities and to insist on effective control over it.

Control over immigration was not, in itself, a new phenomenon. Indeed, throughout the twentieth century successive governments had restrictive legislation at their disposal to check arrivals in Britain. The 1905 Aliens Act was the foundation stone of immigrant restrictions and although it is true that, in its early years, it was exercised in a liberal and humane manner, it nonethe-

less formed a sharp break with the decades of 'open door' policy.
The war stimulated even tighter restrictions in the form of the 1914
and 1919 Aliens Restrictions Acts, subsequently modified by various Orders in Council. But what proved most crucial in the new
legislation of the 1960s and 1970s were the changes brought about
in the concept of British citizenship. Indeed, successive Acts
designed to control non-white immigration directed themselves at
redefining the concept of British citizenship. Conversely the Act
most recently concerned with citizenship – the 1981 British Nationality Act – was essentially designed to control immigration, though
it purported not to do so. The 1914 Imperial Act had determined
that 'everyone born within the allegiance of the Crown in any part
of the empire' was thus a British subject. As countries secured their
independence from Britain after the Second World War it became
necessary to revise the covering legislation. The independence of
India in 1948 prompted the British Nationality Act of that year.

The 1948 Act was a remarkably complex piece of legislation that
divided up all the monarch's subjects into two main groups: citizens
of independent Commonwealth countries, and citizens of the rest
of the empire, described as a united citizenship with the United
Kingdom. Thus when immigrants travelled from, for instance, the
West Indies in the 1950s they did so as citizens of the United
Kingdom and colonies, with full rights of entry and settlement.
It was then the 1948 Act which enabled Commonwealth citizens to
settle in Britain. As immigration grew in the 1950s complaints
increased in number and stridency, but in 1955 the Conservative
government rejected as a matter of principle the concept of controlling immigration. The next Conservative government began to
reconsider its position, largely under pressure from the mounting
complaints. In 1961 it was decided to modify the definition of
citizenship of Commonwealth and colonial subjects, though the
process was also brought about by negotiations for colonial
independence in various colonies. The resulting Commonwealth
Immigrants Act of 1962 limited the right of entry to the United
Kingdom; those with passports not issued in Britain were obliged
henceforth to hold a work permit to secure entry.

The debate on this Bill in Parliament divided on party lines. The
Labour Party bitterly opposed the principles of the Bill and

promised, on return to office, to repeal it. As we shall see, far from repealing it, Labour governments from the mid 1960s onwards stiffened it enormously. No sooner had this Act placed restrictions on citizens of the 'New Commonwealth' than all sides of the political debate came to accept the desirability – and indeed the political *inevitability* – of immigration controls. After 1962 there was never again to be a return to the unrestricted policies of the post-war years. But there were other difficulties in store for the interpreters of the 1962 Act. There were, for instance, people with a U.K. passport issued in the U.K. or in High Commissions overseas who did not fall within the 1962 restrictions. In East Africa, large numbers of Asians had opted for the British passport and citizenship in preference to local nationalities when Kenya, Uganda and Tanzania secured their independence. In 1967–8 it became possible that many thousands (once more, the numbers were uncertain but they were always exaggerated by the politically involved) of East Africans might choose to settle in Britain. Just when the 1962 Act had brought the flow of immigrants to a level that many of the Act's supporters regarded as acceptable, events in yet another of the former colonies threatened to create further antagonism about immigration. The Labour government, which had so strenuously opposed controls only six years before when they were in opposition, rushed to close the door even more securely, this time against the East African Asians. The 1968 Commonwealth Immigrants Act refused the right of entry to those U.K. passport holders not born in the U.K. – or without parents or grandparents born in the U.K. (or naturalized or registered as citizens). Entry was henceforth governed by a strictly limited issue of vouchers. The Act passed through Parliament in a mere three days.

The purpose of the Act was simple: to keep out non-white colonial citizens while simultaneously making it possible for white colonials (whose ancestors were, of course, British) to return 'home' if they wished. Not surprisingly, this was an Act which was widely denounced for its overtly racial character. Indeed its aim (and achievement) was so overtly ethnocentric and punitive of colour that it was hard to deny its racial qualities. The Act and its implementation were blatantly discriminatory. With that in mind a group of Asians brought a complaint against it to the European Commis-

sion on Human Rights in 1970. The Commission upheld their
complaint, concluding that the British government's intention in
the 1968 Act was fundamentally discriminatory. And the critique
by the Commission continues into the 1980s. But, of course, such a
legal critique was to no avail and the judgement was effectively
undermined by being shunted into the complex political machinery of the European Commission.

The difficulties of gaining entry, even for those with a clear right
to do so, were compounded by the 1969 Immigration Appeals Act.
The Act was designed to provide an appeal system for those refused
entry, and the Labour government added to it a clause insisting
that dependants seeking to join relatives in Britain should first
secure an entry certificate. Since these could only be secured
through an interview at the local British High Commission – a
protracted, costly and alien procedure which could often involve a
journey of hundreds of miles – and since the relationship to the
settler in Britain had to be documented and proven, it became a
major obstacle to immigration. Of course the people against whom
this was primarily directed were the families of people already in
Britain. Already separated by great distances and, in many cases,
over a long period of time, such families were often compelled to
live apart by the sheer impracticalities created by the procedure; at
best the coming together of these families was greatly hindered,
delayed and inconvenienced.

The Labour government was largely responsible for this; all that
seemed to have changed was the severity and stringency of each
successive legislative change in immigration controls. And so it
proved, once again, when the Conservative government passed
the 1971 Immigration Act, an Act which granted great discretion to
the Home Office in devising, and revising, the day-to-day rules
governing immigration. The Act was most famous, however, for
inventing the concept and status of the 'patrial', a new category of
U.K. citizenship which traced its roots to parents' or grandparents'
British origins. The remainder, including Commonwealth citizens,
and other aliens, required permission to enter Britain.

It is true that there was specific provision for admitting 'non-
patrials' (those over for short visits, on business, or the Irish and
E.E.C. nationals) but the fundamental aim was to restrict the arrival

of people from the New Commonwealth. Provisions existed for dependants and family to join 'non-patrials' already settled in Britain,
but it was not a matter of *right*, and it was indeed so hedged in by
restrictions and conditions as to make it difficult to comprehend
and often impossible to fulfil. One other consequence of the 1971
Act was to put New Commonwealth workers in Britain on a legal
par with people from other countries excepting the E.E.C. and
subject to similar controls via work permits of a limited duration.
They became, in effect, residents under sufferance, liable to have
their permits revoked for a number of reasons, many of them decided
upon by a procedure both arbitrary and difficult to challenge.

Thus, throughout the 1970s, the prospects of immigrants from
the New Commonwealth undoubtedly deteriorated. The introduction of the status of 'patrial' was clearly aimed at restricting the
numbers of 'coloured' immigrants coming into Britain. And even
for those already here, the new regulations made difficult the task
of reuniting family and loved ones. Equally alarming for that
growing body of opinion which was increasingly unhappy at the
extension of an intrusive state bureaucracy (and policing) into
people's private lives was the nature of the administration of the
1971 Act. Prospective immigrants seeking work in Britain needed a
work permit, issued by the Department of Employment, but would
also be subject to stringent conditions and in some respects to
Home Office approval. Work permit holders were also required to
register with the police. Thus the police were, at an early and
sensitive stage, brought into contact with immigrants; it was the
beginning of a relationship which has, in the past fifteen years or
so, proved one of the most formative (and unhappy) elements in
shaping the immigrant experience.

It would be wrong, however, to imagine that this was a uniquely
'coloured' matter. Indeed, by the late 1970s the largest single group
of work permit holders were Americans, while permits held by
people from other advanced industrial powers give a clear indication of the changing needs of the British labour market. With the
economy in decline, and the levels of unemployment steadily rising,
the economy needed not so much the labouring strength it had so
actively sought in the years up to 1960, but rather skilled, educated
and entrepreneurial manpower. It must also be said that the provi-

sion of work permits was a deeply sexist measure, for the rights of a male holder (for example to bring in dependants who could work) was *not* enjoyed by women. Of course the whole purpose of the work permit scheme, in conjunction with the limitations on 'coloured' immigration, was to cut off the unwanted stream of labour into Britain (which happened by and large to be 'coloured') whilst ensuring the continuity of those labour supplies still in demand.

The door was not entirely closed; it was left slightly ajar and a certain number of immigrants were able to squeeze through – if they satisfied British needs. Britain was prepared to admit and employ skilled and specialized workers, notably in medicine. In 1973 it was calculated that more than one quarter of doctors in Britain were foreign. In certain key areas of the N.H.S. the service would have simply collapsed without this group. In fact this had been true in the late 1940s, with the difference that the labour required had generally been unskilled; this time the requirement was for trained doctors and nursing staff. It is not cynical to remark that while trying to keep out 'coloured' workers and settlers, British regulations since 1971 have nonetheless made ample provision to welcome those whose skills might be useful to the country. Once more the observer is faced by a striking continuity in British responses to immigrant labour; whenever it is needed, it will be encouraged and welcomed. By the 1970s, however, the nature (and health) of the British economy had so changed that it was necessary to seek skilled rather than praedial labour. And in addition there had developed irresistible political and social pressure to limit or to stop non-white immigration. It must also be noted that this inflow of skilled (especially medical) workers placed a severe strain on many of those poor Commonwealth countries which could ill afford to lose their expensively trained doctors to a prosperous western nation. The British were not alone in this, of course, but the relatively high material rewards for doctors throughout the western world provided an irresistible attraction for successive generations of doctors. Furthermore, since so many of them had been trained in western medical schools (at least for part of their courses), there were additional reasons to quit the less rewarding positions available in their homelands. The British thus came to be a serious threat to many of the health services of the poorer Commonwealth countries, a drain on their resources which they could ill afford.

Throughout the history of post-war immigration the determining factor had been, overwhelmingly, the economic attractions of life in Britain. Conversely the British had encouraged or tolerated that immigration because of their own economic needs. But the legal changes inaugurated by the 1962 Act served to change not merely the influx of immigrants but, equally important, they redefined the very concept of British citizenship. The Act of 1968, by stripping that citizenship from tens of thousands of East African Asians, created a group described as 'stateless in substance though not in name'. Many, it is true, were allowed into Britain. There were some 83,000 between 1968 and 1975 and of course the 28,000 Ugandan Asians admitted in a two-month period in 1972 who were fleeing from the vicious tyranny of Idi Amin. But the emergence of the concept of patriality was, in many respects, a logical progression of the legislative changes initiated since 1962. Whether it was openly admitted, or merely tacitly accepted, British immigration laws throughout the 1960s and 1970s gradually began to close the door on non-white immigration. Given the vast expanse of the former British empire and the myriad peoples who, at one point or another, had a perfectly legitimate right to British citizenship, any redefining of that citizenship would inevitably penalize untold numbers of people. The fact that such changes penalized most heavily the non-white citizens of the Commonwealth makes it hard to deflect the criticism that such legislation was overtly racist. It was, quite simply, designed to limit and keep out coloured immigrants. Yet how was British society, whose Parliament had enacted with precious little opposition such discriminatory laws, to treat the hundreds of thousands of New Commonwealth citizens and their British offspring? So many groups cried out for legislative protection, but to offer it would (and still does) involve a logical contradiction. To legislate for better or more harmonious race relations seemed rather odd coming from a Parliament and political parties nonetheless prepared to countenance discrimination in their own immigration policies.

*

The reader who has persevered with this argument so far will be aware that immigration in the broader context of British history is not primarily a matter of race. From the 1950s onwards, however, the political debate about immigration concentrated increasingly (and in many cases, uniquely) on the related questions of race and colour. 'Race relations', though variously described, became an object of growing concern. Indeed it was in many respects the mirror image of the difficulties of and arguments about immigration. With the growth of a substantial, non-white population there developed a host of complex relations between black and white. In the light of Britain's imperial past – and knowing the history of racial attitudes in Britain – it should come as no surprise to learn of the flowering of racial antagonisms in Britain since 1945. At most levels of society, non-white immigrants found themselves confronted by discrimination at work, in housing and education, or merely at the level of daily social intercourse.

It may in retrospect seem ironic, but it was widely assumed by many prominent spokesmen and politicians in the host society that whereas racial discrimination existed in other parts of the world (in the U.S.A., and South Africa, for instance), Britain was unusually free of this scourge. Of course the very history of British imperialism and of the varied experience of ethnic groups in Britain in past centuries clearly argues to the contrary. In fact certain individuals raised their isolated voices both against discrimination and in favour of legislation to outlaw it. As early as 1951 attempts were made in Parliament to outlaw discrimination in public places, and attempts to persuade Parliament of the need to legislate were made with growing frequency in the 1950s and 1960s, notably by the Labour M.P. Fenner Brockway. More and more people were won over to the idea, not merely because of the simple demographic growth of the black population, but, more directly, because of the mounting evidence of overt hostility towards the immigrants. This became an inescapable feature of British society in 1958 following the riots in Notting Hill and in Nottingham. Of course the *existence* of discrimination was not in doubt in the minds of immigrants themselves; they after all were exposed to it, often on a daily and institutionalized basis. The key task was to persuade the British (and white) decision-makers first of its existence and secondly of the necessity or desirability of doing something about it.

What made the case for legislation against racial discrimination so pressing in Britain was the complete absence in British law of any legislation which specifically safeguarded individuals' rights. Unlike other Western European countries, Britain has no 'Bill of Rights' (though there are a myriad other laws and common law judgements which, in a cumulative sense, often provide many of these safeguards). The new Labour government of 1964 set out to establish safeguards for the non-white communities through the Race Relations Act of 1965 which declared as unlawful discrimination through 'race, colour, ethnic or national origin' in public places. Supervising the procedures was a Race Relations Board under the supervision of the Home Secretary. But it soon became apparent that not only were the number of complaints about discrimination very small, but many fell *outside* the terms of the Act. This evidence also coincided with a growth of social and academic research, all of which illustrated the ubiquity, depth and persistence of discrimination in British life. This accumulating evidence indisputably indicated the existence of discrimination against all groups of minorities, especially in work, housing and in the provision of services and goods. It also revealed that such discrimination was most acute against non-whites. Again, this would hardly surprise the West Indians or Asians, or seem so extraordinary many years later. But at the time it *was* a revelation to the many people steeped in British liberal traditions and values who found it difficult to grasp many of the fundamental truths about the history and sociology of British racial views. By the mid 1960s it was becoming clearer to more and more people that Britain was not only discriminatory in the way it legislated and implemented its immigration rules, but also in the ways it treated (and maltreated) its racial minorities. It thus became clear that the provisions of the 1965 Act were inadequate and there followed the Race Relations Act of 1968. This extended the scope of anti-discrimination to include most notably employment and housing, and power was granted to bring prosecutions. In addition, the Community Relations Commission was established to promote harmonious relations. Not surprisingly, the Labour backers of these changes were keen to claim for the Act a string of beneficial improvements. By the late 1960s, however, there was a veritable research industry, much of it with indirect government financial backing, whose findings presented a contrary picture. One could not deny that there were improvements, but the level of discrimination continued to be unacceptably high. Moreover, it was clear that there were, quite literally, tens of thousands of cases which simply went unrecorded and unnoticed, except of course by the victim.

By 1975 the Labour government had pinpointed the main weaknesses in the 1968 Act and, with these in mind, passed the 1976 Race Relations Act, one result of which was the establishment of the Commission for Racial Equality (C.R.E.). The new Act cast its net much more widely than anything before; it covered acts of private discrimination, for instance, and also *indirect* discrimination. This latter point was influenced by the U.S. where long experience had shown that equal opportunities could be denied by indirect methods. Equally interesting, the Act covered publications, while also applying to certain actions of central and local government departments. Henceforth, although individuals could seek personal redress for alleged discrimination, for certain types of discrimination the necessary procedure was and is of labyrinthine complexity. Similarly, the ability of the C.R.E. successfully to investigate and prosecute cases of alleged discrimination is also hedged in by legal, financial and political restrictions which have the effect of delaying and deflecting the main purpose and thrust of such cases. Subsequently, common law decisions have further emasculated the ability of the C.R.E. to pursue the practice of discrimination as originally conceived.

Perhaps the most adventurous measure advanced by the 1976 legislation was the consideration of publications and the publicly spoken word designed to encourage racial hatred. 'Incitement to racial hatred' thus became a criminal offence, and as such it is for officers of the Crown to initiate the prosecution. Undoubtedly this Act, which attempted to tackle racial discrimination on a broad front and more thoroughly than ever before, was a well intentioned and in many respects a potent piece of legislation. It takes no great leap of the imagination, however, to see that, however well intentioned this Act or any other was, it was not necessarily in touch with social reality. No social historian of modern Britain can adequately reconstruct the history of that nation solely or even largely from the relevant legislation. There might indeed be an inverse relationship between legislation and social practice. We need to bear in mind that this legislation is only one way to the eventual ending of discrimination and to a broadening of opportunities for minority group members. To use the words of Laurence Lustgarten, the most recent student of this legislation, 'the economic, political and moral environment must reinforce the legal commitment. This is very far from true in Britain at present.' Indeed, this author concludes his exhaustive study with the words that the 'spirit of this study has been one of qualified pessimism'. Again, such pessimism is only remarkable when set against firstly the specific ambitions of race relations legislation, and secondly when placed in the context of liberal views about British values and virtues. If we take the broader historical view, it seems unremarkable that British society, for so long the world's pre-eminent imperial power, should display at home many of the residuals of racism nurtured over so long a period of global imperial power. Indeed it would have been surprising if the opposite had been true: that a former imperial power should *not* continue to view non-whites (the descendants of former subject peoples) as inferior. This is not to claim, of course, that recent discrimination is specifically a legacy of an imperial past; but it seems perfectly clear that to forget that past is to dismiss one of the main determinants of a continuing and evolving racist tradition.

The significance of this convoluted legal and social process, which stretches back for more than two decades, has been apparent in a most direct (and often offensive) fashion to those thousands of immigrants and their British offspring who have transformed a number of features of British life. There is, it is true, a great danger of presenting a caricature of social reality by trying to condense and precis a complex phenomenon, but if we begin to consider the legislation enacted since 1962, from the non-white viewpoint, it is possible to sense the origins of much of the prickly antagonism within those communities. Firstly, there has been a concerted, and increasingly efficient, effort to keep immigrants' kinsmen out of

Britain, even to the point of breaking family bonds. Secondly, the legislation enacted to safeguard their various human and social rights has been proved inadequate (though it is also true to say that many imperfections have been corrected in time). But, to repeat an earlier point, the benefits of benign and supportive legislation must often seem lost, when viewed from within a number of communities which have borne the direct and indirect consequences of economic decline since the early 1970s. Ever more severe legislation, the general inaccessibility of legal support, in conjunction with major economic decline and the rise of British Fascism, have served to sow the seeds of discord in wide sectors of the non-white community. Historians are, by training, wise after the event, but it is hard not to see in the formal political response to immigration and race relations that seed-bed of racial antagonism which, when nurtured by more obvious and daily social realities (of poverty, poor housing, unemployment and police hostility), blossomed in the summer of 1981 into the worst urban disturbances Britain had experienced for two centuries.

We should also appreciate that the alienating process of hostile or indifferent legislation over the past twenty years has to be seen against remarkable changes within the non-white population itself. Indeed it is these very changes which even render indelicate the terminology used so far in this book. Immigrant communities in general began to shed their national characteristics; they seemed to become more British, more established in the very society which had taken such pains to reject or resist them. We need, then, to turn our attention to the changing demography of non-white society since the 1960s.

Changes in the census forms make it possible to gain a clearer picture about the ethnic composition of the British population from 1971 onwards. By 1971 the total non-white population in Britain was 1·4 million, the largest single group originating from the West Indies. But one of the most crucial facts was that by that year more than one third of that population (35 per cent) had been born in Britain. With time proportions would inevitably change and would, naturally, have major repercussions in the social and political debate about black–white relations. By 1976 40 per cent of the non-white population had been born in Britain; a year later the non-white population stood at 1·85 million. Of course these figures need to be set in their true perspective. Out of a total British population of 55 million, the black population constituted something in the order of 3·4 per cent.

Of course such comparisons can prove deceptive; even the casual observer can see that one of the most salient features of modern British society is the *concentration* of the black population in certain regions. It is perfectly possible to travel to large parts of Britain and not to see a black face; conversely, there are areas of certain cities where the concentration of non-whites is very striking indeed. Often, these concentrations vary enormously from one specific part of a town to another. We need, however, to be cautious, for there is a danger in lumping together such demographic data that we have about the New Commonwealth-born. Again, casual observation will confirm that there are important divisions and distinctions within and between communities; West Indians, Pakistanis and Indians do not necessarily live in the same area, though this has largely been determined by historial and economic causes.

It is also inevitable that the New Commonwealth population has markedly different demographic features than the host society. It is a much younger population, and in many communities there are more men than women: such features have been determined by the nature and pattern of immigration itself. More important, however, are the obvious consequences these simple social facts have for social relations between black and white, and for the inevitable search for spouses among the unmarried. This (particularly among Asians, where men outnumber women) leads to friction between the Home Office and immigration officials, exacerbating still further relations between immigrants and hosts.

Since 1970 the birth rate in British society has fallen, and this factor has threatened to alter a range of social and economic patterns. What is of interest to us is that this fall in birth rate has also been experienced by the West Indian and Asian populations. The simple truth of the matter (though it is frequently and grossly distorted in political argument by interested groups with a partisan case on race or immigration) remains that the non-white population constitutes a small proportion of the total population. Furthermore, its birth patterns provide no evidence that this is likely to change substantially in the foreseeable future. Coupled with this latter point is the fact that stringent immigration regulations ensure that the rough demographic picture of the present New Commonwealth population will not be appreciably altered by new arrivals. The evidence clearly proves that the immigration Acts since 1962 were successful in their determination to restrict severely the inflow of immigrants from the New Commonwealth. Thus the demographic structure, and future, of Britain's black population can be calculated with a fair degree of certainty in the knowledge that it will not be substantially affected by extraneous forces. One other corollary of the demography of the New Commonwealth population is that even if immigration rules were made even stricter, this would *not* have an appreciable impact on the future size of Britain's non-white population. By 2000 there will be some 3·3 million people in Britain of New Commonwealth origin, something like 5·9 per cent of the population.

However we approach these figures they do not suggest that the white host society is about to be overrun by non-white immigrants and their descendants. This is not to deny the particular difficulties of adjustment experienced in certain parts of a number of major cities, notably in employment, housing, education and the social services. Nor is it to say that, for black, Asian and white communities, there are no problems. There clearly are, for a variety of reasons. But it is important to establish that, by the late 1960s, successive British governments, having effectively curbed the patterns of immigration which had evolved since 1945, were obliged to redirect their attention to the complex questions of race relations within Britain itself. All this took place against the backdrop of major economic decline. The social and political ramifications of that decline, most obviously shown in mounting unemployment, were to prove very serious indeed and were to expose the non-white communities to yet more antagonism and hardship. They were largely to bear the brunt of the worst ravages of unemployment (especially among young adults), as well as, ironically, the brunt of political and racist antagonism from those who saw the immigrants as ideal scapegoats for their own thwarted or distorted ambitions. Race was to become one of the ugliest and most important features in British politics. The word Fascism trips too lightly from the tongue of many people interested in contemporary British politics, but it is hard to deny that one of the most sinister consequences of the political arguments about immigration and race (all in a context of major economic decline and general political uncertainty) was the revival of British Fascism on a scale not seen since the 1930s. In the past twenty years Britain's non-white population has had to cope not merely with mounting economic difficulties and all the obstructions created by Parliament, but also with the verbal and physical abuse created by extreme right-wing politics.

9
Politics and Race

Much of the last chapter was concerned with the legislative changes which have transformed both immigration and race relations since the early 1960s. It is perfectly clear that, however we define it, race had become a political issue in Britain, in many respects one of *the* major issues at national and local level.

We have already seen numerous examples where racial issues had long been a political concern. The riots of 1919, the various amendments to the Aliens Act – and, of course, the complicated story of the relationship between the metropolitan power and her colonial possessions – ensured that race would be a major issue in British politics. But what has made the domestic political arguments about race in the past twenty-five years so distinctive is that it has become a question of *colour*.

It would be quite wrong to claim that the politicization of race was solely (or even largely) the result of politicians' actions and words. There have been certain prominent national politicians who have transformed matters of race into a qualitatively different phenomenon by the emphasis they have placed on the arguments, none more so than Enoch Powell. But we should remember that all politicians are constantly subject to a host of constituency and organized pressures which inevitably play an important role in shaping their public or Parliamentary stances. Nor can there be any doubt that public opinion, as expressed through local pressure groups, began to exert a powerful anti-immigrant (and often overtly racist) influence over local M.P.s. Throughout the 1960s and 1970s public opinion polls revealed a consistently overwhelming national antipathy towards coloured immigrants. In 1963, 1964 and 1966 more than 80 per cent of those asked felt that too many immigrants had been allowed to settle in Britain. Similar figures were recorded throughout the 1970s; by 1978 they stood at 86 per cent. And there was just as much opposition to allowing relatives to join established immigrants. Yet there is also a major irony there for it has been widely agreed by students of political behaviour that the question of coloured immigration had little direct impact on the various general elections in these years, in 1964, 1966, 1970, 1974 and 1979 (notwithstanding certain important exceptions). Given the strength of feeling about race and immigration this may seem unusual, but an explanation may be easily found. It has, for instance, been argued that the electorate believed that there was very little to choose between the two main parties. Indeed, this argument has even wider ramifications for it is claimed the failure of the main parties to respond adequately to public sentiment about immigration led to the falling away of voters in British general elections. The corollary seems to be that the British public would overwhelmingly prefer a much tougher line on race and immigration than has been manifested by either Labour or Tory governments.

There is powerful support for this argument in the extraordinary rise to prominence of Enoch Powell following his public speeches against coloured immigration. Powell in many respects became the personification of an overtly anti-immigration stance, although his speeches on the subject were far more sophisticated than the popular press would have anyone believe. The impression his speeches created of rabble-rousing racism, emblazoned in banner headlines, often disguised a more complex and carefully phrased argument. Nonetheless, Powell was (and remains) a consummate politician who studiously chose his timing and topics, and was fully aware of the way his arguments would be interpreted. As member of Parliament for the immigrant city of Wolverhampton he knew that he had only to tap the deep wells of popular racial antipathy to strengthen his case and his support. Enoch Powell thus placed himself clearly at the head of an extremist, albeit populist, campaign against coloured immigration. It proved, however, despite its public backing, to be his political undoing, for it led to his rapid demotion and ultimate political ostracism from the Tory Party. However popular his stand on race and immigration, it won him little political credit within the ranks of his own Parliamentary party.

Doubtless there are those who would argue that this is yet further proof of the gulf between politicians at Westminster and the man in the street, at least on the question of race and immigration. The man who, if public opinion polls are to be believed, dared to express the widespread sentiments of anti-immigration also paved the way for his own political undoing. The ever-increasing isolation of Powell within the Tory Party, which was further compounded by his vigorous opposition to the European Community, is in itself confirmation of the belief on the part of many people that there was really little difference between the two parties. It was as if there was a consensus between the two sides not to make overt political capital out of the politics of race and immigration. Those who have chosen to do so and who, almost as a matter of definition belong naturally on the right wing of the Tory Party, have traditionally been allowed the licence of the extremist fringe: permitted to have their say but generally ignored.

It seems likely that the gulf between Westminster and 'popular opinion' on matters of race is one of the factors alienating certain sectors of the public from the political process. It is only one of a series of issues which political scientists have pointed to as dividing the political elite from their constituents. The widespread disillusionment with party politics which has spread since 1950 is itself a function of this divide. On the question of race and immigration, however, there is a paradox because both Labour and Conservative governments since 1962 have indeed responded to public unease about immigration by establishing the increasingly complex and difficult controls we examined in the last chapter. There would be few Asians and West Indians who would argue that British governments since 1962 have been soft on immigrants. But there is clearly a massive body of non-immigrant British opinion which feels that this policy has been nowhere near tough enough. It has been argued that the restrictive legislation (of 1962, 1965, 1968 and 1971) has been viewed by many electors as a clear indication that too little has been done too late by politicians, rather than that the situation has always been closely controlled.

That alienation from politics which derives specifically from the politics of race may also derive from much greater difficulties of readjustment on the part of older British citizens. For a younger generation growing up in British cities alongside the offspring of

Commonwealth immigrants, the history and significance of the British empire is remote and largely unknown. For older people, however, Britain's imperial power and her apparent global pre-eminence are not mere historical abstractions. There are, after all, millions of Britons who not only remember (perhaps even fondly) the days when 'Britannia ruled the waves', but there are many who were actively involved, however humble their station, in the politics, policing and governance of empire. This was of course especially true during the Second World War. It was an inevitable consequence of empire that the British should view their subject peoples as inferiors. Although, as we have seen, there were subtle changes in time to the British response to them, this belief in the inferiority of subject races, so popularly held by all classes of Britons, was central to the imperial experience. One result of Commonwealth immigration was that British people had to undergo a change of heart and attitude. Henceforth, the British had to treat as equal those who, until the demise of empire, had merely been imperial subjects. For many this demanded a difficult change in outlook; for others it was quite impossible to accept. Again, Britain was not alone in this dilemma, for other European countries were also obliged to come to terms with post-imperial realities and to treat their former subjects as equals. This posed particular problems for France in relation to Algeria and also to Portugal in relation to her African colonies.

It may be felt that this necessary change of outlook is only of minor importance, yet it may be suggested that it was a key factor in the host society's response to the settlement and growth of non-white immigrant communities. At a personal level, it was not easy for people who, by education, upbringing and outlook, had come to view the world through the distortion of imperial power now to accept former colonial subjects as their social equals and near neighbours. Moreover, what made this readjustment even more difficult for many Britons was the fact that Commonwealth immigration into Britain paralleled the rapid, quite unexpected and inexplicable demise of British global and imperial power. People's loyalty towards and pride in their extraordinary empire were severely shaken by the rapid retreat from imperial greatness after the Second World War. It is easy to see, in retrospect, the cracks that appeared in the imperial edifice long before the Second World War. During the war, the great majority of people were too preoccupied with other problems to worry about the future of empire, but the global and strategic events of those years contributed to the dismantling of the British empire. Similarly, the war hastened the ultimate economic and political decline of Britain. By 1945 Britain faced a bleak future, notwithstanding the euphoria with greeted the prospects of major social changes ushered in by a reforming Labour government. The truth, however, was that Britain's economic base was in a parlous state, run down, antiquated, ill-prepared for economic change, and there was little or no money for vital redevelopment. Yet the facts of military triumph (much of it made possible by U.S. economic and military assistance and by the fighting strength of the Russians) bred an illusion of continuing global greatness. It was very difficult for the British, who had made such individual and collective sacrifices during the war, to imagine that the war had actually hastened the decline of their country and paved the way for the emergence of a new form of global power-politics.

The generation following the war saw the rapid, though reluctant, collapse of the old European empires. Often it involved savage and brutal fighting which, in the short term (and because of the human suffering) made it even more difficult for imperial powers to retreat from their colonial possessions. Malaya, Kenya, Cyprus, Aden, Borneo, Indo-China, Algeria, Angola and Mozambique – in all these countries retreating Europeans fought in vain to keep their colonies. All were ultimately lost along with dozens of other colonies which secured their freedom more peacefully. Furthermore, this process of decolonization was paralleled by the political demise of the major European colonial powers. The rapid emergence of new 'super-powers', notably the U.S.A. and Russia, overshadowed the older powers; Britain's international standing declined just as her imperial influence contracted. Of course in such a complex and fortuitous process, there are no easily defined turning points, no neatly packaged sequence of events which enable us more easily to grasp the complexity of these circumstances. Nonetheless, the Suez crisis of 1956 served to illustrate particularly sharply the realities of post-imperial international power. While the British and the French were able to make a show of international military power, the outcome served merely to underline the shallowness of their international and military pretensions, and their inability to win world opinion over to their side. Bitterly divided at home, grossly overstretched abroad, the British withdrawal from Suez was undeniably one of a power in retreat. But the language and attitudes of imperialism continued to haunt British politics, like the imperial ghost hovering over a political wake. Indeed the frequency with which political leaders had to reiterate their belief in Britain's greatness was indirectly a tacit admission that she was no longer great. Why should the leaders of a great power feel the need to convince the public of the survival of their nation's greatness? In truth, Britain's imperial and global pre-eminence, in common with her economic dominance, was a thing of the past; a historical phenomenon which appeared increasingly anachronistic with the passage of time.

It was, then, this rapid and quite unexpected decline in Britain's fortunes on a wide front which proved so difficult for older Britons to come to terms with. The immigrants settling in Britain's cities were, in a sense, a human reminder of this process, and the transplanting into Britain of people (and problems) was of imperial making. When we consider the politics of immigration within the wider context of Britain's global decline, it perhaps becomes clearer why immigrants aroused such powerful and often irrational feelings and animus. Moreover, this animus was as pronounced among people living in areas untouched by immigration as it was among those who felt their immediate homes or workplaces threatened by the arrival of immigrants. For legions of Britons who saw their country declining in material and international terms, it was easy not merely to explain key aspects of that decline in terms of one of the most obvious and undeniable social transformations around them – coloured immigration – but it was a comfort to *blame* the immigrants for the undesired changes in Britain's fortunes. Not only were immigrants thought by many to be the cause of Britain's problems, but politicians from both Labour and Conservative parties were damned for their failure to see or to remedy these issues by stopping immigration. From 1967 only one man, as we have already seen, proved to be the exception. Enoch Powell, in taking a stand against immigration and thereby excluding himself from the prospects of political preferment, spoke for millions of Britons. For those alienated from politics and politicians, Powell had by the late 1960s emerged as the only honest or representative figure in national politics. For the immigrant communities, however, Powell represented quite a different force: the parliamentary spokesman for that varied and malignant coalition of British interests and attitudes, ranging from the unsympathetic to the deeply racist and even violent, which had begun to coalesce into a threatening force against immigrant communities.

The 'politicization' of race and immigration was then not simply a matter of New Commonwealth immigration into Britain, but rather grew out of a complex process of political and international change. Moreover, the politics of race were also shaped and directed by major events in the U.S.A. In the twenty years after the inauguration of President Kennedy in 1961, American black society underwent a series of important changes and political convulsions, some of the most spectacular of which were projected into British homes thanks to new international telecommunication systems. The rise of the civil rights movement, black voter registration, the extraordinary appeals of Martin Luther King and, of course, the fearful urban riots following his death (many, it is true, had preceded it), brought home to the British both the degree of deprivation amongst American blacks and the power of black demands for their rights. The degree to which the rise of American black consciousness influenced the growth of similar tactics and pressure groups in Britain is harder to define. Nonetheless, the general point remains that black American politics served to compound the general and increasing concern and consideration given to matters of race.

This was also true on an even broader scale, for the relations between Britain and black Africa in the 1960s entered a new and increasingly delicate phase. A number of British colonies became independent during the sixties with the result that full statehood and citizenship were conferred upon millions who had previously been less exalted. And as the empire gradually transmuted itself into a new Commonwealth, where black and Asian statesmen spoke freely and equally with their former governors, the politics of race developed another unmistakable dimension. There were now powerful international statesmen quick to speak to their British counterparts on questions of race, on matters of international racial concern and even on issues of domestic British politics. It is a simple though nonetheless important point that British politicians had, from the early 1960s, increasingly to pay heed not only to their constituents but to international forces, more especially from within the Commonwealth. Such a dramatic turnaround demanded delicacy of handling from those who had, until recently, treated as anything but equal their erstwhile colonial charges.

This was especially true in relation to South Africa which, with the rise of a new international commitment to racial equality, found itself increasingly isolated from most agencies of international cooperation. South Africa withdrew from the Commonwealth in 1961 and thereafter the British were plagued by the sensitive questions of relations with the South Africans. Indeed if proof be needed of the growing strength of non-white pressure on Britain in these years, it is to be seen in graphic form in the altering of British links with South Africa. It is true that the economic ties between the two countries remain unusually strong, but it is equally clear that in most other, more visible and more political dealings the British have been obliged to sever their ties with South Africa. And this is because of South Africa's racial, and racist, policies. It is easy to see why this happened. If we look at the list of newly independent former British colonies it is possible to appreciate the increasing pressure brought to bear upon the British by their new Commonwealth partners. Whereas in the 1950s only three colonies had been granted independence (the Sudan, Ghana and Malaya), in the 1960s there was a veritable stampede towards independence. Between June 1960 and September 1968, twenty-seven colonies became independent nations or joined up with independent neighbours. By the late 1960s they had become a sizable and highly effective lobby, a countervailing force to the freedom of action of their former masters, both from within the U.N. and the Commonwealth itself.

To put the matter simply, on matters of race – domestic or international – the British could no longer act as an unrestrained and independent agent; there were strong, increasingly powerful qualifying forces, most notably within the Commonwealth. It is difficult to assess the ease or difficulty with which the British adjusted to these changes, to this less powerful and less independent role. But there is clear evidence to show that it was a painful process which, like the transformation in attitudes and values towards immigrants themselves, was bitterly resisted by large numbers of people. There was no excuse for this resistance to the inevitable or the truculent refusal to face the unavoidable facts of the global and racial changes of the 1960s, but it is imperative that we recognize and accept it as a fact of British life in those years. Outnumbered in the Commonwealth by colonies they once 'owned', committed to 'multi-racialism' in a variety of international organizations, notably the U.N., playing host to legions of coloured immigrants they had once needed but now could do without, the British exhibited a multiplicity of confused and sometimes contradictory political and social responses to the varied questions of race. Nominally committed to racial equality at home and abroad the British nonetheless established a series of discriminatory laws; openly multi-racialist abroad, they continued to succour and benefit from one of the most discriminatory of regimes in the world, South Africa.

Another issue should be discussed when analysing the politics of race since 1960. The British people's immediate awareness and knowledge of race and racially related matters has been determined in large part by media coverage. So far, care has been taken to suggest the degree to which the British were the inheritors of complicated historical and socially determined values of race and empire. It is not to contradict this to claim that, in addition, racial matters have been given the kind of coverage by the media, and even within that broader area of popular entertainment, which has scarcely done anything to dispel the older racial images and stereotypes. Research in the 1970s has confirmed a fact which seems clear enough from a casual assessment of media coverage, namely that any such coverage is intended to present immigrants and black people in general as a threat and a problem. And so the argument comes full circle. As Britain experienced rapid economic, political and social decline, so the baffled populace saw the non-white population in Britain as being responsible for this confusing social revolution.

The tendency to blame immigrants both for the decline in

fortunes and for the problems of contemporary Britain reach their
ultimate and mindless apogee with the rise of British Fascism.
Throughout the 1960s leaders of the various right-wing movements
in Britain consciously used race and immigration to rally support
to their cause and to try to produce a practical coalition of British
Fascists and neo-Fascists. By 1967 the National Front became the
national federation for a string of small but voluble and vociferous
Fascist groups. Ideologically, its principles are abundantly clear:
nationalist, authoritarian and racist. Indeed, British Fascists openly
blame the development of a racially mixed society in Britain for
Britain's decline. Above all else the blatant racism of the National
Front helps to recruit new members and supporters. Again and
again, spokesmen for the National Front return to the central theme
of race in their ideological cry: 'If the British people are destroyed
through racial interbreeding, then the British nation will cease to
exist.' Their solution is quite clear: in the (admittedly unlikely)
event of a National Front government taking office, 'an immediate
repatriation policy would be implemented and they [immigrants]
would simply be sent home!' At the heart of the bizarre assertions
of the National Front lies an unshakable belief in the theory of a
Jewish conspiracy: by encouraging the spread of miscegenation the
Jews are preparing to dominate Britain and other countries. The
argument is summed up with offensive clarity by one Fascist leader:
'If Britain were Jew-clean she would have no nigger neighbours to
worry about.' Such views might easily be consigned to the dustbin
of history were it not for the fact that they recur with unnerving
regularity, appeal to a small but nonetheless fanatical core of
British Fascists and prove the inspiration for regular and even
escalating attacks on Jews, blacks and Asians. In February 1981 a
Parliamentary committee was able to document 250 attacks of this
kind in the previous eighteen months, and many more simply went
unrecorded.

The National Front complains bitterly of the treatment it receives
in the media largely, they argue, because of Jewish influence. Yet it
is in many respects the image of the National Front, more especially
that created by their public meetings and marches, which has
brought them a public prominence their numbers scarcely merit.
Surrounding themselves with the trappings of British ceremonial,

especially the widespread use of the Union Jack, protected by ranks of local policemen, the National Front has taunted its political and racial opponents through marches and rallies on sensitive occasions or in sensitive quarters. These were the tactics of Mosley's Fascists in the 1930s. Not surprisingly, perhaps, these organized and provocative taunts have often had the result they sought: a violent retort from the left and from non-white community organizations. In the process, the anger of the newspapers is often deflected from the virulence of the National Front to the actions of their opponents. This often has the bizarre effect of portraying the Fascists as the victims of unwarranted aggression, particularly when ranks of policemen are used to safeguard the National Front's right to march or speak. The end result is, of course, a political victory for the Fascists for it has been consistently true that such reporting has tended to denounce their opponents and to generate a sympathy for the rights of the National Front. 'The threat to law and order,' wrote George Gale in the *Daily Express* in August 1977, 'comes almost entirely from the Fascist left.' Such views must seem bizarre in the extreme to those Indians, Pakistanis or West Indians subjected to capricious assaults on their homes, families and persons.

Politically, the National Front has failed to make an appreciable impact in national politics; at General Elections its candidates fail to gather more than a nominal number of votes. At local or by-elections, however, it tends to fare better. Nonetheless it would be wrong to seek to assess its influence through the formal accumulation of votes. Its greatest success has been its own internal buoyancy in the 1970s, its eye-catching (albeit venomous) tactics and its ability to seduce Chief Constables and even the Home Office into providing the movement with the necessary facilities for its public campaigns. There is also a case to be made that the crude nationalism of the National Front has been absorbed by the right wing of the Tory Party. Viewed from the black, Asian and Jewish communities, the story of the National Front since 1967 is a chilling reminder of earlier experiences and a shocking indictment of British official policy. While speaking of multi-racialism and of racial equality, successive British governments have sought to safeguard the activities of racists and Fascists. Clearly, refusing permission to march or meet is not to be easily conceded. Yet again and again, it has appeared to immigrants and their friends that the police and the Home Office have proved more effective in protecting the National Front than immigrants under threat of attack. It is, in short, a story which, if not documenting the success of the National Front, nonetheless compounds the suspicions, the doubts and the alienation of hundreds of thousands of non-white British people.

It would be false to claim that racism in Britain is the preserve of a small core of Fascists. There is an abundance of evidence to show a much wider support for racist arguments, at all social levels and even in areas of the country untouched by local immigration. Indeed research in the 1970s suggests that racism is a widespread phenomenon in Britain, and appears to be at its strongest among unskilled working people. The animus among such people cannot easily be explained in terms of a long-term historical tradition, but is more easily answered by reference to contemporary social and economic problems. Coloured immigrants, naturally, want all the basic material requirements of life around them, and it is their demands on local employment, housing and education and social services which form a recurring complaint among their antagonistic white neighbours. It is a common feature of immigration (into Britain and into other countries) that immigrants are obliged to endure the worst of material conditions and the least rewarding kinds of work. Yet they are generally blamed for many of the disadvantages they are obliged to inherit: poor work, poor housing, poor pay and poor schooling. Of course it needs to be reiterated that such a complexity of forces is often very specifically local and the consequent antagonism created is often an equally local political force.

Local political parties, responding to the local changes, have been tossed hither and thither on the question of immigration and race. Firstly, local people have expected their parties to take a tough line against immigration, a task which local Labour Party groups have found more difficult than the Conservatives. But with the growth of significant ethnic groups, blacks and Asians have themselves become politically active, seeking to influence local affairs either directly through the major local parties or indirectly through ethnic pressure groups campaigning locally. Dislike of local immigrants derives in large measure from very specific – and,

again, very local – issues: council house policy, the wider difficulties
of housing, local unemployment, the 'pressures' on local whites to
quit their neighbourhoods and even the dislike of immigrants'
life-style. In the past decade, as Britain has stumbled ever more
clearly into a major economic recession characterized by massive
unemployment, it is easy to see how these various objections would
be heaped upon the immigrants and their descendants. Of course
such feelings tend to ignore the fact that the non-white communities have fared much worse than the whites; levels of black
youth unemployment are, for example, appreciably higher than
white. Notwithstanding such evidence, it has been this undeniable
(though constantly changing) subterranean urban discontent
among working people which has provided the National Front
with its limited support. Yet the discontent, which at its most
extreme takes an overtly racist form, is not channelled solely or
even mainly into the National Front. Indeed much of this hostility
towards blacks does *not* take an open, political form. Resentments
towards the 'coloureds' feeds upon the related distrust of the two
main parties – Conservatives and Labour – which are held to be
responsible for bringing about the problems in the first place. Thus
the arguments seem once more to come full circle; the politics of
race may well have served to compound the political alienation in
modern Britain, though to what degree it is difficult to assess.

In the case of traditional Labour voters this may have been
compounded by the campaign in 1976 by the unions and the Labour
Party to counter what is regarded as working-class racism. It may
well have served to confirm the widening suspicion that organized
politics (and trades unions) are hopelessly out of touch with the
feelings of the nation at large. Clearly race and immigration do
not provide a complete explanation for encroaching political alienation among growing numbers of people. In certain areas of the
major cities they may well offer the clearest guide to the spread of
distrust towards both major parties, though this is not to claim
that the racial perceptions which lie behind this phenomenon are
true or reasonable. Once more, however, as in so many historical
settings myth can prove as influential as reality. When enough
people come to believe that the immigrants and their descendants
are the cause of prevailing social and economic problems, and

when that belief is explained by the failures of party politics, there is created a volatile social and political mixture which augurs ill both for political and social tranquillity.

So far the discussion about politics and race has concentrated on the host society. There is another side to this story: the political response of immigrants to living in Britain. Black and Asian political activity has thrived, not merely in proportion to the increasing demographic strength of the various communities but, more directly, in response to the misfortunes and political antagonism heaped upon them especially in the 1970s. It would be wrong to see this response as purely defensive but nonetheless the need to counter the mounting difficulties has proved vitally important in shaping non-white politics. At its broadest point this has merged (notably with the Anti-Nazi League) into a broad coalition of opposition which cuts across ethnic lines. There have been, it is true, a number of other anti-racist organizations but they remain relatively small and marginal and have largely failed to produce significant improvements for their cause. Furthermore the existing host institutions (unions, political parties, professional organizations, local authorities) have consistently failed adequately to heed the demands of their ethnic members. Thus there has been, on the part of ethnic communities, an increasing disillusionment with the effectiveness, goodwill and intentions of white pressure groups and institutions even to begin to tackle the major problems facing the ethnic communities.

Ethnic communities have, since the 1970s, spawned a myriad organizations – self-help groups, publications and the like – often for very parochial or transient issues. Despite (and sometimes because of) efforts to integrate ethnic struggles within a broader campaign (let us say for union matters), the most striking feature of black and Asian local politics has been its specific sectionalism; the need to protect a particular group of workers, to defend a geographically restricted area, to argue the legal case of one individual or group. The development of ethnic organizations, for instance in the workplace, may seem a fragmentation of effort but it is clearly a logical and effective ploy to counter conditions not of their making. But transcending this often small-scale fragmentation has been the contrary process, notably among West Indians and

British blacks, to create an Afro-Caribbean cultural and political style which embraces both pan-Africanism and the cult of Rasta-farianism. The end result is what has been described as an 'intense black cultural nationalism'. At certain crucial points this Afro movement has converged with the development of specifically Asian political responses, because Asians, like blacks, have been propelled into their own particular politics and pressure groups by the difficulties of the 1970s. Discrimination, hostility and violence have become the causes of a political unity, often most effective at the local level, between immigrant groups and their British-born children divided by a host of cultural and ethnic distinctions.

This has, for instance, been a striking feature of black and Asian responses to the educational disadvantages created for their children; cooperative, collective agitation has often been success-ful in revising a number of educational policies which took little or no account of the particularities of their children. Similarly, ethnic communities have worked together with great effectiveness when tackling the grievances of policing, law enforcement and the periodic injustices of certain immigration rulings. And in addition there has been a proliferation of housing action groups, defence committees, local youth and community projects, nurseries, job-creation projects, hostels, and advice centres which are organized, staffed and controlled by black community groups themselves. Of course we need to recall that this varied community politics is not peculiar to the ethnic communities but has in fact been one of the most striking innovations in British politics in the past twenty years. It is particularly important and effective within (and for) the ethnic communities. Given the essentially *local* nature of such poli-tical activity, it has the effect of creating an amazing kaleidoscopic impression of a great range of political ideologies, cultural forms and ethnic and national groups all seeking to speak for and serve the interests of their own particular constituents. If a national unity is to emerge from these various groups (themselves constantly changing) it seems likely that it will be created from the need to counteract those national and malignant forces – expressed in their worst forms through the National Front – which seek to do such harm and to heap such indignities upon the non-white population.

If we take the long-term view, it seems plausible to argue that the most effective steps to safeguard and advance the interests and well-being of non-white communities is an effective coaliticn of highly organized local ethnic groups, working in conjunction with friends elsewhere to secure political and legal safeguards. This was, after all, the effective tactic employed in combating slavery in Britain and in ending it in the British empire. Both ended as a result of cooperation between black and white. The alternatives suggest continuing and perhaps incurable grievances and a society flawed and fissured not merely by social class but also by lines of colour and ethnology. It is not intended to argue the case for a melting pot, or to support the decline of important cultural and ethnic distinctions, but there is a case to be made that material and social progress is unlikely to be made if a policy of cultural or ethnic separatism is followed. To secure racial and social equality will require much more than effective community politics. Like the ending of servitude and the coming of colonial independence, racial justice demands all-round acceptance.

10
A Mosaic of Communities

Although this book has tried to present a story of immigration into Britain which stresses the unusually varied backgrounds and nature of the immigrant communities, observers and laymen tend to lump all immigrants into one generic group. In fact this is a natural tendency when commenting from the side of Britain, the host country. But it is also true that the lumping together of utterly different ethnic, cultural or religious groups into an undifferentiated mass can itself unconsciously display a variety of misconceptions and prejudices. Clearly, it would be absurd to claim that Greek Cypriots should be grouped with Jamaicans for any other reason than that they are settlers and residents in the same land. Yet many of the same objections apply, though less obviously so, towards categorizing groups which seem naturally linked by the common denominators of region or nationality.

West Indians provide a classic example of this problem, for their homelands stretch in an arc of more than 2,000 miles, from Florida to South America, encompassing a multitude of islands whose differences create particular loyalties and commitments which sometimes transcend the attachment to the region. Whereas the typical white British person is unaware of the important differences among West Indians, the truth inevitably is more complex. Not only are there the substantial barriers of race among West Indians, notably between Asians and Afro West Indians, but the fierce island attachments are generally ignored by outsiders. Blacks who look alike to the British will prove to be Jamaicans, Barbadians, Montserratians, Trinidadians or others. The post-independence history of the British West Indies has been shaped in large measure by the separate and conflicting island identities and interests which have often proved too strong or brittle to mould into regional political or economic unity. The tensions between and within those islands survive to this day in a myriad ways: within Caricom, the regional university, and even within the controlling body of West Indian cricket. It would therefore be quite wrong to overlook such different island characteristics when we consider the nature of West Indian life in Britain.

The numbers of settlers from the Caribbean have traditionally been drawn unevenly from the islands. Although Jamaica provided the largest number, in absolute terms, it is by far the most populous British island. Some of the smaller islands have, proportionately, sent a much higher number of settlers to Britain. By 1960, for instance, Jamaican emigrants to Britain constituted 9·2 per cent of that island's population, whereas from the tiny island of Montserrat (total population 12,167 in 1960) emigrants to Britain represented 31·5 per cent of the island's population. From Trinidad and Tobago and from British Guiana (now Guyana) the flow of emigrants amounted to less than 2 per cent of the combined population.

Whereas the bigger islands could manage a significant drain of manpower without much noticeable effect, the smaller islands could not so easily bear the loss without some social and economic consequences. Ironically, in the case of Montserrat money sent back from immigrants in Britain had, by 1960, become one of the island's major sources of income, yielding a greater income than some of the major local industries. Money from Britain and from other areas of emigration was vital in supplementing low and irregular local wages. Conversely, it was the earnings of emigrants in Britain which enabled other low-income members of an immediate family to embark on the relatively costly voyage to Britain. Thus large numbers of Montserratians arrived in Britain thanks to the efforts of relatives, a factor which strengthened local bonds of attachment and loyalty. And such family and community ties have traditionally been strengthened by the nature and location of residence in Britain (overwhelmingly in London). Clustered not only in the same *parts* of the capital, new arrivals tended to group themselves in houses or streets close to the earlier settlers from their home island. Furthermore, immigrants, particularly those from Montserrat, tended to marry people from their own island. This served to reinforce the loyalty and commitment to the home island

and to reinforce the distrust and dislike towards West Indians from other islands.

Such commitments to island loyalties are reinforced in a number of other ways: by religion and church attendance, by financial self-help organizations and a myriad social organizations. But there are, as we shall see in a later chapter, contrary and countervailing forces which blunt or deflect any attempt at island identity. And none are more powerful or more obvious than the changing values and outlooks inevitably shared by the children of immigrants. For Montserratians in London, like migrants all over the world, it becomes progressively more difficult to maintain the attachment to the homeland with the passage of time and as new generations grow up with less secure roots in their parents' home islands.

It is a reasonable point to make that the size of a Caribbean island – and Montserrat is not 40 square miles in area – might be crucial in shaping loyalties among emigrants in Britain. It is in fact a particular species of parochialism (in the strictest sense) which might be a less compelling social factor among people from a larger island. Jamaica is comparatively large, a mountainous and luxuriant island with a host of urban settlements, the largest of which, Kingston, is a major city by any standard. Whatever the reasons for the migration of Jamaicans to Britain, it has been calculated that by the end of the 1960s more than a quarter of a million Jamaicans lived in Britain. Inevitably perhaps they came from all walks of Jamaican life, from the countryside, from Kingston, and those who gravitated towards the city from all over the island. Like any society, Jamaica has shaped a host of distinctive cultural values among its people, values which were transported into Britain and to other parts of the world. We need also to recall that Jamaica's is a complex social structure, differentiated in a number of ways by colour, class and occupation. What seems to have shocked Jamaican settlers in Britain was that the British did not accept or even know about the particular levels of status, skill or achievement already attained by arriving Jamaicans. Jamaicans were, in British eyes, an undifferentiated group of poor black immigrants. And, whilst black Jamaicans formed the majority of their home population in the Caribbean, in Britain they found themselves outnumbered by the white host society. While these

points may seem obvious and scarcely worthy of note in British
eyes, they were startlingly unexpected and unwelcome by the
Jamaicans. Even before settling down, Jamaicans (and of course
other black settlers) found they were downgraded and degraded
in the eyes of the host society.

Overwhelmingly, Jamaicans undertook the tasks which the
British did not want to do; the dirtiest, most tedious, the least
rewarded. There were exceptions of course but, by and large,
Jamaicans found themselves in the role of British helots. And
whatever disgruntlement stems from this fact has been reinforced
by the open discrimination – in housing, education and the social
services –which have been the undoubted lot of all black immigrants. Detailed research into these issues has frequently confirmed
what any black immigrant (and his children) could report at first
hand: namely the widespread, ubiquitous and all-pervading existence of discrimination against black people in Britain. For many
older Jamaicans this may have seemed to be a reprisal for that
series of rebuffs which were built into the economic and social
structure of colonial West Indian society and which have been
removed in the years since independence. How to combat them in
British society remains extremely difficult. Not surprisingly then, a
very substantial proportion of Jamaicans in England (upwards of
one half) have shown a determination to return to Jamaica, should
economic and social circumstances allow. Indeed, it seems likely
that life in Britain was viewed only as a temporary expedient among
many emigrants from Jamaica. But the harsh realities of British life
have often served to give this long-term ambition an even sharper
and more urgent edge.

Like so many immigrant groups, Jamaicans have found it difficult to maintain many of the essential features of Jamaican life and
society. Marriage has been perhaps the most obvious of changes
among Jamaicans. Whereas in the island it often tended to be
considered after the birth of a number of children, the invisible
pressures to conform to British norms, in conjunction with powerful economic forces in the form of tax allowances, have served to
alter marriage and family patterns among Jamaicans in Britain.
Marrying earlier, less frequently preceded by (or substituted by)
common-law marriages, Jamaicans in Britain have noticeably

veered towards the creation of family units which are more obviously British than Jamaican. Of course the forces behind such
changes are complex and cannot be explained by a conscious desire
to imitate or emulate British patterns. The simple truth is that
circumstances conspire to make people accord with prevailing
norms. This seems clear in the case of Jamaican women who, at
home, would have a wider network of family, kin and neighbours
to help with the care of their children. In Britain, such networks
are nothing like as prevalent and make it important for women to
rely, in their absence, on other systems of support and help. Social
and economic conditions thus determine, to a very large degree,
the enhanced importance of a family unit and life style which has
come to approximate more closely to the British than to the traditional Jamaican. But this is not to claim that the process amounts
to a conscious deliberate assimilation; it does not.

Just as these changes have been moulded by social pressures at
large, so too have patterns of life, labour and leisure within
Jamaican families in Britain. For instance, husbands and wives
seem to spend more time together in England than is the custom in
Jamaica. Again, the explanation may lie in the general absence of
kin and the associated networks, with the result that women turn
to their menfolk for help and companionship whereas in Jamaica it
would have been found among other relatives, notably other
women. But we must also put this in its economic context. Many
Jamaican women play an important economic role within their
families in Britain; they are not utterly dependent on the wages of
their husbands. In Britain man and wife are more economically
interdependent with all the consequences which inevitably flow
from the restraints, open or subtle, which the one can exercise over
the other. There is, however, the great danger that, by reducing to
simple generalizations a complexity of patterns to be found within
any sector of the community, we run the risk of offering caricature
rather than serious analysis. After all, when we consider the enormous range of family types and experiences within the host *British*
society, it is easy to see how risky are generalizations which fail to
recognize or do justice to the unusually complex array of social
experiences in family life. Moreover, family life has been undergoing notable changes in all walks of British life (although remaining

firmly wedded to the nuclear model); Jamaican immigrants have grown accustomed to changes in their family lives over the past generation. Indeed, this may be proof that wider social and economic forces are reshaping the malleable outline of British family life, be it immigrant, working or middle class. And if this is true, it is further evidence that immigrants are not perhaps consciously imitating, or assimilating, so much as being pushed in the same direction as other members of British society by factors no one can control or predict.

Many similar points need to be stressed when we consider almost all other immigrant communities. Indians, like the West Indians, cannot easily be labelled as one neat group, as the host society would no doubt like to see it, which comes anywhere near representing the extraordinary complexity of Indian society. Again, the point is simply made; Indians come to Britain from all over the vast sub-continent and inevitably reflect the rich diversity of language, religion, caste and region of their homelands. Their sense of identity clearly has its roots in the commitment to the Indian political and national framework and in the common experiences they share when confronted by the obstacles of the white host society. But such forces for collective identity are, again, normally transcended by stronger, more specific attachments.

Just as many in host communities fail to notice the very considerable differences between West Indians – simply regarding and treating them as an undifferentiated group of blacks – so it is the case with Indians. Like the generic term 'West Indian', 'Indian' is a descriptive general term which rides roughshod over an extraordinary complexity of differences. There are obvious differences which the hosts recognize – Sikhs, for instance, can hardly be confused with any other group – but generally the British tend not to differentiate between indigenous groups. A cursory glance at the geography of India, or a mere passing acquaintance with its history, will hint at the human diversity which has, through immigration, come to be reflected in a number of British cities. Equally, although there is a crude popular awareness of the differences between India, Pakistan and, more recently, Bangladesh, there nonetheless survives the tendency to lump together all people from the sub-continent into the misleading and inaccurate term, 'Indian'.

Some of Britain's most striking ethnic communities are those created by the Pakistanis, the largest numbers being from the Punjab and Kashmir, generally from rural communities which have had a long tradition of migration. They settled in cities where work was available – notably Bradford and Birmingham – and where local men had established tentative roots after the Second World War. A pattern quickly evolved. Pakistanis would work for a number of years before entering into a marriage arranged by the head of the family, returning to Britain to establish the home before wife (and possibly children) would follow when appropriate.

Just as in West Indian families, Pakistani family life and structure did not fit the definitions of 'normal' family life generally entertained by British immigration officials and Home Office regulations. This posed problems from the very beginning for dependants of settlers in Britain. The Pakistani allegiance to the head of the family (normally the father at home) has served to ensure that loyalties remain securely rooted in the homeland. This may explain the initial weakness of Pakistani politics in Britain.

The greatest force for change, obviously a common factor among many other communities, is the settlement of wives and children in British cities. Try as they might to insulate their womenfolk from what they consider to be corrupting influences of British life, there are crucial forces which make this difficult and sometimes impossible. The need for women to work (breaking down male dominance – again, like the West Indian example), the exposure of children to British education and culture (in its wider sense) and the relative material prosperity of British life all place a strain upon the Pakistani way of life in Britain. And as an immigrant's family settles more securely into a British city and as his children grow up unmistakably British in many key respects, the aspiration eventually to return home withers and often dies.

It is important to stress once again just how heterogeneous is the British Pakistani population and how difficult it therefore is to generalize about that population. But it does seem clear that Pakistani immigration to Britain has had a major effect on both countries. In part, this has proved to be a matter of status, but, more substantially, it involves the remittance of British earnings. However unsympathetically Christian Britain is viewed (from a country of strong Muslim faith) the material well-being created by life in Britain has a transforming effect on the home village as much as on the immigrant settlements in British cities. Nonetheless, Pakistanis in Britain tend to maintain the differences of region and class which, among their fellow countrymen, mark them off one from another. They may appear, in British eyes, to be mere Pakistanis but among their own folk, more specific geographic, ethnic or social distinctions take precedence. The end result is that, even within the heart of a British city, the values, customs and principles of a specific village or rural life shape and determine local Pakistani life.

It would be wrong to imagine that life continues unchanging and unchanged, albeit in a different setting. Distance from the family head and from the code of village customs and restraints serves to create a greater degree of independence among the menfolk. For women, however, it has been argued that in many cases life in British cities has served to make stricter the cultural and religious controls over their lives. Many are cut off from the activities they traditionally share with other women in their home villages and find their lives more severely limited than in Pakistan. It is important to remember that since this is a very recent phenomenon (women have joined their menfolk relatively recently and therefore their families are very young) it is impossible to predict future developments. And the most unpredictable and determining force is likely to be the rearing and education of children and how these British-born will adapt to the cultural patterns shaped by their parents in the setting of British urban life. As we shall see later, schools and the education they provide for second-generation immigrants are at the centre of a continuing political and social debate which involves major issues for all immigrant children. The tussle (in some areas more a tug-of-war) between the communities, expecting schools to provide for the specific cultural and religious needs of their children, and between British interest groups, seeking to oblige *all* children in Britain to conform to existing educational patterns, is now a perennial feature of British urban life. Perhaps the key issue is the related matter of language and religion. The commitment to Muslim culture will demand of educational authorities (and of course, of the children involved) utterly different facilities and commitments than, let us say, the demands for revisions in the education among the children of West Indians. To claim that their needs are the same or even similar, solely because their communities are part of an exploited immigrant class in a white society, is to create from a mosaic of communities a social unity which, in certain ways, simply is not there.

This point can be made without invoking the sharpest of contrasting images among immigrants; it is no less valid when we examine other, different kinds of communities from the Indian sub-continent. One of the most distinctive of Indian communities is that of the Sikhs, some of whose religious principles have been severely challenged by the insistence, on the part of numerous British institutions, that everyone should conform to local rules. British schools insisted that Sikh schoolboys should wear caps, not turbans, bus companies have similarly expected Sikhs to remove their headwear. And, of course, English law expected Sikhs to don crash-helmets. At its worst, these and many other examples reveal that blend of arrogance and insensitivity to other cultures which has been a characteristic of British dealings with many immigrant groups since British imperial history began.

Sikhs, from the Punjab, had established a reputation for themselves as enterprising and effective traders and merchants throughout South East Asia by the late nineteenth century, spreading even as far as East and South Africa, Australia and California. Sikhs settling in Britain from the 1950s onwards came primarily from families of moderate means; not poor, but anxious to elevate their families' status and material well-being. Once more, however, we need to recognize the distinctions *within* the Sikh community which, despite the official commitment to equality of all men, has come to be divided into occupational groups very much like castes. Pedlars were the Sikh pioneers in Britain, and they were rapidly followed by other Sikh entrepreneurs lured from the Punjab and East Africa by stories of bright economic prospects in post-war Britain. Success and prosperity enabled pioneers to send for other members of their families. There rapidly grew (notably in Leeds) a basic network of aid: contacts, friends and relatives for new arrivals. Food, lodging and work were generally found for newcomers and as numbers increased so too did the sophistication and the spread of the Sikh networks. Astute investments, notably in property, led to the rapid and widespread increase in Sikh prosperity in Britain, with consequent further economic diversification and the means of bringing into Britain relatives from the Punjab and East Africa. Largely because of their commercial success, Sikh families have managed to re-establish themselves in Britain far earlier and more rapidly than other communities from the subcontinent. Thus the Sikh communities have been more 'advanced', and able to recreate many of the customs and institutions of life in the Punjab, much of it centring on the Sikh temples. It would be quite wrong, however, to imagine that all Sikhs are involved in entrepreneurial activity, or that all are commercially successful. Similarly, we need to remember that there are a number of other Asian communities – Ismailis and Gujeratis, for example – who have made an extraordinary commercial impact on modern Britain.

The numerical expansion of Sikh communities and their economic successes have meant that traders and shopkeepers have been able to satisfy all the distinctive consumer demands of the community. More significantly, perhaps, Sikh shops have, along with others from ethnic communities, helped to create a British taste and demand for Indian goods and foods. Indeed, one of the extraordinary changes in domestic British life, in the short span of one generation, is that exotic cuisine has become so popular. Along with the Chinese and some European immigrants (notably the Italians), Indians have utterly revolutionized British eating habits just as they have transformed the face of the local high streets, now dotted with Chinese and Indian restaurants and take-away food shops. Much of Indian cooking has been pioneered and developed by Sylhetis, from Bangladesh, who had earlier specialized as cooks on British ships. Ironically enough, many Indian restaurants in Britain are owned not by Indians (in the strictest sense) but by Sylhetis from a country which has only recently won its independence from Pakistan. (Indeed, a very large number of the cooks and waiters in all Indian restaurants are Sylhetis.) And, in addition to this impact on catering, there has been a quite extraordinary Indian impact on British retailing. Corner shops, sub-post offices, newsagents have been taken over by Indian businesses and families.

Indeed, there are streets in many major cities where the great majority of local small shops are Indian owned and run.

As the Sikhs have become more prosperous they have followed a path well trodden by British and immigrants alike, moving out of their initial, poorer homes into more prosperous areas, and often selling their old properties to less prosperous (Indian) immigrants. The parallel with Jewish history in Britain is very striking, right down to the geographical areas of first settlement and then re-settlement. But there are unsettling factors which make Sikh commitment to life in Britain less than enthusiastic. There has traditionally been a powerful and openly declared ambition among older Sikhs to return home; they see life in Britain as a temporary means towards a better life in the Punjab. But, however weakened by the passage of time, this resolve has been periodically reinforced by outside elements. Arguments about repatriation advanced not solely by the best known or most extreme British politician tend to unnerve Sikhs and other races, especially those with haunting memories of the Ugandan nightmare of the early 1970s. Similarly, the physical assaults on Asians of all types have had an equally unsettling effect, strengthening the resolve of many to return eventually to the Punjab.

The violence which became so commonplace in the 1970s was indiscriminate, with attacks on Asians of all kinds, and in most Asian communities in a host of British cities. Murders, terrible beatings and fire bomb attacks on Asian homes and property left scars on more than just the immediate victims. There have been similar attacks on black society, but the Asian communities more than any other incurred the wrath and violence of organized and spontaneous extremism. The outrage at such violence often united people previously separated by ethnic or religious beliefs. It became clear to the Asians and certainly to their enemies that Indians had, in a number of cities, formed a distinct unity, and from that startling awareness there developed a number of political initiatives and organizations which sought to provide short-term safeguards and long-term pressure groups.

One of the most troubled areas was Spitalfields in London, where a large Bengali community had been systematically subjected to violence and spasmodic attacks on their property. Close to the City of London, Spitalfields can boast some of the worst features of social deprivation anywhere in Britain. Furthermore, it is an area close to the old docklands which had for centuries provided a home (however wretched) for successive waves of foreign settlers. French Huguenots, Eastern European Jews and, most recently, a new generation of settlers, lascars, Indian sailors from Sylhet and elsewhere who had joined their ships in Calcutta and Bombay. Early settlers provided lodging for their itinerant kinsmen, numbers of whom increased during the Second World War. Slowly but unmistakably Brick Lane became the focal point for a growing Bengali community, spilling out from its original area of settlement but maintaining strong trading and cultural links with the old centre. Not until the violence of the 1970s (which spawned the term 'Pakibashing', an odious term reflecting an even more odious practice), did the Bengali community in Brick Lane and Spitalfields generally begin effectively to organize themselves politically and to forge links with sympathizers who could demand protection and rights for the immigrants.

The history of Spitalfields, however, provides some very revealing insights into the wider phenomenon of British history. While it has recently become known as a Bengali area, it has, over the centuries, been Irish, French and Jewish. Moreover, a similar pattern has developed, though with local peculiarities, in many other parts of the country. In Bradford and Leeds, we have seen, cheap and decaying areas of the towns acted as magnets to new settlers anxious to advance their economic claims. At different periods, Jews and Sikhs bought up old properties, later moving out to better areas and selling their homes to new arrivals. Much the same happened in Manchester's Moss Side, where the Poles and Irish were gradually displaced by new arrivals of West Indians and later by Sikhs. Of course each city, or each community within each city, has its own distinctive history and any attempt to create a new generalization which explains all immigrant patterns will crumble against a host of local or ethnic characteristics.

Enough has been said in the past few pages to illustrate a simple point, obvious enough to the people concerned but which is so often overlooked by the British. Even among the 'Indians' in Britain there is an unusual range of ethnic, cultural and religious differences which divide them into distinct sub-cultures. Whenever unity has emerged it has generally done so in response to particular social or political crises. Even then, tensions and divisions between the communities have frequently manifested themselves; for instance, during the war between East and West Pakistan, the troubles between India and Pakistan and the internal Indian political crisis during Mrs Ghandi's 'state of emergency'. It is quite natural that these and other periods of crisis should find a reflection here, among people who, though living in Britain, maintain strong links and loyalties not only to a particular nation state, but also to a much more specific and even parochial region within it.

Large numbers of the Indian community have settled in Britain to work in the expanding catering and restaurant trades. But if one ethnic community more than any other is famous for its catering role it is surely the Chinese, a role they have created in dozens of other countries around the world. In Britain, the Chinese more than any others have revolutionized British cuisine and eating habits. As far as is known, most Chinese in Britain are connected in some way with catering, although as the numbers of Chinese here have increased other occupations and services have developed to provide for the distinctive social and economic needs of the Chinese. Thus we have a range of Chinese shops, insurance and banking services, travel agencies and entertainments and, inevitably perhaps, weekend Chinese schools. But with the exception of the communities in London and Liverpool (London's Soho is a relatively recent development) the Chinese have tended to be dispersed throughout the country.

Of the 100,000 or so in Britain in the 1970s, the majority were from Hong Kong, many of them from the villages in the rural hinterland of the colony. In common with West Indians and Indians, the earnings of the Chinese in Britain are economically vitally important to their communities at home. And like other groups (notably the Sikhs) the logistics and costs of emigration, accommodation and work are organized by earlier migrants. In many respects the Chinese in Britain remain the most distinctive, less well known to the host society, more closely knit and acutely aware of their collective identity. It has even been argued that the Chinese are the most unassimilated of all ethnic groups, but militating against this fact is the recent and rapid development of a second generation who must, inevitably, undergo the transforming experience of growing up and being educated in and by a British society. This factor, together with the uncertainty of the political future of Hong Kong, may serve to break down the initial cultural resistance developed by the Chinese in Britain. Of course in this they have exhibited only a different *degree* of a similar and natural response of all settlers and immigrants, namely the maintenance of loyalties and commitments to the broader cultural forms (language, religion, kinship ties, etc.) of the native homeland.

A fact often ignored – though it should be stressed – is that immigration and foreign settlement in Britain are not solely a matter of colour. The fact that over the past twenty years it has increasingly been *perceived* to be a question of colour is a remarkable insight into British perceptions and values. Yet, as we have seen frequently in this book the period since the Second World War witnessed large-scale non-coloured settlement in Britain. From Europe and the Mediterranean, from the old white colonies and dominions of South Africa, Australasia and Canada, and from the U.S.A. no less than from the New Commonwealth, substantial numbers of people have settled in Britain in the past forty years. There has developed a veritable mosaic of communities, each distinctive, each changing slowly, and many of them owing loyalties to another region of the world, but each drawn or propelled to Britain by forces which, in time, begin to impose new and unexpected features on the settlers.

In a book of this nature it is obviously impossible to do full, or even partial, justice to the extraordinary richness and diversity within Britain's immigrant societies. Omissions and simplifications are bound to be as striking as some of the cases studied. It is perhaps worth a cursory glance at some of the communities whose story goes unrecorded in other parts of the book. There are often elements in the history of even the smaller immigrant groups which provide insights into the broader phenomenon of settlement in Britain. In the case of the Cypriots, for instance – both Greek and Turkish – the pattern of settlement is another reflection of colonial rule. Although small numbers had arrived earlier, the great bulk of Cypriots settling in Britain came in the 1950s and 1960s; the 1,075 of 1931 had forty years later grown to 72,665, though with their

British-born offspring the true figure may well have been double that. Living overwhelmingly in London the Cypriots, lured primarily by the economic attractions of the period, may appear to be a relatively small group. But as a proportion of their island population they present quite a different impression; one Cypriot in six lives in Britain. With an almost equal proportion of men and women, and therefore able to maintain their traditionally firm commitment to Cypriot family life, Cypriots have kept their identity through a host of social and religious organizations and through the preservation of strong family and economic ties with their native land. Cypriots were instrumental in establishing and then expanding the new-found British taste for Greek cuisine; in common with a range of other immigrants, they have helped to transform some of the tastes and social habits of the British. But Cypriots have always been particularly concerned about maintaining their children's cultural identity, to ensure that it is not lost in the process of growing up and being educated in Britain. Consequently, a number of private and evening schools and classes were established to teach the language and to maintain the Greek Orthodox religion (which has more than fifty churches in Britain, primarily in London). There is, however, evidence to suggest that the second generation's commitment to Cypriot religion and cultural forms is less firm than their parents would like.

Similar problems are experienced by a number of other immigrant communities. Among Poles for instance, faced by a noticeable decline in their numbers (from 135,000 in 1960 to perhaps 105,000 in 1976), the problems seemed especially acute, because unlike other communities they had an older age structure and fewer new arrivals. The Polish community, however, was an overwhelming and fiercely Catholic community, for whom their own churches and related schools came to provide a complex social web for Polish people throughout Britain. Like other political refugees, however, the experiences of the Poles do not necessarily reflect a broader immigrant experience. After all, many Poles (unlike, say, West Indians or Asians) did not choose to quit their homelands, but found themselves stranded by or drifting to Britain on, the tides of war. In many respects this clearly created acute frustration; to have fought so bitter a war so valiantly, to have incurred such terrible losses, to have wandered through most theatres of that war and then to find their homeland captured by another alien regime was a source of great distress to thousands of Poles. But the un-happiness at the fate of their country has been partially counter-balanced for many by the virtues of living in a free society. It is impossible to listen to the testimony of Poles who escaped from the horrors of wartime Poland to the relative tranquillity of Britain not to appreciate the extent to which numbers of settlers in Britain value their adopted home. This should not make us complacent. But it is an undeniable fact that, whereas many post-war immi-grants and their children have a string of legitimate complaints against Britain, European wartime refugees tend to tell a different story. This is, of course, an understandably relative phenomenon; however bleak post-war Britain, it provided for many thousands of Poles a stable home, a peaceful society and the opportunity to rebuild lives and families shattered by the war. Although public hostility grew towards Polish settlers when the war ended, this was a minor irritation compared with all the traumas of earlier years.

The Poles settled primarily in the cities, overwhelmingly in London, but also in Birmingham, Manchester and, on a smaller scale, in Bradford, Wolverhampton, Leeds, Nottingham, Sheffield, Coventry, Leicester and Slough. Others went into the mines and on to the farms, where labour was especially short after 1945. In many respects the sophisticated Polish social system derived directly from that established during the Second World War, much of it based on ex-soldiers' organizations. One key theme (as with the Cypriots) has been the efforts to maintain the Polish language, partly through newspapers but, more importantly, through schools for children of Polish settlers. Such schools provided language and cultural tradi-tions as well as sporting and social activities for the young, en-couraging a commitment to the idea of being Polish. This identity, although clearly difficult to maintain in the face of countervailing pressures on the young, is helped by the way Poles keep up their family ties in Poland itself. Indeed ties with the Polish homeland have, if anything, been strengthened in recent years by unforeseen political turmoil which has given Poland such renewed inter-national prominence. The economic crisis in Poland, the upsurge of a grass-roots democracy and resistance, exemplified by *Solidarity*

– and the quite remarkable impact of a Polish Pope – have all served to revive the 'Polishness' of émigré Poles everywhere. Extraordinary work has been done by Poles in Britain to raise funds, provide food, clothing and medicine for their troubled homeland, and this has been true of second-generation Poles as much as their elders. Of course the Poles have a ready-made network for this and other ethnic activities, for they have a framework of seventy-three Polish parishes in England and Wales and four in Scotland. What will happen to this Polish community in future is quite impossible to predict. But it seems perfectly clear that the breakdown of Polish identity and of the related social organizations in Britain, openly predicted in the early 1960s, quite simply has not happened. It would perhaps be equally foolish to make similar predictions for the next twenty years.

The purpose of this chapter has been not to offer a glimpse of all the varied communities in Britain so much as to suggest their diversity. They form a veritable mosaic of contrasting forms and hues. All have their own distinctive cultural identities; at certain points some very different communities become related to each other (normally through political exigencies). All have changed, by the very fact of being in Britain and all have, in certain important ways, brought about changes in the host society. Their history, and their contemporary story, is not however uniform. Nor are those communities devoid of major problems. Indeed, one of the recurring themes in this book has been the persistence of certain points of conflict between settlers and hosts. Further study of those conflicts will provide insights not simply into the immigrants' peculiar difficulties but also into those of the British themselves.

II
Points of Conflict

The history and modern sociology of immigration and settlement in Britain is, in many key respects, a story of disputes between settlers and hosts. Indeed so frequent, widespread, and so recurring are such conflicts, in almost any historical setting we care to examine since the seventeenth century, that it is tempting to offer generalizations on this theme. It is perhaps an inevitable consequence of the intrusion and settlement of outsiders that hosts will express doubts and dislikes, will reveal objections towards the newcomers. Clearly, this is not true for everyone but it seems sufficiently widespread among enough people to suggest a common denominator in the history of population migrations. But the process of upheaval and resettlement creates conflicts not only with the host society. It seems equally clear that conflicts and tensions are also generated among immigrants and settlers; between those in Britain and their kin in the home region, between immigrants and their British-born offspring and between different ethnic communities.

It is likely that conflicts of some kind inevitably attend the process of settlement in a foreign land. There is, for example, sufficient evidence from other societies which have been shaped in large part by immigration (the U.S.A., Canada and Australia, for example) to suggest that tensions between settlers and settled (however we define them) is inescapable. In the case of Britain since 1945 such conflicts have become centred increasingly on the immutable question of colour and have, in almost every walk of British life, become institutionalized into overt or subtle forms of racial discrimination. There is in fact strong evidence that in many important ways both host and immigrant communities tend traditionally to see the development of immigration as a series of conflicts, some more serious than others, some more soluble than others. Nonetheless the centrality of conflict is self-evident – and recognized – on all sides. It may be felt that there is little difference in such an analysis between other conflicts within British society and while it is not intended to enter the (largely ideological) debate about such broader conflicts, it appears clear that the conflicts generated by immigration and settlement have their own distinct qualities and consequences.

From one ethnic community to another there is a recurring complaint about their dealings with British officials. For many thousands, the difficulties of dealing with British bureaucracy began even before they reached Britain. The protracted procedure for securing passports, entry vouchers, visas and work permits traditionally brings potential immigrants into contact with British High Commissions and their officers. Long before shuffling into those slow-moving and rather daunting lines at British airports, settlers to Britain have learned to face extensive questioning and scrutiny about family, friends, economic status and motives. British immigration regulations and controls may seem (to those obliged to suffer them) to be both labyrinthine and confusing, but they are no different from many other countries. Indeed, it is a reflection on the massive movement of peoples around the world that such bureaucratic restrictions create obstacles for most outsiders seeking to enter a new country, even if only temporarily. This does not however invalidate the basic point that immigrants' initial experiences of British officialdom are generally daunting; the contact with men in uniforms at immigration checkpoints is only the beginning of continuing and recurring irritations between hosts and settlers. In essence it is unavoidable that vetting and control of immigrant people should be part of any state's machinery but it is a matter of deep and abiding complaint that such machinery is, by virtue of its controlling legislation, discriminatory. No less serious are the periodic complaints from ethnic communities and from welfare agencies anxious to safeguard the interests of immigrants, that immigration officials often transgress their powers, ignoring or violating immigrants' rights. Few would have believed it possible or likely that, as part of immigration controls, British authorities would take it upon themselves to institute 'virginity tests' for potential female immigrants. But it is now clear that such outrageous procedures, however unusual or infrequent, were put into practice.

It is possible to exaggerate the significance of the fact that the first British contact with immigrants is conducted by people in uniform. But it is abundantly clear that uniformed people are thought to pose serious difficulties for ethnic communities in Britain. Indeed settlers in Britain from the horrors of Nazi Germany have expressed their initial dislike of uniformed British officials. They soon learned, however, that the men inside those uniforms did not behave as others had in German-occupied Europe. There is a more substantial point to be made about British bureaucracy. It is the agency for, by and large, a very efficient state; the very efficiency of the modern British state makes it intrude much more into the lives of everyone than before (certainly before 1939 in Britain). For immigrants from Third World countries, where national poverty undermines the ability of the state to intervene effectively and control its own affairs as it would like to, contact with the British system is in fact to come face to face with a qualitatively different state bureaucracy. To argue for the greater efficiency (and therefore for the greater intrusiveness) of the machinery of the British state is not to decry or belittle the bureaucracies of other New Commonwealth countries. But it would be unreasonable to expect poor countries to be able to afford the complex, sophisticated and highly technological bureaucracies of advanced industrial nations. Quite apart from the presence of expensive technology, notably computers, Third World nations cannot afford to train, administer or man the levels of state bureaucracy, at the levels of comparable efficiency, so commonplace in the West. Thus, at its simplest, immigrants from the Third World find themselves confronted by and subjected to a bureaucratic scrutiny quite unlike the ones they may have encountered before. Furthermore this contact – intrusive, sharp-eyed, rigorous and impersonal as it seems – continues long after the immigrant passes through the immigration control and out into British society.

Of course similar experiences, with their attendant round of questioning on sensitive matters, are often repeated when New Commonwealth settlers return to Britain after holidays or visits home. It is, quite simply, not a single, 'one off' experience. Furthermore, there is a continuing irritation among ethnic communities about fresh immigration cases which regularly cause social and political disquiet. As we have seen, a number of ethnic communities have only recently begun to send for wives and children. Often the marriages are traditionally arranged; often too the network of immigrant familial and kinship ties do not conform with the perception of family life or dependency links on the part of immigration officials or Home Office regulations. Thus, we find these regular but unhappy encounters between officials and settlers periodically repeated, with the cross-examining of immigrants about their relationship with people in Britain and in their homeland. Of course, these dealings have been shaped by the nature of the particular laws and regulations, themselves politically determined. But, whatever their provenance, however understandable their intentions, their cumulative impact is to exacerbate the feelings of mistrust and dislike on the part of immigrants towards British bureaucracy and officialdom.

It would be pleasing to report that such conflicts end when people have passed through immigration controls. Of course this is not the case. On the contrary, immigrants and their offspring embark on a life in Britain which seems fraught with obstacles placed in their path by British officials. Nowhere is this more strikingly the case than in the relations between the police and the ethnic communities. In almost any social context we choose to examine, the ethnic communities enter into and endure some of the worst features of urban deprivation in Britain. Bad housing, low pay, poor health services, poor education – immigrants run the gamut of British social deprivation. Living in the poorer quarters in run down areas of British cities, ethnic communities attract the attention and presence of the local police which has, for almost a century and a half, been the lot of the urban poor. Almost as a matter of definition, the poor are seen to be a police problem, and this is as true of the Irish in mid-nineteenth-century Liverpool as it is of West Indians in London today. We need not slide into a simple social determinism (i.e. that all the individual and collective problems of the poor in urban life are socially predetermined and beyond the ability and the power of the people concerned) to argue the case that many ethnic groups are as much the victim of social circumstance as they are the objects of extra-vigilant scrutiny by the police. Moreover, this vigilant (and often crude and insensitive) policing exists not simply because most of the ethnic communities are poor, but also because, in innumerable ways, their lifestyle and cultures conflict utterly with the values and approaches of the police. The 'unusual' features among the ethnic communities serve to enhance police curiosity and suspicion.

Criticisms of the police are most acute and persistent in the black community, where, it is claimed, police harrassment – especially of black youth – is commonplace. We should remember that unemployment is especially high among young blacks and large numbers with plenty of free time often gather together in ways which attract police attention. When in the summer of 1981 major disturbances erupted in a number of British cities, notably in Liverpool and Brixton, the violence was primarily a reaction against the police. It is true that the riots were not uniquely black. White youths took part in most of them and in Liverpool they seem to have been in the majority. Unemployment had, by 1981, become no respecter of colour. But the riots were overwhelmingly anti-police. The way the riots were reported, notably in the press, created a great deal of misunderstanding although it is true to say that the subsequent report by Lord Scarman brought some clarity back to the discussion. And he too drew attention to the central role of anti-police feelings.

There was and continues to be a tendency to interpret the 1981 troubles as 'race riots' in the classic American style, of black versus white. In truth, the English riots were quite unlike, say, the riots which followed the murder of Martin Luther King. There was looting and considerable damage to property and vehicles (the majority of them police vehicles) and the riots spread from their initial targets to other victims, sometimes the ambulance and fire services. But in essence the attacks were on the persons and the property of the police. Such violence – 247 were arrested in Brixton alone – may seem out of all proportion to the alleged insults and injuries suffered by the blacks. It does however provide us with an indication, however extreme, of the profound feelings of, and the once latent antagonism shared by (primarily young) blacks towards the police. Of course it has also to be said that not everyone agrees with this assessment. For many, the riots were the fulfilment of Enoch Powell's infamous prophecy, couched in classical imagery in 1968, which predicted future violence in British cities. In reality, the origin of this tension was more prosaic. It is true that there were unacceptably high levels of certain street crimes in a number of ethnic areas, but the police response – whether 'swamping' or the capricious impact of the Special Patrol Group – served largely to inflame the tensions without solving the problems of crime.

It is perhaps unreasonable to expect police officers not to display the range of prejudices (on race or other matters) to be found in society at large. If, as seems clearly to be the case, Britain is a deeply prejudiced society in a number of ways, it will certainly follow that her policemen will be similarly prejudiced. In fact there is evidence to suggest that the police, especially in London, are more fundamentally tainted by racial prejudice than the society they serve. Attitudes towards blacks of an almost eighteenth-century crudity, which would have graced the dinner table of any slave holder, have been shown to be widespread among recent police cadets. It is true that since the 1960s a number of police forces have incorporated some basic lessons on 'race relations' in their training programmes, a process accelerated since the 1981 riots (alongside new training in riot control), but it is undeniably a difficult and uphill struggle.

Lord Scarman was in no doubt of the parlous relations between the police and the black communities and was adamant about the need to improve them by changing the training (and disciplining) of policemen and ameliorating the prospects for young blacks, notably through 'positive action'. There is, however, little political credit to be accumulated by investment in such issues, especially in times of recession and in a society which, as we have seen throughout this book, is less than benign in its fundamental attitudes towards its ethnic communities. In a society which tolerates discrimination in almost every walk of life, it is hard to see how pleas for progressive and liberal changes can make much headway, unless given the strength of unrelenting and pertinacious political backing. Here, however, we come full circle because however benign and harmonious their public utterances the two major political parties are, in the eyes of the ethnic communities, party to and responsible for many of the discriminatory legislations and practices (primarily immigration controls) which are so resented. Thus, at the time of writing (1983) the police and the ethnic (especially the black) communities gaze at each other with incomprehension and scarcely veiled mistrust and dislike. Indeed, so ingrained have these mutual dislikes become that it is hard to see a flicker of optimism on either side. The policing and law enforcement of ethnic quarters of British cities have resolved into a state of permanent and grudging conflict.

In the press and in the political debate about 'law and order' in British society, the early 1970s saw the mysterious evolution of a new crime and of a new group of criminals. Behind these new concepts – given wide publicity by the media – lay distinct racial and social assumptions on the part of the people who fashioned the concepts. 'Mugging' and 'muggers' quickly established themselves as clear-cut phenomena; street crimes and criminals largely, if not overwhelmingly, carried out by blacks, or so it was reported. It is however abundantly clear that the statistics for crimes allegedly committed by different racial types are perceived of and accumulated in a remarkably crude way.

Similarly, there emerged in these discussions the concept of 'black youth' which is couched in terms of that group's 'natural' criminal proclivities. In large measure the capricious use of the 'sus' laws by the police ensured that such racial assumptions would indeed be fulfilled; it was very easy, thanks to 'sus', for police officers to transmute innocent blacks into street criminals by the simple process of arresting and charging them. Examples are legion of innocent blacks, naturally upset and offended by police scrutiny, responding in a way which enables the police successfully to level another charge against them.

The concept of 'mugging', a term without any legal or dictionary definition when it first reared its head in England in the early 1970s (my own Oxford dictionary describes 'mugger' as a 'broad-nosed Indian crocodile'), was imported from the U.S.A. Almost instantaneously mugging became *the* major crime threatening the social fabric of British cities. This allegation was carefully promoted by the media and by the Met. (which was at the time deeply involved in a battle of an altogether more serious kind against the ranks of corrupt officers within the force). One need not be cynical to appreciate how concern about 'mugging' deflected attention from the more alarming threat of a thoroughly corrupt London police force. Courts quickly took up the cry against the muggers, magisterial denunciations echoing through the media. Thus was public attention quickly and effectively focused on the criminal activity of certain sectors of black society. Yet subsequent trials, revelations and detailed research have shown how, even on its own terms, the concept of mugging as a particularly black phenomenon is absurd. Firstly the racial categories used by the police will not bear close scrutiny; secondly it is perfectly clear that the police do not classify the racial type of all offenders. Whites tend not to be categorized, blacks invariably do. Not surprisingly, the figures begin to look extraordinary.

By the mid 1970s the British had, overwhelmingly, come to accept that mugging was a persistent urban crime carried out by blacks against older white people. Furthermore, the Met., now under the guidance of Robert Mark – long-accustomed to the benefits of good liaisons with the press – carefully cultivated its relations with local and national newspapers, feeding the editors with titbits of cautionary evidence. Inevitably, such evidence quickly surfaced, often in sensational form, in the press. Indeed, it has been forcefully argued that the belief in a particularly strong wave of black crime even entered the Scarman Report of 1981. There is little doubt that whole sectors of white British society had by the early 1980s come to accept a series of dubious propositions about crime and black society. Moreover many of these propositions hinged specifically on racial assumptions; on the beliefs that blacks were, in certain important ways, naturally prone to crime and lawlessness. Of course many of the same allegations had been made of the Irish in the eighteenth century and of the Jews in the early twentieth century. What is extraordinary is that even in the 1980s criminal behaviour (itself of course in need of careful definition) can be associated with ethnic, racial or national types. Whereas many (if not most) might seek the roots of criminal activity in particular social or personal circumstances, in much of British debate about certain crimes there has been a tendency to revert to explanations which would not be ill suited to nineteenth-century racial theory. The 'natural' disorderly nature of Jamaicans, the inclination towards violence among West Indians in general are often all put in a context of Caribbean history which seeks to explain these personal and national characteristics in terms of the residual experience of chattel slavery. Such concepts are at best ill conceived, at worst malicious. But they – and the gamut of more complex assumptions with which they are associated – are more revealing of the person or group adhering to them than they are of the social issues they purport to explain. Nonetheless, a key point to be made here is that, since the early 1970s, there has been planted in the British mind an unshakable belief that crime is associated with black society.

The blacks have in fact become *les classes dangereuses*, that threatening, little-known and subterranean class so widespread throughout nineteenth-century urban society and which was considered to be a menacing force which might easily sap or undermine the peace and well-being of propertied society. To argue in this way might be seen as offering a crude and simple view of relations between black and white in modern Britain. That is far from the book's intentions; but the depressing evidence about the recent history of the relationship between black society and the forces of the law, expresses, in very large part, its own inexorable logic and draws its own conclusions.

The conflicts between black and white about policing and the administration of the law are only among the most obvious of such conflicts. Less volatile, but contentious nonetheless, has been the issue of the education provided for children of West Indian (and other immigrant) parents. Again, although it is tempting to describe these educational difficulties in general terms there are marked differences between different communities, the most striking being that between the English-speaking people and the non-English speakers, with all the complex religious and cultural associations which those languages represent. It is in fact a common feature of most immigrant communities that education in the language, religion and customs of the parents' home society is consciously used to maintain that cultural identity which parents seem anxious to pass on to their children. Where local education authorities have failed to do this, there have invariably followed private schools, classes and instruction. This seems to be more easily arranged when a religious organization provides the particular community with a ready-made framework, personnel and literature. Poles, Chinese, Sikhs and many others have been able easily to provide a sound educational system of passing on their own distinctive language and learning to British-born children.

For the non-English-speaking people, the encouragement of language skills in the parents' indigenous language is viewed as the central and determining factor in establishing cultural identity. Of course, among British-born the particular accent or intonation of the parent – be it Irish, Greek, West Indian or whatever – gives way to the prevailing accent of the social class or region into which the child is born. It is a simple but important point that a blind person listening to such people could rarely detect the ethnic or national origin of the family. Yet language can provide an unmistakable guide to the broader cultural identity. Many young West Indians are determined to maintain the verbal style and vocabulary of the Caribbean (though in truth it varies greatly between the islands). Many black Britons can move between what are, in effect, two distinct languages: one, the more formal English demanded by British society, the other, their indigenous language which though often viewed as *patois* is recognized by many as a distinct language.

The question of language has become both an educational and political issue among the ethnic communities. For people with utterly different languages from English – Polish or Urdu, for example – the main, perhaps the sole, means of maintaining that language (and all that it represents) is to provide formal education. The political controversy normally arises when demands are made for such language tuition *within* the local state schools, rather than through voluntary or weekend classes. In communities where a particular immigrant group is demographically strong, pressures have grown to persuade local authorities to provide training within the normal school system. It takes no great imagination (and it requires no prejudice) to appreciate that such demands have the makings of fierce social and political controversy, at the heart of which lies a series of conflicting values about how immigrant groups should conduct their lives and prepare for the future.

Arguments about language seem clear-cut when the languages are indisputably different, as are, say, English and Urdu. Less obvious, though sometimes more troublesome, is the problem of variants of English itself. It is now accepted by some linguists that Creole English – black English – spoken in different ways by West Indians, is quite a distinct language from English itself. Both in the West Indies and in Britain it has become clear that to insist upon formal English has been to demand of pupils *two* languages, one possible factor in the troublesome arguments about the educational achievements of West Indian children in British schools. For local authorities to provide appropriate language tuition – or education through a language other than standard English – is not only expensive and difficult (at a time of dwindling resources) but creates, in a particular form, more general arguments about the very nature of education which the state ought to provide for its children. Indeed it is not to stretch the case too far to suggest that the development of immigrant communities has posed a series of challenging intellectual as well as practical questions about the very nature of education in hundreds of British schools. If a particular language is to be provided in school why not the historical and cultural context of that language? Indeed arguments about language are often merely a specific form of a more general educational argument which has developed in the past twenty years about the nature of education for immigrants and their children. For many thousands of second-generation children whole sections of formal British schooling seem especially tangential and unrelated to their lives and aspirations.

Nowhere is this more striking than in the study of history. There are, as we noted at the beginning of this book, serious intellectual objections to much of the history provided through formal schooling. Changes have, it is true, transformed history teaching in recent years, largely under pressure from a new school of social history. These convergent pressures – the demands of social history and those from immigrant groups seeking a history which is more 'relevant' and revealing of their own past and culture – have cumulatively created an urge for a different kind of history in schools. In a number of schools with large numbers of second-generation children there have been a number of pioneering and remarkably interesting efforts to present schoolchildren with a different kind of history. The subjects covered – the history of the Caribbean, of

Africa, of slavery and the slave trade, of India – are all perfectly 'respectable' in themselves and clearly provide a point of contact for many pupils normally indifferent or hostile to more traditional history. There is inevitably a resistant and begrudging reaction on the part of many people (educators, politicians and publishers) to such a transformation in historical curricula, a resistance which is often rooted in ignorance of the importance of newer historical fields and in an inflated and often uncritical attachment to more conventional historical studies.

In recent years this has become a political issue; part of the determination expressed by senior policy-makers and advisers to return to 'well tried' and proven patterns of learning and teaching, a return to the older substance of, say, history, which it is claimed served Britain so well for many decades. In truth, the substance of history teaching during the century since the establishment of compulsory education has always been exposed to serious and fundamental criticisms of substance, purpose and style. It would of course be absurd to claim that history in British schools has been crudely ideological in the sense that is commonplace in totalitarian states. But there is a strong case to be made that the bulk of school history has sought to present a limited and less than impartial view of Britain's history. Indeed, long before the demands for, say, black or Indian history, there was a wealth of criticism of history teaching from those who saw in it few traces of the white *British* common people.

There can be little doubt that school history has for decades presented a particular story of British (indeed largely *English*) history which has consistently ignored or distorted huge areas of social experience. Equally the image of Britain's global and imperial pre-eminence had traditionally been portrayed to millions of British schoolchildren as a godly crusade by which the white men took the benefits of white civilization into the primitive and barbaric regions of the world. At the heart of the teaching about the empire lay an enthnocentric view of the world which, however comprehensible in its time and place, proved influential in shaping the political and racial outlook of untold legions of British people. Indeed, much of the history of Britain's imperialism was presented in terms of the unique qualities of the British 'race', a concept which, however specious, had quite profound ramifications. It was given a new lease of life in Winston Churchill's history of the English-speaking people and also in a number of his famous war-time speeches, which frequently returned to the theme of 'this island race'.

Careful research into the curriculum of history teaching in the late nineteenth and twentieth centuries has provided a wealth of detail about the nature and direction of the ethnocentricism and racism which informed practically all school textbooks in geography, literature and history. While other Europeans were dismissed as less worthy and exalted than the British, it was for non-white peoples that such school texts reserved their sharpest barbs. The 'barbaric peoples of Asia' were often contrasted with Christians ('from whom better things might have been expected'). Africans tended to be sympathetically portrayed only because of the lingering British guilt about slavery and the slave trade. Few doubts existed about West Indians, however: 'lazy, vicious and incapable of serious improvement or of work except under compulsion . . . He is quite happy and quite useless and spends any extra wages he may earn upon finery.' The British Empire, it was commonly argued, brought the prospect of converting to Christianity to millions of subjects labouring under the weight of their various 'superstitions', 'certainly more than 300 million human beings all bowing down to gods of wood and stone'.

Similar arguments recur again and again in a host of British school texts. Furthermore, they were often used in the schools throughout the empire and colonies. It is then perfectly understandable that newly independent Commonwealth nations should seek a different kind of history curriculum in their nations' schools. But it is equally clear that such literature, however modified and qualified its form, would prove inappropriate at best and offensive at worst for children of immigrants in Britain. Yet this is only the most obvious of a series of criticisms which have been levelled at (in this case) the history curriculum in British schools. It needs also to be stressed that the educational survivals of 'traditional' history are, in fact, quite inappropriate for most children. In fact, recent demands for changes in the substance and aim of history teaching are merely variations on an older theme: to make history in schools more attractive to pupils. This is not to be done, however – as is so often alleged – by discarding the fundamental principles of truth, critical assessment and careful reconstruction but by examining areas and themes which are so often ignored. The rise of social history in the past twenty years has made considerable strides towards rectifying the in-built imperfections of history teaching. But it is important to emphasize the ever-changing nature of history; were it to remain static it would quite simply wither and lose its intellectual appeal and its wide attraction.

There is then absolutely no intellectual reason (excepting ideological and political objections) why school history should not provide a broad historical context which makes intellectual and contemporary sense for a wide range of pupils. Indeed, the most powerful case for changes in the substance of history teaching in schools – to provide, for instance, African, Caribbean or Indian history – is that it is as important, as relevant and intellectually challenging for all British children (and adults) – whether of immigrant of indigenous families. It is as important for white children to know of their nation's involvement in the slave trade or the British dominance of India as it is for children whose parents came from these regions. The history of the British empire is, after all, an incredibly complex story which bound master and slave, Briton and colonial into a symbiotic relationship which shaped their separate identities and their mutual relationship from that day to this. To demand a more 'multi-cultural' and a more varied view of history is not to seek to discard the older virtues generally claimed for history but rather to embark on the very process which has ensured the survival and the continuing fascination of history and its ability to respond to changes in the intellectual climate. In general, those who resist demands for such changes seek to defend a number of intellectual and educational qualities which have long been in dispute. And at heart they are proffering an ideological argument which seeks to defend values which were challenged *long before* the rise of modern ethnic communities. Ironically, however, those proponents of changes in school curricula (to take account of newer communities) are themselves often accused of arguing an ideological case. Yet consciously to deny the children of, say, West Indian parents access to the history of that region itself demands a decision which is as ideological as it is educational. Thus what appears to be a straightforward and simple matter – the teaching of history – has opened up an extraordinarily complex intellectual and political debate (much of it masquerading as educational policy) which challenges some of the central and broader precepts of compulsory schooling itself.

There are in addition other educational problems specific to certain communities. Since 1971 there has been a great deal of concern about the performance of West Indian children in schools. Even allowing for the low income and status of their families, it is often claimed that their scholastic performance is lower than it ought to be. The evidence is, however, uncertain though there is undoubtedly an *assumption* that blacks fail to achieve educationally, an assumption which naturally creates a great deal of resentment. There are unquestionably failings and deprivations in the schooling system. Poor people have for a century been denied a fair share of the educational facilities and opportunities in Britain. Now that substantial sectors of the urban working class in certain areas of British cities are black, they too have become the victims of that social neglect in education and other sectors which has previously been the preserve of the white poor. But whether this factor alone provides an adequate explanation remains an open question and a continuing conflict between the black community and white society.

It is scarcely surprising that, in a period of major unemployment, people leaving school with poorer (or no) formal 'qualifications' will be among the most prominent of the unemployed. Young black adults fare badly in the increasingly competitive demand for jobs, to say nothing of places in further or higher education. The figures are distressing and were able to impress themselves on Lord Scarman's report as a factor in the Brixton disturbances. Something like 55 per cent of black males under nineteen in the Brixton area were unemployed by the early summer of 1981. Of course what makes these figures more serious is that they cannot be explained uniquely in terms of educational disadvantage. In employment, as in most 'public' walks of British urban life, non-whites are hemmed in by complex layers of overt or subtle prejudices which deny them equality of treatment and opportunity.

It is not proposed to document the full nature or incidence of discrimination or disadvantage, for it is sufficiently and abundantly proved in volumes of recent research; research which merely confirms in depth what most non-whites in Britain could easily vouch for. Indeed so obvious is this fact of modern British society that in July 1983 the new Home Secretary, Leon Brittan (who is himself a descendant of an immigrant Jewish family) asserted to a Hindu audience in Bradford, 'It is a hard fact that ethnic minorities suffer disproportionately from unemployment; there is incontrovertible research evidence to back up individual experience of discrimination in recruitment or selection.' When such sentiments have penetrated to the highest levels of the Home Office, and can be carried in *The Times* under the headline 'Prejudice a daily reality . . .' it seems unnecessary to repeat them here.

It would, however, be misleading to imagine that this is merely a matter of work. There are, it is true variations *between* the ethnic communities (inevitable, given their geographic and occupational differences) and between the sexes. But the central fact of discrimination in employment is clear enough. It is also present in the complicated matter of housing and accommodation, a topic which, again, has attracted a great deal of academic scrutiny in the past twenty years. In moving into and acquiring the most run down and unattractive properties, immigrants were propelled by a number of forces. Firstly, there was the natural and unavoidable need to live cheaply among their kinsfolk, a fact encouraged by the discrimination shown towards them by private and public property markets. Sociologists continue to argue about the weight to be attached to these factors; but the argument is normally about the relative importance of discrimination, *not* about its existence. In 1979, for instance, research in Handsworth showed that whites were disproportionately successful as applicants for home improvement grants. Here, as elsewhere, the non-whites suffer such deprivations not solely through discrimination but through subtle changes in the housing market (or labour market) which manage to outflank and render impotent the legislation to prevent discrimination.

There are, then, a series of interlocking discriminations which render the lives of ethnic communities more difficult and frustrating. It would be impossible to offer predictions about the likely outcome of such conflicts (and others) either on the development of ethnic communities or on their relations with the host British society. But it is relatively easy to see potential (and existing) dangers should these disadvantages be visited upon the children of immigrants. It is bad enough that settlers should be victimized in such complex though comprehensive ways but it raises a qualitatively different element when the victims are British-born. The summer of 1981 provided an unpleasant example of one type of response. It is not suggested that this is the only (or even the most likely) response, but simply that the grievances of ethnic communities – long unnoticed and unheeded – are of a distinctive and pressing kind, many if not most created or exacerbated by the host society. These and other points of conflict must be resolved for the future well-being of all concerned.

12

The Changing British

It is to be expected that the settlement of large numbers of immigrants and the growth of distinct ethnic communities in Britain will
have ramifications far beyond the confines of those communities.
Older British people will remember the time when a non-white face
was unusual. By 1976, Britain was home to the following numbers
of people: 604,000 West Indians, 636,000 Asians and 531,000 from
other New Commonwealth countries. Of course they are not scattered evenly throughout Britain but are to be found, overwhelmingly, in concentrated communities in a small number of major
conurbations. At the most obvious levels, Britain has changed its
urban and demographic make-up in proportion to the growth of
these communities. Although non-whites still form only a relatively
small proportion of the total population, it is now possible to
speak of Britain as a multi-cultural society quite unlike during any
other period of British history. While it is obviously the case that
immigrants and their offspring are *not* to be found spread equally
thoughout all social classes but, as we have seen, are grouped
primarily in the poorest of social categories, their impact has been
profound, far beyond the social and geographic limits of their own
communities.

The British are without doubt undergoing a number of changes
in their personal and collective lives brought about by the presence
and influence of these varied national and ethnic groups. Some of
the changes are obvious for all to see; others are more subtle and
less easily detectable. It is possible for instance that changes are in
train in the way the British perceive themselves and their role in the
world. Although it is the case that prejudices and discrimination
continue to be persistent features of British life, it is uncertain
whether such vices will continue unchanged in the future. It is
clear, for instance, that attitudes to non-white people have under-

gone a series of complex changes over a period of many centuries and there is no convincing reason to feel that similar or different changes will not continue in the future. To put the matter simply, the British in 1980 have quite different perceptions of the black or the Asian than they held in, say, 1780. Who could have foreseen, for instance, that the complex and economically important slavery empire of 1780 would, within half a century, be utterly overthrown? It was impossible to imagine that the concept of the black as *a thing* (the central ideological principle of the slave trade) would, by the early 1830s, have been pushed aside by a changing economic and social outlook which insisted that the black was indeed 'a man and a brother'. These changes did not, however, constitute a process of continuing improvement. Within another generation, further changes had overtaken the British view of non-white humanity and by the mid-nineteenth century new forms of racial theory once more relegated blacks to the lowest levels of humanity. All this is well known and well documented, but for our purposes these relatively swift and extreme swings in racial outlook offer the clear suggestion that there is nothing immutable or fixed about the British perceptions of non-white humanity. Of course it is perfectly possible to claim that, at certain points, the British have moved from a benign and sympathetic view to one of malignance and hostility. This seems to have been the case in British attitudes towards India after the Great Mutiny of 1857. Equally, it would (obviously) be wrong to suggest that these various changes in attitudes were universally common; at any period we can find evidence of racial attitudes which form the polar opposite to what may appear to be the predominant or most influential views.

Attitudes to race and to colour are slippery concepts to describe and to categorize. There is, however, one key area where such British views are clearly undergoing change, if only because there is a concerted effort to change them. While it is true that since the 1960s the law has been harnessed to the task of enforcing a certain set of attitudes towards racial minorities, it is likely that the most important transformations will be produced by education. Educators generally tend to overestimate the importance of their work and we need to be cautious about educational changes, if only because they operate in a context where contrary social forces are also at work. Recent work has made important findings about the extent to which racism, for instance, is powerfully embedded in and advanced by the media. Nonetheless, large numbers of schools and their governing authorities have taken steps towards revising their curricula, employing specially trained personnel and creating supervisory roles to ensure non-racist education. This is, naturally enough, an enormous task, much of it requiring the kind of funding which is increasingly scarce. More appropriate literature and the discarding of overtly racist texts are crucial, a change already underway in a number of schools and educational authorities.

Here, however, one is likely to confront naïve ideological arguments about censorship or political editing. It is not suggested that *Othello* or *Tom Sawyer* be dispatched down the Orwellian memory-hole because they might cause offence. But it is important to provide a historical and sociological education which is faithful to the tenets of scrupulous teaching, making modern British society comprehensible to all sectors of society while equipping them with the skills needed to cope with that society. If schools, and the colleges and universities which ultimately service those schools and train their staff, are unwilling to or cannot embark on this task, or if their political masters deny them the funds to achieve it, it is likely that the task will fall to the 'self-help' and community groups. If this happens, the central difficulty is that they are likely to preach to the converted. Pressure groups operating within local politics and education have already made important strides in changing the nature of education and in establishing important checks on the older and inadequate curricula. What is quite impossible to predict is the degree to which these changes will alter the attitudes of future generations.

At its crudest, this may strike some people as a rather unattractive and naïve lunge at social engineering. In fact, it is in essence no different from the way in which British education has been changed over the past century. Schools have traditionally reflected and reinforced contemporary morality, values and dominant attitudes, and as those qualities are slowly transformed that transformation is to be seen in changes in the schools. In an obvious though structural fashion this is, after all, what happened following the 1944 Education Act, the more recent drive to put secondary schooling on a comprehensive basis and the raising of the school leaving age to sixteen. It is not sinister, left wing, subversive or authoritarian to argue that schools ought to change in order to reflect and encourage the vital transformations in society at large. Whether the outcome will be what the proponents of change expect is of course quite another matter. Indeed, the persistent frustration of the ambitions of educational reformers throughout the twentieth century has been an unhappy epilogue to their various schemes. How far schools can expect to create a more liberal and tolerant outlook among pupils remains to be seen; indeed, there is a powerful lobby which would deny that they should even try to do so. Given the remarkable demographic and ethnic changes in British society in the past thirty years, it seems reasonable to feel that such qualities, far from being old fashioned or increasingly irrelevant, are indeed the very guarantee of future well-being and stability.

Any changes brought about through educational reform would obviously be long-term and unpredictable. There are, however, other transformations which have already begun to affect the British. We have already mentioned the culinary influence of immigrant groups whereby Greek, Chinese, Indian and other foods and restaurants have become a feature of most British cities. In fact there is a neat though largely fortuitous coincidence, for food rationing ended in Britain in 1953 at about the time immigration began from the West Indies and India. Material prosperity aided the rapid changes in British diet. In addition to the more 'exotic' foodstuffs from Hong Kong and India, the British began to eat much more (and increasingly varied) European foodstuffs, a fact explained by the expansion of foreign travel, the widening European retailing of foodstuffs and the dramatic expansion of domestic refrigeration and freezing facilities. But pride of place must go to the Chinese catering trades which by the mid 1970s had established more than 2,000 restaurants and take-away shops throughout Britain, with an annual turnover of £27 million. 'Chow mein' and sweet and sour pork were familiar to seven out of ten people in a survey of 1976, beaten only by pizza as a well-known 'foreign' dish.

Eating out had, by then, become one of the major forms of British leisure and although the majority of eating places are not foreign, it is clear that the opening of Indian and/or Chinese eating places

proved instrumental in encouraging others to follow. Anyone who
can remember trying to get a meal on a Sunday evening in 1960 in,
say, Oldham or Stoke-on-Trent, will need no reminder of the beneficial impact of these ethnic restaurants, notwithstanding the degree
to which they have modified their cuisine to suit British tastes.
Similarly, many of the older and traditional British eating institutions were taken over by the newcomers. Indians, Pakistanis and
Greeks often bought existing fish and chip shops, adding their own
distinctive foodstuffs to the customary offerings. Curry and chips
might sound like the worst of all culinary worlds but it is nonetheless readily available throughout British towns. And if further proof
is required of the penetration of foreign foods, we need only recall
that items of Chinese or Indian food regularly appear on the menu
of school dinners. Similarly the trend is confirmed by the way both
Chinese and Indian meals or ingredients are now packaged as
'convenience' foods (one of the most important changes in British
diet in recent years) and can be bought at most corner shops or
supermarkets. Initially, such foods could only be bought at specialized (normally ethnic or community) shops but it is a sign of their
widespread and growing acceptability that they now line the shelves
of strictly 'British' shops.

In one aspect in particular West Indians have come to exercise
an extraordinary influence on Britain, indeed, around the world.
West Indian music and musicians have perfected a series of musical
forms which have become globally popular in themselves, but have
also permeated a multitude of non-Caribbean groups and styles. It
is well known that the Jamaican Bob Marley became not only the
first 'super-star' from the Third World but his overtly Rasta lifestyle
gave the Rasta movement international attention it had earlier
lacked. In addition, Marley's music was consciously political both
in the general sense of speaking for the oppressed blacks everywhere, but also specifically through his political affiliations in
Jamaica. Like it or not, Bob Marley established himself as a political
figure (or figurehead), a fact more than confirmed by the indecent
haste of politicians to associate themselves with his funeral cere-
mony. Marley himself considered his concert to celebrate the
independence in Zimbabwe to be the highlight of his short-lived
career. Clearly his music spanned black society throughout the

world; in Africa, the Caribbean, the Americas and in Europe, where his following, although centred on black communities, was also to be found throughout white society. So pervasive was Marley's influence (although in fact he was only the best-known of a rich West Indian, especially Jamaican, popular musical culture) that throughout the late 1970s and early 1980s some of the most successful white groups openly copied the basic musical structure of reggae and even the distinctive vocabulary of the Caribbean. A stranger listening to recent songs by Wings and the Police – both British – and by the Australians, Men at Work, could be forgiven for suspecting they were West Indian.

In some respects this is hardly surprising, since many British rock stars travel to the West Indies both for ideas and for actual recording sessions. The use of West Indian session musicians in the West Indies is clearly designed to imprint prevailing Caribbean styles on the music. Of course it could be argued that, in part, this is a well-established pattern which goes back to the 1960s. One characteristic of the transformation of popular music during and after the extraordinary impact of the Beatles was the positive enthusiasm for experimenting with musical forms but, more specifically, to incorporate 'ethnic' music and instruments. By the late 1960s the Beatles not only incorporated instruments and musical forms from India into their music but also spent time in India (in a period when India was thought to hold out revealing and unique experiences for large numbers of young Europeans and North Americans). Whatever the confused philosophical impulse and effects, there can be no doubting that those years saw the elevation of certain Indian musical forms and performers to the level of international fame. It never reached the heights later achieved by Bob Marley, but the point nonetheless remains valid: 'ethnic music' (though the phrase is both crude and somewhat condescending) directly entered and shaped popular western culture over the past twenty years.

Such an argument does, however, tend to ignore the degree to which popular musical culture had long been influenced by 'external' forces, none more potent than black music from the Americas. It is quite impossible to understand the history of British popular music since the First World War without considering the impact of black American music, from jazz to blues. Even many of the

other American musical influences, especially rock, were themselves shaped by black musical traditions. It is symptomatic that
many British popular musicians have explored the ethnic roots of
black American music and have incorporated their interpretation
of it into their own music. But this is quite a separate phenomenon.

In any such discussion about the impact of ethnic, primarily
black, music there is a danger that any writer will unconsciously
slide into that caricature of black musicality which is as ancient as
the early commentaries by Europeans on black society in Africa
and the Americas. As early as the sixteenth century, and regularly
thereafter, white observers frequently remarked on the blacks'
'natural' interest in music. African music and instruments quickly
entered the culture of the slave quarters of the Americas. It was at
once feared (as a means of conveying messages and rallying crowds)
and also enjoyed; something with which slaves could occupy their
free time relatively harmlessly. But however it was viewed it was a
widespread assumption among the whites that blacks were
'naturally' musical. Such an assumption, though commonplace
today, rests on a number of false premises. It may be true that there
are powerful social factors within certain black societies which
ensure the continuity and spread of local black music, but this is
primarily a *social* and not a *natural* phenomenon. Blacks are no
more naturally musical than Welsh miners; the fact that both create
distinctive musical forms can only be explained in their particular
social contexts. It seems likely, however, that there is a powerful,
self-fulfilling prophecy at work – the belief in black musicality
feeds upon itself, encouraging new and younger people to take up
what has become a potent (and sometimes lucrative) musical form.
Furthermore, the belief in black musicality has been given an added
boost by the electronics revolution; cheap radios, tape recorders or
records have enabled millions to listen to and imitate the dominant
black musicians, and even to aspire to their success. Bob Marley's
fame would not have been as extensive and universal, particularly
in poor black countries, without the cheap transistorized gadgets
which had flooded those societies, primarily from Asia.

Black musicality has partly contributed to that pride in black
achievements which is often exaggerated because it stands in sharp
contrast to the overwhelming frustrations and thwarted ambitions

in so many other areas. Along with black sporting prowess, it is a phenomenon which is indisputable but which contains its own obvious and serious dangers. For many young blacks, in Britain and elsewhere, to excel in sports or music has its own danger of providing an unsatisfactory alternative to success and endeavour elsewhere. Certain critics have even argued that such achievements, or striving towards them, are in part a determination not to achieve academically in school. If black society – or rather particular *peer group* pressure – values musical or sporting achievement and *not* educational success, there are powerful internal forces nudging young blacks away from learning and towards music or sports.

In fairness this has been a noticeable pattern among large numbers of British working-class children for many years. Those who were particularly good at soccer, and hoped to make a career from it, simply drifted away from formal learning within school, a tendency encouraged by clubs interested solely in their sporting skills. The end result is that, for every successful sportsman (in this case soccer player) there are literally dozens of failures with nothing to show for their ambitions but a lack of education, qualifications and prospects. This is a very well-worn path; especially in Scottish working-class communities where it has been trodden by untold armies of youths for the best part of a century. The illusions of sporting fame and fortune are, in large part, a disruptive force which often serve to delude large numbers of youths about their own best interests. Worse still, so staggering are the rewards for the talented and lucky few that the pressures to abandon everything for sport or music are now even greater than ever. The warning signs are clearly marked.

The withdrawal from prevailing British values of work and industry is encouraged among certain sectors of black society by a number of distinctive factors. The rapid spread of the Rasta movement, which positively encourages the withdrawal from the conventional work ethic – in conjunction with the very real bleakness of working prospects – serves to compound the drift from work. Whereas West Indian parents travelled to Britain for any kind of work, and by and large spent their working lives doing things the British did not want to do, large numbers of their children see no reason why they should continue the tradition. There are then powerful converging forces which encourage young blacks to opt out of a system which many of them regard as not of their making and which seems to offer them few real benefits.

But there remains the distinctive pleasure of black cultural life centred on music, which has become both a means and an end. Furthermore much of that music is suffused with or directly influenced by the ideals of the Rasta movement. The purpose here is not to argue that music has become the 'opium' of large parts of the black community, however true that may be for some. The point is to see the phenomenon in its broader context, for black music is of major importance in black society and, in its impact both on Britain and other societies. This is an extraordinary achievement for people traditionally discarded in the role of white society's helots. It is no small achievement to be widely acknowledged as the creative proponents of important musical culture; an achievement which needs to be set against the low esteem in which whites traditionally hold black society. But, to repeat a point made earlier, the commitment to music contains both obvious, and sometimes invisible, pitfalls. The white stereotype of the amiable black uniquely animated by and good at music has haunted relations between black and white for centuries. Like all stereotypes, it needs a kernel of observable reality to gain any credibility or acceptability. The risk is that the stereotype will, by virtue of the recent and continuing prominence of Afro-Caribbean music in Britain, serve only to limit and restrict the legitimate rights and expectations of young blacks. The British are becoming accustomed to blacks as labourers, musicians and sportsmen; for blacks to aspire solely to these roles will create a self-fulfilling prophecy which, in its turn, can only limit the expectations of British black society.

Whatever the dangers, there can be no doubting the dramatic and relatively sudden impact of black sportsmen and women in Britain. Black sportsmen had made an impact in various sports long before the twentieth century. In the early nineteenth century for example, two of Britain's most prominent boxers, Bill Richmond and Tom Molineux (though both born in North America) were black. But it was in the U.S.A. where black sportsmen first came to prominence, though they were for years effectively excluded from a number of national games dominated by white

Americans. It is not surprising to learn that when society openly excluded blacks from most social and economic fields it also kept them out of white sports, odd as this may now seem when we look at the composition of American baseball, basketball, football, boxing and athletics. Today, when blacks dominate many American sports, it is difficult to imagine the indignities heaped upon even the greatest of their sporting heroes in the recent past, none more so than Jesse Owens.

Despite the national and international fame and wealth of the most prominent of black U.S. sportsmen (less so women), many of the risks already mentioned in relation to British black society have long been evident in the U.S. While it is often glibly argued that sporting prowess offers one certain way out of the ghetto, it is rarely noticed that failure at sports is the one sure way of staying in it. This may well prove true for British blacks. Like their working-class predecessors, the encouragement towards sporting endeavour – by peer, family or school pressures – serves to isolate young blacks from other areas of activity and development. In the fiercely competitive world of athletics, soccer or cricket there is, increasingly, little time for anything but training and physical development. Nonetheless British sports have been transformed in the past twenty years by the rise of black sportsmen and women. It is now common to see major athletic events won by British blacks. Again and again, the British athlete stepping up to receive a medal at international events is black.

Even more dramatic perhaps is the rise of black footballers. Twenty years ago they were extremely rare in professional British football and were rarely British-born or raised. Today there is scarcely a professional club without its own black players; some have a large number while a number of famous clubs regularly field two or three in their team. Naturally enough English blacks have already won places in the national football squad, as they have within the national M.C.C. team. In most of the major spectator sports black sportsmen have, within a very short space of time, risen to the very top. Significantly, however, this has not been the case in sports which require extra social factors and which may well lack the esteem in black communities: for instance golf, racing and tennis. Given the structure of all these sports in Britain, it is not surprising that they have yet to attract black sportsmen. These (and others) apart, there can be no denying the unusual achievements of black athletes, achievements out of all proportion to their numbers in society at large. It is possible that the process of spotting and selecting promising athletes begins in the schools and it has even been argued that some schools unconsciously encourage black sporting excellence at the expense of more 'academic' work. Of course their very success renders top-flight sportsmen quite untypical. Not only in physique and motor-skills but, equally crucially, in application and persistent industry, successful athletes inevitably distance themselves from their social context. More than that, it is quite illusory to imagine that, because blacks have in so brief a period made such an impact on British sport, that sporting prowess provides an obvious route to success. By definition, only a small minority can ever become (to say nothing of remaining) successful; the rest are doomed to failure. Of course it is perfectly legitimate to argue the case for athleticism for its own enjoyable ends. But in that case, there is no need to invoke the success of the famous athletes. The sad truth is that ambitions towards a professional and lucrative athletic career are, with very few exceptions, bound to be thwarted. It would be harmful for the long-term interests of the black community if the myth persists that black athleticism is in itself a distinctive quality which enables the meanest to aspire to worldly success. Athletic success is in many ways a lottery. And a lottery provides no real key to future salvation.

When we examine the kinds of sports at which blacks have excelled in Britain, it is possible to see how discrimination and deprivation operate even within sports. The truth is (and again this is commonly reported by black athletes) that blacks have to be *especially* good to make the initial (and the continuing) impact in British sports. Again and again, successful black athletes testify to their determination to succeed in order to 'get back' at a system which makes their life difficult. Moreover, there is general agreement among black athletes that they have to be extra good to be chosen in preference to a competing white. This seems to be true both in the U.S. and in the U.K.

There is an additional quirk to the discrimination in sports, for it seems that in team sports blacks are rarely given the positions of authority. In American football and British soccer, they are normally expected to occupy a subservient role and to do as the captain says. Furthermore, as we have seen, the initial *access* to sports varies enormously and blacks tend to gravitate towards those which are cheap or readily available. Once embarked on a particular sport, a black athlete has to operate within the constraints established by officials, trainers and managers, among whom are to be found some extraordinary ideas about what blacks can or cannot do. On top of that, there is evidence that when faced by competing performances sporting officials (overwhelmingly white) will invariably choose the white athlete, unless the black is clearly superior. It is true of course that the assessment of performance at, say, soccer or boxing is largely a subjective phenomenon, but black athletes are themselves in no doubt that the odds are greatly stacked against them in the subconscious minds of the officials controlling their chosen sport.

More easily described, largely because it is so obvious and audible, is the overt racism which black athletes face from British sporting crowds and even from other athletes. Soccer seems to be worst of all, for reasons which lie deep in the modern sociological transformation of the soccer crowds and the outlook of certain sections of their younger members. Black footballers are widely barracked and booed. In grounds where, over the years, such chanting has been perfected to a fine point of obscenity, clear-cut racist chants are regularly picked up on television or radio. Old Trafford's rhythmic shout of 'coon', directed at one of the country's finest players, is as unavoidable as it is distressing. Other fans have the grotesque habit of throwing bananas at an equally prominent black player. Nor is racist abuse reserved for visiting opponents for even local fans indulge in the racist baiting. When a team does badly or mistakes occur, the black player automatically becomes the target for the home crowd's abuse. Such obscenities are, however, counter-productive, for the personal testimony of the players suggests that it merely serves to stiffen their resolve and increase their efforts to play well.

Clearly, it would be easy to exaggerate the wider significance of such overt racism within one particular sport. Soccer is after all undergoing a process of major change which is slowly transforming the nature of the game and changing its relationship to its traditional supporting roots. Nonetheless, the racism within British soccer is a reflection, however distorted, of a number of cruelly harmful forces within certain sections of modern British society. There is an irony here for while blacks have established themselves among some of the finest of modern British athletes – in this case foot-ballers – their successes have been rewarded not merely by lavish material returns but with an abundance of racial abuse. They can furthermore expect similar abuse, face to face and less audible to the outside world, from their competitors on the field.

More surprising perhaps is the extent of such racial antagonism in boxing, more so because it is a sport which has had a long history of black success in the U.S. and in the U.K. Once again, the people involved tell a different tale; black boxers provide an abun-dance of shaming evidence about the racial abuse to which they are subjected inside and outside the ring. At times the racism of the boxing fraternity has been even more venomous and violent than that of the football fans. In boxing and in other sports the athletes also have to face the complex and sometimes subtle prejudices of their friends: coaches and managers who openly accuse them of the 'black vices' of laziness, lack of application and industry. It is not surprising that such views exist among sports officials – after all such views are widespread in society at large – but again they tend to be counter-productive, goading black athletes to even greater effort and concentration. Of course it is also possible that such judgements may be *deliberately* directed at athletes by coaches and managers, ever anxious to goad and needle them into better perfor-mance. In fact it seems that racial assumptions are employed, con-sciously or otherwise, in the coaching of British black athletes. This is, once again, further proof (if more is needed) of the depths of racist assumptions common throughout modern British society. Again and again the image of the 'naturally skilful' (but lazy) black, of the naturally musical and carefree black, is invoked by certain sectors of British life for their own benefit or entertainment. Like all assumptions and attitudes, it is impossible precisely to tabulate or represent such views about blacks in any clear-cut or scientific fashion (though as we have seen earlier, antagonism to black society is graphically portrayed in various recent opinion polls on political issues). There is, however, an amazing amount of parallel evidence of all kinds which points us once more in the same direction – towards the central, unavoidable and ubiquitous *fact* of racism established in all walks of British life.

It may be true that the British now have some remarkably talented black sportsmen and women but their successes do not shield them from the racist barbs of white society at large. It may be countered, however, that sport – either among participants or spectators – is not a perfect reflection of society. But it is possible to accept this point without deflecting the main thrust of the argument, namely that the racism to be found in Britain (notwithstanding its uneven spread and location) is directed at blacks everywhere. The black unemployed incur hostility (and are thought to be the source of major urban problems) and even the successful sportsmen, with all the material trappings of success, are abused. And all are the objects of a curious set of assumptions and beliefs about 'natural' black qualities and vices on the part of large sections of white society. For anyone familiar with the long-term history of black settlement and the history of racial attitudes there is a sense of *déjà vu* about many of the modern British responses to blacks. It would be quite wrong to suggest that the British have not changed, or cannot change again in the future, but the continuing links with racial attitudes from the past are as striking as the changes.

Many of the points mentioned so far are fairly obvious, familiar if only because they are visible and unavoidable. Anyone can see these changes in Britain brought about by black settlement. Of course, not all the changes are by any means as clear, as has already been mentioned in relations to attitudes. There have in addition been a number of changes in the religious patterns in Britain brought about by immigration. We need to set those changes in the context of much longer-term transformations in patterns of traditional religious beliefs in Britain. But within that context, a number of relatively new (for Britain) religions have established themselves.

Interestingly, some of them have taken over older, redundant churches and converted them to suit their own purposes. At a number of points earlier in this book the complex issue of religion has been touched on. Again, it is important to recall that until very recently all but a sympathetic minority of Britons viewed exotic religions as merely the superstitions of primitive people. Part of the impulse behind Victorian and Edwardian imperialism was in fact to lure non-Christians from their existing faiths and convert them to what was regarded as the one and true faith. When we recall the extraordinary numbers of British missionaries from all churches and sects who sallied forth to all corners of the globe to convert the 'heathens' to Christianity, it is difficult not to be impressed by that powerful ethnocentricism which for years rode roughshod over the religious sensibilities of other peoples. Thanks to immigration, the British can now see a number of these religions in their own cities. Hindu, Muslim and Sikh temples now dot the urban landscape of those particular communities. And of course an important mosque breaks the skyline around Regent's Park.

Among Asians living in Britain, religious affiliations cut across what we normally view as national categories. The very great bulk of Pakistanis in Britain are Muslim but Indians are either Muslim, Hindu or Sikh. It is clear even without a detailed knowledge of Indian history that these religious ties often conflict with national allegiances. In Britain, the largest religious group among Asians are the Muslims, 40 per cent (in 1977), followed by 29 per cent Hindu and 25 per cent Sikh.

In these faiths, as with many others, the distinctions are not merely a question of religious observances on particular holy days. These faiths provide a broader cultural framework which can determine every facet of daily life and can demand specific forms of dress, food, courtship and marriage, family and kinship ties and much more besides. It is in this wider cultural context that the British have come face to face with practices they do not always comprehend or sympathize with; hence, as we have already seen, the clumsy clashes at schools or amongst employers over Sikh headwear. In fact the insistence that 'outsiders' should conform to British Christian customs (however defined) has been a persistent feature since the Reformation. Persecution of Catholics, fear of whom was revived by the massive Irish settlement in the 1840s, and particularly distrust of and hostility towards Jews had long been common. Throughout the late nineteenth- and early twentieth-century years of Jewish immigration, a series of objections (some of them legal) were directed at certain aspects of the Jewish faith.

Although a *modus vivendi* was ultimately arrived at, it emerged slowly and, on the British side, reluctantly.

Then, as more recently (in relation to newer, especially Asian immigrants) there was a commonly expressed view that people coming to live in Britain should become like the British. Apart from begging the question precisely who and what are the British, many of the early settlers in Britain did not initially come with a view to permanent residence. Among large numbers of Asians there was the initial conviction that they would eventually return home. In their 'exile' their religions and cultures provided something important and familiar to which they could relate, and support and comfort in a strange land. Moreover, there were innumerable aspects of Christian Britain which were positively unattractive. Even had it entered their heads, there were few attractions for pioneer immigrants to abandon the faith of their ancestors for what they viewed as the unattractive qualities of a Christian British life.

The truth of the matter is that the British have been obliged to change in a number of ways their attitudes to 'exotic' religions. Most obviously, the schooling system has to make provision for the particular demands of religious groups, as indeed had already been the case for their Jewish pupils. Holidays, meals, religious instruction, dress have all had to be adjusted under the simple demographic impact of the children of immigrants. This is not necessarily to argue that a greater understanding or tolerance was generated; it *may* have been, but that is hard to prove. What is abundantly clear is that many of the habits and the structures of daily life of many Britons have, willingly or not, been altered in a number of ways by the presence of non-Christian communities in their midst, especially in the schools. The British have in fact come to accept the consequences of having within their cities that mosaic of communities mentioned earlier.

There was never any real possibility of success for the arguments that ethnic communities should drop their particular distinctions and become 'like us'. It is true that similar arguments are to be heard regularly in modern Britain but they have, by and large (and with the important protection of the law), been pushed aside by the more realistic, practical and ultimately beneficial acceptance of

religions and ethnic differences. It is in this sense that Britain has,
in many urban settings, become a multicultural society though this
is neither to deny the overwhelming dominance of a Judaic-Christ-
ian culture, nor to ignore the powerful (primarily political) objections to the tolerance of other cultures and religions within it.
What remains to be seen is the way these newly-arrived religions
will thrive or change as their demography undergoes the natural
transformation from immigrants proper to second generation.
There is, at the moment, little evidence to suggest that their appeal
will diminish among the British-born. They have after all survived
many other, even greater migrations and resettlements both within
the Indian sub-continent and as their followers travelled and settled
throughout the Indian Ocean and the Pacific. Britain is, then, likely
to remain the home of thriving Asian religions as long as their
human base continues to thrive as distinct communities. In the
process, British life has been unusually enriched and diversified by
the infusion of religious, social and ethical qualities and concepts
which had previously remained the preserve of exotic and
geographically-distant people.

If we take the example of the impact of Jews on Britain in the
past century, it would be difficult to deny (unless one belonged to
the Fascist fringe) the exceptional transformations brought about in
Britain by Jewish communities. There is no reason to feel that a
comparable process will not follow the more recent settlement of
immigrants from even further afield. Whatever precise changes
British society will experience remains obscure but it is perfectly
clear that there can be no return to the society of the 1940s. In
common with many other western European countries, and of
course with the U.S.A., Britain has become a society unalterably
infused with a variety of national, ethnic stocks, with a number of
different colours and new (for Britain) religions. It is a process of
change which quite simply cannot be reversed through its future
direction and pace remain uncertain.

13

Born British

It is a straightforward matter to describe the development and growth over the past thirty years of those significant non-white communities which dot the urban landscape of modern Britain. Much less easy is the task of peering into the future (in this or any other matter). There are, however, certain trends which are reasonably predictable, if only because their embryonic outline can be seen today. It is possible to suggest for instance the future demographic trends of Britain's ethnic communities. In 1961 the New Commonwealth population of Britain was in the region of 673,497. A decade later it stood at 1,341,000 and by the mid 1970s had reached 1,771,000, something like 3.3 per cent of the total population. At a number of points throughout the book it has been stressed that such bald figures mask as much as they reveal, but even the absolute numbers (themselves a continuing source of disagreement) provide some indication of the transformation which large numbers of Britons have seen in their own lifetime. The restrictions on immigration are now so strict that it is very unlikely that any major change in these figures will be brought about by fresh arrivals from the New Commonwealth. There will be, it is true, a continuing trickle as dependants and families manage to satisfy the stringent conditions of entry and join their (normally male) relatives in Britain, but this will be a mere drop in the ocean and will not appreciably affect the overall balance of population.

More significant still are the predictable changes *within* the existing ethnic population, changes which quickly make redundant even the vocabulary used to discuss these communities. The concept of 'immigrants' (used in a non-pejorative sense) becomes inaccurate – and even offensive – with the emergence of a British-born population. In 1971 some 65 per cent of the ethnic population in Britain had been born abroad and only 35 per cent in Britain. In 1976 these figures had changed to 61 and 39 per cent respectively and as the figures constantly change, and as older generations give way to new ones, the relative balance inevitably shifts. By the end of the 1980s, a majority of the ethnic communities will be British-born, and the process will continue inexorably. Immigrants tend almost as a matter of definition to be unusual; their age structure and sex distribution is unlike both the host society and the societies from which they came. Immigrants to Britain over the past thirty years have confirmed these trends, being much younger and, by and large, initially largely male. These central facts have important consequences for the present and future. Throughout the 1960s and 1970s there was a marked imbalance between the sexes, but by 1976 it had evened out among West Indians though it still remained predominantly male (58 per cent) among Asians.

The ethnic communities are, similarly, younger than British society at large; among West Indians and Asians the proportion of children is higher and that of older people lower than in British society today. But these figures will inevitably level out in time and come into line with the age structure typical of white society. On top of this, it seems that the birth rate among Asians and West Indians is falling gradually and will soon be comparable with the rates now common in white society. Such figures – which are often grist to the mill of different and conflicting political arguments – when viewed in their long-term setting, show that the ethnic communities are slowly but unmistakably settling into patterns which are British, or rather their demographic features are becoming increasingly indistinguishable from those of the host society. What makes this fact less clear, and thus enables it to be used for controversial political arguments, is the *concentration* of the ethnic communities within a relatively small number of urban areas. When local school class-rooms, local crime statistics, local unemployment levels, local housing matters are dominated by non-white people, it is a simple (and for some an irresistible) matter to extrapolate from the local to the general. We have already seen that this has been a striking feature of the arguments about urban crime, but it has also been true of arguments about ethnic demography.

Some political opponents of immigration have sought, quite simply, to cut completely the trickle of dependants into Britain.

Even were legislation of such an inhuman dimension enacted it would affect the future ethnic population in only the most minor of ways. Realization of this fact has, with other various factors, persuaded a number of observers to consider and to promote 're-patriation' for members of the ethnic communities. Demands for 're-patriation' (a meaningless concept for those actually born in Britain) are not, however, new. If, once more, we take the broader historical view, it is possible to detect similar reactions at earlier periods, notwithstanding the utterly different demographic context. As early as the 1590s Queen Elizabeth I issued an edict against imported blacks: 'there are of late divers blackamores brought into this realm, of which kind of people there are already here to manie . . .' Elizabeth therefore advised 'that those kinde of people shoulde be sente forth of the land . . .' A few years later, the same complaint recurred about blacks 'who are fostered and powered here, to the great annoyance of her own liege people . . .' Almost two centuries later in response to the large black community in late eighteenth-century London, a more organized scheme was devised to solve England's black 'problem' by shipping the blacks back to Africa. The abortive Sierra Leone scheme of 1787, which proved disastrous for the small band of blacks who volunteered to embark from London, was flawed from the start. Conceived as an attempt to remove the 'black poor', it was a scheme characterized by confusion, corruption and indifference to the fate of the blacks.

The only effective point of comparison with recent demands for repatriation is that all are conceived of as a solution to domestic British 'problems'. Repatriation is concerned not with the well-being or fate of the people inevitably involved, but simply with removing them to their homelands. Of course repatriation tends to ignore the fact that, in removing people or encouraging people to move, children are inevitably involved; people who are British-born and who have no direct or personal experience of their parents' country of origin. This does not in itself necessarily mean that such children will not or cannot settle in, say, Jamaica or the Punjab. But the ease or difficulty of such an upheaval or transition is not of course in the mind or consideration of those advocating repatriation. The central impulse behind the various repatriation schemes advanced by a number of British politicians is simply to rid Britain of people viewed as aliens. The statistics clearly show, however, that only a massive movement of people could make any dent in the substantial ethnic communities in Britain, and such a major upheaval is quite inconceivable.

It must not be thought that only right-wing politicians want to see members of the ethnic communities leave Britain. Many of the settlers themselves are even keener to leave than their political opponents would dare to hope. This ought not to be surprising, not least because large numbers (though it is impossible to offer a precise figure) came to Britain with no real intention of staying. Most striking perhaps among the Sikhs, the determination to return home looms large in the outlook and philosophy of large numbers of settlers. Again, this was a common feature in any number of societies characterized by immigration. Even in the U.S.A. – its history and society shaped in a remarkable degree by the ebb and flow of migrations and settlement – there were very large numbers of people who returned to their European homelands after short and (for them) lucrative visits to the U.S.A. There were even regular patterns of movement to and fro across the Atlantic as people (mainly men) stayed for a while in America before returning to Europe with money to pick up their lives again in their native region. In Britain, as in the U.S.A., however, even among settlers with diminishing prospects of going home, the conviction that they would some day return has proved a forceful and unshakable belief. Thus what for many was initially a reasonably accessible possibility has been transformed over the years into a distant but nonetheless potent myth.

This belief in returning 'home' can obviously serve a host of functions. It provides an aspiration and a means of enduring personally difficult conditions; men separated from family and kin for years can take comfort in the prospects of going home. It also reinforces the commitment to the culture and values of the homeland (serving, at the same time, as a critical contrast to British life). For many, the prospects of return become dimmer with the settlement of family in Britain, especially as children begin to grow up, and – however strictly maintained the commitment to their indigenous culture – as they develop into British children, teenagers and young adults, the practical problems of returning home are greatly increased. After all, the migration to Britain involved for most a conscious decision to break out of the particular difficulties of home and to seek a better (i.e. materially more rewarding) life in Britain; simply at the level of economic well-being it is often difficult to make the transition back to the homeland. There are, obviously, many thousands for whom such a return is quite impossible. Few East African Asians are tempted to return to Uganda; many Hong Kong Chinese feel too uncertain about the colony's future to contemplate a permanent return.

Notwithstanding such difficulties and despite the obvious practical difficulties of uprooting children born in Britain many immigrants do return home. Throughout the 1970s for instance a significant number of people quit Britain for their homelands. At a number of points more left than arrived from a particular region. While 9,000 West Indians arrived in Britain between 1971 and 1973 some 14,000 left. A year later there were 2,000 more departures than arrivals. There is no doubting the acute upheavals such movements normally create, although we can easily exaggerate both their impact and the automatic hesitation about moving because of the presence of children. After all, many thousands travelled to Britain with their children (a fact which may go some way towards explaining the educational difficulties of some children). Furthermore, going 'home' remains an ambition for large numbers of people who were born in Britain, particularly among West Indians who have been progressively disillusioned with their treatment and their everyday lives.

There are few parts of the British West Indies today where one will fail to find people recently returned from Britain. In one remote corner of rural Jamaica in Christmas 1982 the author located no fewer than twenty-three Jamaicans who had returned home from Britain. Many had left for a combination of reasons, not least the recurring complaint about the British weather. Most had been able to buy their own plot of land and to build a home on it. Some had even diversified into a local business – a betting shop, a local store and a village bar. Others had returned with marketable skills which had subsequently been put to use in Jamaica in occupations such as insurance agent, mechanic on the local sugar estate; others had managerial experience. Some had returned to the island they only vaguely remembered from childhood days. British education and training had stood a number of them in good stead in securing fairly lucrative local professional work (in accountancy and airline operations, for instance).

There are, undoubtedly, many other Jamaicans in the same area who have spent time in Britain. Moreover, this does not include many others who have spent time abroad elsewhere, especially in the U.S.A. and Canada. What is striking is this 'homing instinct', the zeal to quit the alien world of Britain for more fondly remembered regions of their youth. Furthermore, in this case (and in countless others) the area to which they returned is a relatively isolated part of Jamaica, with few obvious economic opportunities, save of course those of buying a plot of land and fulfilling a characteristic Jamaican ambition of building a home of one's own.

Many of these particular Jamaicans returned home with their children, some of whom had been born in Britain and who knew of Jamaica only indirectly. It would be impossible to categorize the responses of these offspring to resettlement; they were, as we might expect, varied. They ranged from the smoothest of transitions to the unadaptable, with all the varied consequences such reactions would have, both on schooling and within the wider family. Yet it is often forgotten that such varied reactions to migration characterized the *earlier* move from Jamaica (or elsewhere) to Britain. In general, however, even the young did not regret the move back to the country they considered their home. Nonetheless, however significant a theme such returns to the homelands have proved to be, they form in numerical terms a strictly minority phenomenon. While many more save up for a visit or a holiday with family in their native land, the passage of time makes it increasingly difficult for many immigrants to Britain to uproot their families, yet again, for another speculative move back home. However strong the myth of return, it is normally overwhelmed by economic and social realities which secure the people to their lives in Britain. There are a number of obvious factors which may persuade more people to uproot and return. First and foremost are the growing difficulties of unemployment which, as we have seen repeatedly, afflict the ethnic communities most seriously. Secondly, and more difficult to predict, is the corrosive effect of all-pervasive discrimination. The ambitions of parents in, say the 1960s, may have turned to dust when they see the bleak prospects facing their offspring in and beyond the 1980s. It is also true, however, that the economic prospects in many of the Commonwealth nations are, if anything, no less daunting. The queues at British High Commissions of local people seeking the requisite documentation for travel to Britain provide a continuing reminder of the apparently limitless zeal among armies of Commonwealth citizens to seek a better life in Britain.

In Britain itself, the emergence of a second generation, of Britons born into a particular ethnic community, has profound significance for the future not merely of that immediate community but also of the wider host society. We have already seen how a number of cultural and social values have been transformed, in the crucible of British society, among immigrants themselves. This is even more pronounced among their offspring. How could it be otherwise for children born and bred not in the Punjab but in Bradford, not in Jamaica but in Hackney or Moss Side, not in Uganda but in Leicester? The change in values and attitudes among this second generation is, understandably, remarkably different between the various communities. It is also a subtle process, often taking unexpected and unpredictable forms. It would be wrong, however, to claim that being born and bred in Britain will inevitably convert such children into Britons like any other, even allowing of course for the spectrum of social and geographic differences among the British themselves.

There are substantial differences between the offspring of different communities. Among blacks the comparison they tend to make with their lives is not that so often at the forefront of their parents' minds – between life in Britain and the Caribbean – but between their own condition and the generally superior circumstances of white society at large. Little work, dismal prospects, educational provision which seems at best irrelevant, all of this, and more, when compounded by the various and ubiquitous acts of discrimination, has concocted a volatile mixture of bitterness and frustration. In its turn this serves to drive young blacks into their own distinctive urban cultural forms; into their own meeting places where black music, language and organizations provide a sympathetic environment and a relief and a barrier from the world at large. And there are in addition very strong peer pressures for young blacks to seek their pleasures among their own kind. Of course this has also been a noticeable feature of working-class life in British cities for a century and a half, perhaps even longer. For people living in poor, socially deprived working-class districts there has too rarely been the opportunity or occasion for breaking out of the immediate social environment. In this, blacks are little different from earlier generations of working-class youths, except of course for their colour which is widely accepted, by blacks themselves, as the central cause of their persistent deprivation. And although there are unquestionable regional variations in this pattern – between, for instance, London, Manchester and Liverpool – there are important national forces which create a sense of identity from remarkably varying experiences. Above all else, it is the overt hostility of white society in general, but also the perennial animosity of the police, which help persuade blacks from many different parts of the country that they share a common identity with each other.

Among the British children of other ethnic groups the sense of identity tends to be shaped by other cultural forces. Nothing seems to be more potent than religion (in its wider cultural setting). Sikhs, Muslims and Hindus need no external pressure to create their own distinct sense of identity within British society. For their second generation, however, there are undoubted difficulties. This has been shown, for instance, to be especially the case with girls from Islamic (notably Pakistani) families, where family insistence on particular and strict codes of habit often conflicts with the cultures of other girls in local schools. Such children adapt in different ways but it seems that most are capable of a flexibility which might appear surprising to outsiders. In social life, education and, subsequently, in marriage the offspring of Islamic communities are on the whole able to accept the restraints and demands of their culture without unduly distancing themselves from their non-Islamic peers. Much the same story is true of second-generation Sikhs. Indeed, the 'rebellion' which they and others sometimes display towards their parents may be no more widespread or significant than that so commonly experienced by most parents of adolescent children. This is not to say that difficulties do not exist between the generations in Asian families, but outside researchers and observers have been led to expect major cultural conflicts between the generations. And this expectation has more often than not been exaggerated.

For many children of Asian families the future is not viewed with that pervasive bleakness so common in black, primarily West Indian, communities. This is not perhaps surprising for, while it is undoubtedly true that hostility and discrimination have been directed equally (in some cases more vigorously) against Asians, the economic context for many Asian communities is quite different. There is, for example, a powerful insistence among Sikhs that children should work hard, within the family businesses, academically and within the broader Sikh community. Whatever economic difficulties face the offspring of that community stem largely from the downturn in the economy as a whole, rather than from a particular form of discrimination. Even when faced by economic difficulties, Sikhs are able to turn elsewhere for more secure business, for their international links often provide economic opportunities and a wider trading outlook than would be the case for many other trading communities.

Much the same seems to be true of the Chinese in Britain, among whom there is that striking belief in the principle of hard work so visible in other Chinese communities around the world. To an important degree it is possible to provide second-generation Chinese children with viable economic opportunities and a reasonable future because so much of the Chinese economic activity is family based. Children are generally brought up within the context of family-based economy in much the same way that children in pre-industrial rural England were unquestioningly expected to work within the family unit. We have already seen that because so many Chinese enterprises are family based they are able to undercut or push aside competitors. Children and wives do not require formal wages; hired hands clearly do. Like the Sikhs, the Chinese in Britain attach great significance to education, a belief in the necessity of a cultural upbringing which is difficult to disentangle from the broader ethic of industry and willingness to work long hours. Chinese children in this country inevitably have no need for their parents' language, a short-coming remedied in London (where the largest concentration of Chinese live) by evening and weekend classes in

Chinese. Because the Chinese have created their own thriving economic empire, centred on the catering business, there is little unemployment among younger Chinese. Of course their numbers still
remain relatively small and any incidence of unemployment would
accordingly be minor, but the Chinese themselves are prepared to
argue that their well-known application and industry traditionally
protect them from unemployment. This, clearly, is an insufficient
explanation and we may need to probe the particular structure and
nature of the Chinese community for a more convincing one. We
know that in cases of distress or economic misfortune, Chinese
rally together and contribute money and assistance to the distressed
person or families. Such cooperation, together with the Chinese
reluctance to approach British bureaucracy, has the effect of making
the British Chinese relatively self-contained and self-sufficient.

The relationship between Chinese in Britain and those in their
homelands in Hong Kong has, in common with all immigrants,
changed quite markedly over the years. In some respects the ties
have strengthened, partly because cheap jet travel has brought
these two distant regions closer together. Although recent immigration rules make it more difficult for new immigrants to join
the Chinese in Britain, the political uncertainty surrounding Hong
Kong's future is likely to encourage yet more people to quit the
colony for Britain and elsewhere. In the meantime, the children of
Chinese settlers are rapidly forming a distinct ethnic group, particularly in London, unmistakably Chinese but the great majority
lacking their ancestral language. How much the broader distinctive
Chinese culture will survive, when effectively distanced from the
homelands, no longer refreshed by new arrivals and lacking the
seminal language, it would be idle to predict. There are cases
elsewhere which suggest what might happen, for in the Caribbean
and in the U.S. (among many other places) the Chinese have developed their distinct form of *local* Chinese culture which, though
recognizably and obviously Chinese, nonetheless has its own
distinct peculiarities. The prospects of adaptation rather than assimilation face the Chinese in Britain.

Throughout the book so far the concept of ethnic or racial
'identity' has been used in a way which might give the impression
that it is a static and unchanging concept. This clearly is not the

case for, with any group, that sense of identity changes across time and from place to place. This change in both personal and collective identity can clearly be seen when we consider a number of the various immigrant groups to Britain. If we take the case of West Indians, whereas an older generation of settlers had clear cultural affinities with a particular island and had a perception of their role in Britain which, by and large, did not preclude any kind of work, this is much less true of their offspring. Although young blacks are doubtless committed to a loyalty to a particular island, more striking still is their sense of *collective* identity and interests within Britain. What galvanizes this identity is, as we have seen, that ubiquitous burden of disadvantage and discrimination which pervades British society and which it is claimed is directed specifically at young blacks. The long-term consequences are, once more, difficult to predict but it is indisputable that the British responses (legal or political) which seem to have been borne stoically by an earlier generation of West Indians will prove unacceptable to their children. And much the same is equally true among the offspring of other ethnic groups.

What is perhaps more striking about many, if not most, second-generation children is their refusal to accept the debasing stereotypes long used by British society and accepted by the immigrants themselves. Of course the images, the stereotypes and roles which minority groups play out in front of their 'betters' contain the very qualities which those minorities need for their own well-being and survival. Slaves throughout the New World were infamous for their 'personality' traits which, though described by whites, were copied and perfected by slaves for their own use. There were, for example, great advantages in being thought stupid and lazy. In the case of modern West Indians, early settlers in the 1950s seem to have accepted the British stereotype of the black as an unquestioning beast of burden, happy to work (often in dreadful conditions) because of their 'natural' physical and social qualities. The British-born show no inclination to adopt the roles long expected of them by white society. This clash is not merely a result of economic forces. There have, after all, been many societies where the lower orders have tolerated their menial status, returns and prospects, however widespread acts of resistance or rebellion might have been.

In Britain, the overriding tranquillity of the working class over a period of almost two centuries has been a historical and social phenomenon which has regularly attracted the bemused curiosity of historians, notably those who expect to see resistance and defiance among the lower orders. Indeed, it is hard to imagine how society could have survived (and, by and large, thrived) without the widespread acceptance of social and economic roles by people in all social classes.

The accepted picture seems, however, to be changing in at least one crucial area. Young blacks are beginning overwhelmingly to reject the role collectively allotted to them. Such a rejection takes many forms (opting for the Rasta movement, a coalescing into the autonomous world of black culture, a desire to go home to the West Indies) but its prospect augurs ill for both black and white society. There are many black youths who refuse to accept the economic life-style of their parents. Many of the factors which suggest themselves – a desire for material improvement, a 'brighter future' and the like – have, it is true, been present in working-class communities for many years but this has not prevented offspring from inheriting the low status and income of their parents. Nor can it be explained purely in generation terms, of one, younger generation rebelling against their elders. It is perfectly true that many young blacks have rejected many of their parents' values and life-styles; their industry in menial jobs, their membership of fundamentalist and non-conformist churches, their general commitment to a hard-working life-style. At school and afterwards, young blacks often veer sharply away from values and styles which, though undoubtedly those of their parents, were, equally, shaped by British inerests. This is not to argue that older West Indians were the mere dupes of insidious British values and interests for they used their churches, industry and commitment for their own good as well as for the benefit of others. The difference may well lie in what these different generations recognize to be their own real interests. Immigrants travelled thousands of miles to be labourers; they also chose to join and even establish their own churches. In both these cases and more there were very real material or social benefits to be had. For many young blacks this seems not to be the case. Buffeted and rejected by one blow after another large numbers of young blacks turn their backs on the commitment to employment, so important among their parents, and seek or are lured to alternative life-styles.

What accentuates the frustrations of untold numbers of young blacks is the yawning gap between the social and material ideals which Britain espouses, and the reality of their own situation. This is, again, true of many other groups. It has been a persistent (though changing) feature of plebeian life throughout industrial Britain. And it is, naturally, a striking feature of women's experience in Britain. For young blacks, however, the gulf between promise and reality is even greater. This is not simply a matter of material prospects though it is inevitably true that the poor, ill-educated and unemployed can have no realistic hope of the material benefits so proclaimed and valued by all social classes, of home-ownership, the material possessions of life and the increasingly costly pleasures of modern Britain. In addition to this undeniable fact there is a cruel distance between a number of the principles and ideals in which the British take such pride, and the daily reality for young blacks. Nowhere is this more striking than in the question of the law. However imperfect the legal process, whatever its biases towards the propertied and against the poor and dispossessed, English and Scottish law has served to safeguard personal and political liberties. But it is impossible to convince many young blacks that the law, however we examine it, does not operate against them. Legislation itself, notably the widespread misapplication of the 'sus' law, the behaviour of the police, the conduct and outlook of court officials and the judiciary, the difficulty of gaining access to decent legal advice and, more recently, revelations about the proportion of blacks in British jails all confirm blacks' assumptions that the law is the white man's law. 'Freedom before the law' is likely only to raise a crude belly laugh; 'equality before the law' will merely invoke the inescapable illustration of discriminatory immigration rules. Clearly the imperfections of the legal system, and whatever flaws it contains particularly for the blacks, need careful analysis and explanation. It cannot satisfactorily be explained solely by a general theory which veers towards the conspiratorial. Furthermore, it is an uneven story for the law has been used (and continues to be used) in a number of ways to safeguard or secure black interests, even if, in general, it fails to do so. And this has been true, patchy as the historical picture is, since the anti-slavery campaign of the late eighteenth century. Nonetheless the law, in its broader setting, is perceived to be unfriendly to the blacks.

The disenchantment with British life, so widespread a feature of life among young black adults in British cities, has been accentuated by a host of external forces. The Rasta movement and its music exert a continuing, apparently growing and disenchanted influence. Similarly, though less easy to plot because the trajectory of its movement is so invisible, has been the example of black politics in the U.S.A. since the 1960s. 'Black power' in all its forms proved to be an influential force well beyond the U.S.A. and although the demographic strengths of black society are greatly different (in the U.S. blacks form a group of more than 20 million) the tactics, vernacular, imagery and apparent successes have provided an inspirational filip for many blacks in Britain. Indeed it is striking that many of the black political and social responses to the academic debate about black society in Britain have many of the characteristics and qualities of the comparable arguments which troubled the U.S. in the late 1960s.

It is possible, however, to overstress the U.S. influence at the expense of the Caribbean. Nonetheless the basic argument remains valid: wide sectors of young black society are profoundly disillusioned with white Britain and with their role in Britain, notwithstanding the range of considerable achievements of many black youths. How long such profound and collective unhappiness can be contained is impossible to say. Nor is it clear that the 'positive action' proposed by Lord Scarman will be acceptable (to British politicians) or prove advantageous to blacks even if it were promoted. Whatever the future, there is now in existence an unusual, even a unique situation, where a substantial minority of the nation's young (in some specific urban regions this amounts to an absolute majority) reject the values to which they are expected to conform and live by. It is hard indeed to conjure forth a comparable historical phenomenon in Britain. Thus Britain faces the reality of being an urban society, not only troubled by the manifold ramifications of industrial decline but also embracing substantial (and young) communities who see few virtues, benefits or compensations to life in Britain. The flip and all too common response that they ought in that case to go home needs to face the unavoidable and central fact that home is Brixton, Handsworth or Moss Side. Yet it needs also to be said that there is now powerful evidence of widespread alienation among white youths, notably among the long-term unemployed.

However disenchanted many young blacks, the same is not true on anything like a comparable scale among the British children of other ethnic communities. Asian families exercising a tight and restrictive influence over their children seem able to inculcate the highly competitive qualities in their offspring which serve them well when they begin to work. Naturally, there are exceptions to this rule, but so severe are family and community pressures that only the most unusual offspring is able to break away from the particular life-style. Furthermore the Asians, like the Chinese, have around them that complex network of economic and social ties which, for many, provide a greater economic security than many other groups can reasonably expect. Many have chosen to reject, or have been unable to gain access to, this ethnic network, seeking instead their economic and political future among their white peers. But this, again, is unusual. Even when making allowances for this rather exceptional group, the overriding point remains valid; that the outlook and prospects for young Asian adults seem much less bleak than those among the West Indians. There may well prove, in the future, to be a coming together of black and Asian youths and young adults into political and industrial organizations to advance their own particular interests. At the moment, however, and notwithstanding the existence of a multitude of organizations designed to that end, the differences and gaps between these young people are more striking than the similarities. It is in fact another reminder of the fundamental flaw in viewing, talking about and describing immigrants, and even their British-born offspring, as a single undifferentiated group.

The difficulties of Britain's ethnic communities and what is for Britain the relatively new phenomenon of coming to terms with substantial numbers of *indigenous* ethnic Britons can be plotted by the rapid and widespread growth of academic, journalistic and governmental investigators. Much as it may be disliked by many people within the communities – however much it may smack of anthropologists exploring the workings of unknown people – it is a tendency which is both inevitable and, on the whole, enlightening. It may be countered of course that surveys and investigations can only document what the people involved could have told at first hand. Even if this is true it is important for everyone that the realities of life within the ethnic communities should be widely known. This is after all no less true for any other social quarter in British life.

There has thus been a quite extraordinary outpouring of research and writing about Britain's ethnic communities, from which this book is an obvious beneficiary. Yet is is quite remarkable that the very great bulk of that work has concerned itself with male society. In the pre-occupation with nationality, race and social class, commentators have paid relatively scant attention to gender differences. There are a whole range of social characteristics common to both female and male. Indeed, many aspects of discrimination and unemployment afflict females more seriously than males. It is generally true that, in a society accustomed to thinking of the 'breadwinner' as the male head of the family, female unemployment is rarely accorded the economic or social importance of male unemployment. In the ethnic communities, like many other working-class communities, female earnings are vital for the well-being, sometimes even the existence, of the wider family groups. The economic collapse of a number of major British industries has produced high levels of unemployment among women in ethnic communities, a fact which compounds the economic distress within the family produced by adult unemployment and the receding prospects of employment for the younger members. On top of this, large numbers (the actual numbers remain inevitably imprecise) of black and Asian women have been forced into work of a remarkably exploitative nature typified by long hours, minimum wages and poor conditions. Occasionally their work has become a national *cause célèbre* which brings rallying to their side organized labour and other sympathetic pressure groups. But it is proving increasingly difficult, at a time of rising unemployment and contracting opportunities, to guarantee and maintain the conditions of employment, for white or black, which normally prevail in times of economic buoyancy.

It would nonetheless be reasonable to claim that female labour has, in recent years, been proportionately more important for ethnic communities than for British families. In the mid 1970s, before the onslaught of mass unemployment, of employed women 81 per cent of New Commonwealth immigrants worked full time, compared with 62 per cent among the British. There is other parallel evidence to corroborate the importance of full-time work among Asian and black women (and therefore, of course, of vital importance for their families). The contraction of factory production, particularly acute in many of the regions where immigrants settled, and the associated decline in a number of service industries have undoubtedly made deep inroads into the employment of immigrant women.

It would be mere speculation to try to assess this and the related economic ramifications of economic decline in the families and communities of various ethnic groups. But it takes no imaginative leap to see that it is and will continue to be corrosive and harmful. Many people who came to Britain initially to better themselves and to shake off the economic disadvantages of their homeland now find themselves enduring conditions which are, if anything, no less disadvantageous. Indeed, they may well be regarded as more oner-ous than conditions in the homeland because they are suffered in an alien land. For many people, it was only full-time work and the prospects of material improvement which made life in Britain toler-able in the first place. When the prospects of material prosperity recede and disappear, the basic attraction of life in Britain may well also evaporate, as it does for those thousands of Britons who quit their homelands for a new life overseas. This does, however, bring us full circle. The prospect of quitting Britain is much less immediate and tangible for the British-born.

Any discussion about those born British from the ethnic com-munities must end as it began with the central and unavoidable reality of demography. In earlier centuries the non-white com-munities in Britain very quickly disappeared through altered demo-graphic circumstance. They were, in any case, relatively small and predominantly male. Quickly swallowed up into an expansive white society, the blacks of eighteenth-century Britain were soon lost from sight. What makes the present – and future – so utterly different are the numbers involved and the balance between the sexes (or a balance soon to be reached in those communities still dominated by males). This balance, the youthfulness and the fertility of the ethnic communities will, short of an unpredictable political cataclysm, ensure the healthy development and growth of significant ethnic communities within Britain. They will remain in a numerical minority, overall if not in their own immediate locale.

One worrying feature is the fact that whole sections of these communities are likely to remain in an unending and seemingly unmoving state of social and urban deprivation. When we examine the post-war history of the U.S.A. we begin to catch glimpses of a possible future for Britain. It will never be fully like the U.S.A., if only (and again) for demographic reasons. But in the sense that substantial ethnic communities have become ensnared in a complex web of (primarily urban) deprivation from which it is proving ever more difficult to escape, the parallels are depressingly familiar. Moreover, the economic ability and the political resolve to combat these sapping disadvantages are simply not in sight. It is not intended to suggest that an apocalyptic future lies in wait, but it is very difficult indeed not to feel dispirited by the lack of optimistic signs. Historians are, it is true, chronically and professionally incapable of prediction and the purpose here is *not* to suggest that, on the basis of a largely historical examination, future events will unquestionably unfold in a particular way. There are, however, few signs that life for many of Britain's ethnic communities will improve. What the reaction to this will be on the part of the British-born only time will tell.

Conclusion

The British Nationality Act of 1981 made a crucial change in the traditional nature of British citizenship, by revoking the right of *jus soli*, citizenship for anyone born in the U.K. The specific restrictions of that Act were aimed at reducing still further the right to British citizenship of people from the non-white Commonwealth. Not surprisingly it was denounced as an overtly racist measure in Parliament, by pressure groups and, of course, throughout the non-white Commonwealth. Thus, by the early 1980s Britain had a new Act which effectively closed the door to non-whites, yet kept open another legal door for 6 million patrials, and 200 million in the E.E.C. The 1981 Act marks the most recent step towards ever more discriminatory legislation governing immigration and citizenship. And while it is true that it was the work of a Conservative government (which also tried to claim a political monopoly over the nation's patriotism) and while it is also true that Labour bitterly opposed that Act, the record of earlier Labour governments left little room for congratulation. Trying to discuss those changes in British life which culminated in that Act is bound to leave a sense of unease; an unease compounded by the depressing nature of much of the evidence and the general direction of the argument. Moreover, the events described in this book unfolded in a period of marked material and social decline in Britain. It is important, however, to ask whether it would have proved a different problem – less depressing an outlook – for an author covering a comparable, earlier period but writing in, say, the early summer of 1914 or 1939?

In many respects the problems would have been similar. In 1914 and 1939, major social and economic problems taxed the British people, none more troublesome and intractable than the persistence of a thick layer of urban working class in conditions of appar-

ently unchangeable wretchedness. Yet set against this obvious fact
was a contrary and contrasting phenomenon: of wide sectors of
British life (more striking of course as one glanced up the social
scale) untouched by contemporary economic troubles and able to
lead a life of material comfort. There had been numerous determined efforts to improve the lot of the poor and of the deprived,
notably the reforms of Churchill and Lloyd George before 1914.
But it was the establishment of the Labour government's welfare
state after 1945 which inaugurated the most thorough attack on
Britain's social ills. Yet, in retrospect, it is possible to see in the
optimism of the post-war world – optimistic in the belief that
careful state management would remove Britain's long-standing
urban blights – the seeds of subsequent frustration and disillusion.
However strongly one is committed to the concept of the welfare
state, it would be foolish to pretend that it has purged the nation of
its endemic social problems. The levels of poverty and of inadequate social provisions in all their forms remain remorselessly
high. And all has recently been made much worse by unprecedented
unemployment; a nation with 4 million unemployed and 2 million
illiterate needs to temper its sense of achievement.

What makes Britain in the 1980s quite different from the Britain
of 1914 or 1939 is that many of the worst aspects of social deprivation are now endured by black, as well as white, Britons. This is
not a transient problem. Neither the people nor the difficulties they
endure are likely to go away. The black population is in Britain to
stay; indeed it is becoming progressively more British. And it is
quite unrealistic to discuss their lot without addressing the broader
problems of British society. Originally, I had no specific intention
of writing about the wider social conditions in Britain, but it soon
became apparent that to ignore them would be to overlook some
of the seminal grievances between black and white.

Not all ethnic groups endure these difficulties in anything like
the same measure as the blacks. There are, as we have seen, significant minorities – we have mentioned the Sikhs – who seem able to
create for themselves a rapid improvement in material conditions,
much as poor Jewish immigrants had earlier in the century. There
is, however, a common denominator which binds together the non-
white communities into a common sense of identity, a unity which

transcends most of the myriad differences between them, namely the inescapable climate and practice of discrimination. This book has tried to argue that racial discrimination in Britain and by the British can only fully be understood within the wider historical context of British imperial and global power. As that power declined, however, residual attitudes survived, but were increasingly directed not towards the people of distant colonies and possessions, but towards the ethnic communities emerging in British cities. Clearly this is not to say that racial discrimination would *not* have existed had there been no British empire. But to discuss the racial outlook of the British without reference to that potent and only recently departed imperial past would be to distort our understanding. After all, the very great bulk of non-white people in Britain does indeed originate from parts of the former empire and colonies.

Racial attitudes – benign or malignant – do of course change, and perceptions of non-white humanity have undergone notable transformations with the development of Britain's ethnic communities. But it would take an optimism well beyond this author's to argue that, in the recent past, it has been a change for the good. Whatever efforts are currently underway – through the law, education and the like – to combat discrimination and prejudice, the surviving problems are monumental. No matter how particular communities manage or fail in the main ambition which powered their initial settlement and growth – to improve themselves materially – the task of altering British attitudes to and treatment of those communities will remain.

For a long time, 'assimilation' was an important concept behind many liberal policies toward immigrants: the desire that everyone should become as British as the next person. Experience has shown that the concept of assimilation is not merely flawed, but it is also specifically rejected by people who see it as a process of destroying their own distinctive cultures, a rendering down of all distinctions to the lowest common British denominator. In truth, British life, long before the coming of modern immigration, has been much more varied than is normally recognized. The differences between regions, religions, classes and cities, between urban and rural life have all ensured that Britain has been a veritable mosaic of contrasting cultures throughout the period of industrial society. Such diversity within Britain is, of course, the very fact which prevents many critics from writing about 'British society' as a whole.

Notwithstanding such differences there is, equally, a range of cultural forces which gives shape and coherence to the concept of 'Britishness'. The political and legal framework has developed over a long period. But social unity has also been determined by other less immediately obvious forces. Colour and language are clearly among them. The fact that the British have, by and large, shared a common colour and a common language has proved to be among the most crucial factors in shaping the social unity among people who differ in many other important respects. Even allowing for the remarkable diversity in regional accents and dialects, the British speak the same language, have the same physical appearance and share the broader culture of a dominant Christian tradition, even when they eschew its specific observances. It was into this society that peoples of different colours, creeds and languages settled in growing numbers after 1945.

For many Britons this involved a social change which threatened the basic elements in their perception of being British and living in Britain. Even when we allow for earlier immigrations, Britain had never before consisted of such sizable communities which so often differed in many of those features which the British viewed as basic to their own society. It was natural perhaps that the demand should go forth that immigrants should assimilate, or become 'like us'.

The alternatives are not altogether clear. Nor are those that are particularly attractive in many eyes. There is no doubt (because it is already, visibly in progress) that settlers' life-styles inevitably change when adapting to an alien environment. But there are powerful and understandable efforts (conscious and unconscious) to resist the change and dilution of ethnic culture and life-styles. There is even a trend to withdraw completely from white British society. The urge for separatism, like the desire to go 'home', is a confusing response to the difficulties and rebuffs of life in Britain. But it is unlikely to recede in the forseeable future, more especially when that future contains few glimmers of economic improvement. And this is especially so for the poor and the ill-paid, among whom are large numbers of non-whites. Whichever viewpoint we adopt, it is clear that Britain is entering a remarkable phase in its development. Its future, no less than its past, will be closely associated with the progress and the problems of its non-white people.

Bibliography and Guide to Further Reading

1. A Nation and Immigrants

R. B. Dobson, *The Jews of Medieval York and the Massacre of March 1190*, Borthwick Pamphlet, No. 45, York, 1979.

D. George, *London Life in the Eighteenth Century*, London, 1966.

V. G. Kiernan, 'Britons Old and New', in C. Holmes ed., *Immigrants and Minorities in British Society*, London, 1978.

L. H. Lees, *Exiles of Erin. Irish Migrants in Victorian London*, Manchester, 1979.

R. Loyn, *Anglo-Saxon England and the Norman Conquest*, London, 1962.

F. Sheppard, *London, 1808–1870. The Infernal Wen*, London, 1971.

T. C. Smout, *A History of the Scottish People, 1560–1830*, London, 1972.

2. The Empire and Race

V. E. Chancellor, *History for their Masters, Opinion in the English History Textbook, 1800–1914*, Bath, 1970.

P. Corfield, *The Impact of English Towns, 1700–1800*, Oxford, 1982.

W. Cunningham, *Alien Immigrants to England*, London, 1897.

P. Edwards and J. Walvin, *Black Personalities in the Era of the Slave Trade*, London, 1983.

N. File and C. Power, *Black Settlers in Britain, 1555–1958*, London, 1981.

P. D. Fraser, 'Nineteenth century Blacks in Britain: War Office Records as a Source', paper delivered at 'Blacks in Britain' conference, University of London, September 1981.

V. G. Kiernan, *The Lords of Human Kind*, London, 1972.

D. A. Lorimer, *Colour, Class and the Victorians*, Leicester, 1978.

B. Porter, *The Lion's Share*, London, 1975.

F. Spiers, 'Blacks in Britain and the Struggle for Black Freedom in North America, 1820–1870', paper delivered at 'Blacks in Britain' conference, University of London, September 1981.

J. Walvin, *Black and White. The Negro and English Society, 1555–1945*, London, 1973.

3. The Special Case: Ireland

J. C. Beckett, *The Making of Modern Ireland, 1603–1923*, London, 1981.
F. Finnegan, *Poverty and Prostitution. A Study of Victorian Prostitutes in York*, Cambridge, 1979.
A. D. Gilbert, *Religion and Society*, London, 1976.
S. Gilley, 'English Attitudes to the Irish, 1789–1900', in C. Holmes ed., *Immigrants and Minorities in British Society*, London, 1978.
J. A. Jackson, *The Irish in Britain*, London, 1963.
L. H. Lees, *Exiles of Erin. Irish Migrants in Victorian London*, Manchester, 1979.
D. A. Lorimer, *Colour, Class and the Victorians*, Leicester, 1978.

4. Newcomers, 1880–1914

J. Cheetham, 'Immigration', in A. H. Halsey ed., *Trends in British Society since 1900*, London, 1972.
B. Gainer, *The Alien Invasion*, London, 1972.
J. Garrard, *The English and Immigration, 1880–1910*, Oxford, 1971.
V. G. Kiernan, *The Lords of Human Kind*, London, 1972.
K. Little, *Negroes in Britain*, London, 1947.
J. P. May, 'The Chinese in Britain, 1860–1914', in C. Holmes ed., *Immigrants and Minorities in British Society*, London, 1978.
B. Porter, *The Lion's Share*, London, 1975.
G. Stedman Jones, *Outcast London*, London, 1976.
J. Walvin, *Black and White. The Negro and English Society, 1555–1945*, London, 1973.

5. Wartime and Hard Times, 1914–39

M. J. Craton, *A History of the Bahamas*, London, 1968.
N. File and C. Power, *Black Settlers in Britain, 1555–1958*, London, 1981.
M. Gilbert, *Auschwitz and the Allies*, London, 1981.
A. H. Halsey, ed., *Trends in British Society since 1900*, London, 1972.
C. L. Joseph, 'The British West Indian Regiment, 1914–18', *Journal of Caribbean History* II, May 1971.
K. Little, *Negroes in Britain*, London, 1947.
R. Macdonald, 'The Role of London's Black Press in the 1930s and 1940s', paper delivered at 'Blacks in Britain' conference, University of London, September 1981.
C. Loch Mowatt, *Britain Between the Wars*, London, 1959.
K. Robbins, *The Eclipse of a Great Power, 1870–1975*, London, 1983.

E. Scobie, *Black Britannia*, Chicago, 1972.

A J P Taylor, *English History 1914–1945*, Oxford, 1965.

6. The People's War, 1939–45

A. Calder, *The People's War*, London, 1969.

N. File and C. Power, *Black Settlers in Britain 1555–1958*, London, 1981.

M. Gilbert, *Finest Hour*, London, 1983.

J. Keegan, *Six Armies in Normandy*, London, 1982.

M. J. Proudfoot, *European Refugees, 1939–1945*, London, 1952.

E. Scobie, *Black Britannia*, Chicago, 1972.

B. Wasserstein, *Britain and the Jews of Europe, 1939–45*, Oxford, 1979.

7. The Post-war World, 1945–62

R. Desai, *Indian Immigrants in Britain*, Oxford, 1963.

R. Glass, *Newcomers*, London, 1960.

A. H. Halsey, *Trends in British Society since 1900*, London, 1972.

J. Jackson, *The Irish in Britain*, London, 1963.

A. Marwick, *British Society since 1945*, London, 1982.

M. J. Proudfoot, *European Refugees, 1939–1945*, London, 1952.

K. Robbins, *The Eclipse of a Great Power*, London, 1983.

E. J. B. Rose *et al.*, *Colour and Citizenship*, London, 1969.

B. Wasserstein, *Britain and the Jews of Europe, 1939–45*, Oxford, 1979.

8. Closing the Door: Immigration and Race since 1962

M. Banton, *Race Relations*, London, 1970.

I. Crewe ed., *British Political Sociology Yearbook*, vol. 2, *The Politics of Race*, London, 1975.

P. Foot, *Immigrants and Race in British Politics*, London, 1975.

C. Husband ed., *Race in Britain*, London, 1982; essays in Part II.

L. Lustgarten, *Legal Controls of Racial Discrimination*, London, 1980.

R. Moore and T. Wallace, *Slamming the Door*, London, 1975.

J. Rex, *Race, Community and Conflict: A Study of Sparkbrook*, London, 1967.

J. Rex, *Race Relations in Sociological Theory*, London, 1970.

E. J. B. Rose *et al.*, *Colour and Citizenship*, London, 1969.

Runnymede Trust, *Britain's Black Population*, 1980.

9. Politics and Race

M. Banton, *Race Relations*, London, 1970.

M. Banton, *Racial and Ethnic Competition*, Cambridge, 1983.

D. Butler and D. Stokes, *Political Change in Britain*, London, 1969.

I. Crewe ed., *British Political Sociology Yearbook*, vol. 2, *The Politics of Race*, London, 1975.

R. Hepple, *Race, Jobs and the Law in Britain*, London, 1968.

C. Husband ed., *Race in Britain*, London, 1982.

A. Lester and G. Bindman, *Race and the Law*, London, 1972.

R. Miles and A. Phizacklea eds, *Racism and Political Action in Britain*, London, 1975.

B. Porter, *The Lion's Share*, London, 1975.

M. Walker, *The National Front*, London, 1977.

10. A Mosaic of Communities

M. Banton, *Racial and Ethnic Competitors*, Cambridge, 1983.

A. Dummett, *A Portrait of English Racism*, London, 1973.

R. B. Davison, *Black British*, Oxford, 1966.

S. Patterson, *Dark Strangers*, London, 1963.

C. Peach, *West Indian Migrants to Britain*, Oxford, 1965.

J. Rex and S. Tomlinson, *Colonial Immigrants in a British City*, London, 1979.

D. J. Smith, *Racial Disadvantage in Britain*, London, 1977.

J. L. Watson, ed., *Between Two Cultures*, Oxford, 1977.

J. Zubrzycki, *Polish Immigrants in Britain*, The Hague, 1956.

11. Points of Conflict

M. Barker, *The New Racism*, London, 1981.

V. Chancellor, *History for Their Masters. Opinion in the English History Textbook, 1800–1914*, Bath, 1970.

D. Dabydeen ed., *The Black Presence in English Literature*, Wolverhampton, 1983.

A. Dummett, *A Portrait of English Racism*, London, 1973.

M. Green, *Dreams of Empire, Deeds of Adventure*, London, 1980.

C. Gutzmore, 'Black Youth . . .', paper presented to conference at University of Hull, July 1983.

S. Hall, *The Empire Strikes Back*, London, 1982.

S. Hall *et al.*, *Policing the Crisis*, London, 1978.

S. Hall, *Culture, Media, Language*, London, 1980.

R. Moore, *White Racism and Black Resistance*, London, 1975.

A. Phizacklea and R. Miles, *Labour and Racism*, London, 1980.

K. Pryce, *Endless Pressure*, London, 1977.

The Scarman Report; The Brixton Disorders ... Report of an Inquiry by the Rt Hon. The Lord Scarman, London, 1981.

M. Stone, *The Education of the Black Child in Britain: The Myth of Multiracial Education*, London, 1981.

B. Sutcliffe, *British Black English*, Oxford, 1982.

S. Zubaida, *Race and Racialism*, London, 1970.

12. *The Changing British*

J. Burnett, *Plenty and Want*, London, 1979.

W. Baker, *Sports in the Western World*, Totowa, New Jersey, 1982.

E. Cashmore, *Rastaman*, London, 1979.

E. Cashmore, *Black Sportsmen*, London, 1982.

Ethnic Minorities in Britain, Home Office Research Study, No. 68, London, 1981.

Ethnic Minorities in Britain; statistical background, C. R. E. London, 1979.

C. Husband ed., *White Media and Black Britain*, London, 1975.

P. Willis, *Learning to Labour*, London, 1977.

13. *Born British*

S. Allen, 'Perhaps a Seventh Person?', in C. Husband ed., *Race in Britain*, London, 1982.

M. Banton, *Racial and Ethnic Competition*, Cambridge, 1983.

E. Cashmore and B. Troyna eds, *Black Youth in Crisis*, London, 1982.

Ethnic Minorities in Britain, Home Office Research Study, No. 68, London, 1981.

K. Pryce, *Endless Pressure*, London, 1977.

J. Rex, 'West Indian and Asian Youth', in E. Cashmore and B. Troyna eds, *Black Youth in Crisis*, London, 1982.

J. Walvin, *A Child's World. A Social History of English Childhood 1800–1914*, London, 1982.

J. L. Watson ed, *Between Two Cultures*, Oxford, 1977.

Index

MORE ABOUT PENGUINS, PELICANS
AND PUFFINS

For further information about books available from Penguins please write to Dept EP, Penguin Books Ltd, Harmondsworth, Middlesex UB7 ODA.

In the U.S.A.: For a complete list of books available from Penguins in the United States write to Dept DG, Penguin Books, 299 Murray Hill Parkway, East Rutherford, New Jersey 07073.

In Canada: For a complete list of books available from Penguins in Canada write to Penguin Books Canada Ltd, 2801 John Street, Markham, Ontario L3R 1B4.

In Australia: For a complete list of books available from Penguins in Australia write to the Marketing Department, Penguin Books Australia Ltd, P.O. Box 257, Ringwood, Victoria 3134.

In New Zealand: For a complete list of books available from Penguins in New Zealand write to the Marketing Department, Penguin Books (N.Z.) Ltd, P.O. Box 4019, Auckland 10.

In India: For a complete list of books available from Penguins in India write to Penguin Overseas Ltd, 706 Eros Apartments, 56 Nehru Place, New Delhi 110019.

A CHILD'S WORLD

A SOCIAL HISTORY OF ENGLISH CHILDHOOD
1800–1914

During the 19th century more than a third of the English population was fourteen or under. Put more graphically; there was no escaping from children. Their noise and play were a constant feature of life, they cluttered up streets and houses and haunted the historical documentation of the time. At one end of the spectrum they underpinned the Victorian ideal of the family, at the other they provided cheap, pliable labour for the industrial revolution.

There were enormous differences between children of different classes, ages, sexes and localities, but even under the harshest conditions children managed to inherit, create and pass on their own stories, songs, street-games and mythologies.

Their experiences shaped society as we know it and this Pelican is a unique and fascinating study of a hitherto neglected area of our history.

Published in Pelicans

INSIDE THE INNER CITY
Paul Harrison

The early eighties have seen the breakdown of Western economies, the erosion of welfare states and the disappearance of social consensus. Nowhere have these processes cut more deeply than in the inner city, where industrial decline, low incomes, high unemployment and housing decay are fuelling crime and racial tension to create our most daunting social problem.

Combining interviews and eye-witness accounts with his own penetrating analysis, Paul Harrison provides a grim portrait of the human costs of recession and monetarism. From dying factories to social security offices, from single mothers to street thieves, it offers a unique insight into the stark realities of deprivation and social conflict in Britain today.

INSIDE THE THIRD WORLD
Paul Harrison

The Third World is increasingly in the news. Superpower confrontations and north–south negotiations have joined the old stories of famines, wars, coups and revolutions. This book fills in the background to those events.

It provides a comprehensive guide to the major problems behind mass poverty and political instability: from climate and colonialism, through land hunger, exploding cities and unemployment, to over-population, hunger, disease and illiteracy, placing them all in the context of national and international inequalities.

The wealth of facts and analysis are brought home in first hand, often harrowing accounts of the realities of life for poor people and poor communities in Asia, Africa and Latin America. It is the tragic story of three-quarters of humanity.

Published in Pelicans

WE HATE HUMANS
David Robins

Every year the renewed wave of 'soccer hooliganism' revives the Great Debate: make parents responsible? Fence them in? Ban the professional game itself? Needless to say, the fans remain as impervious as ever. Theirs is a world which has its own history, enjoys its own rights and obligations and obeys its own logic, a logic of violence – which is also highly exportable.

The author spent seven years researching his subject, and his book tells the story of the youth 'ends' through the vivid descriptive speech of the fans themselves. Black and white, they are united against the law, and their voice is the unique voice of the Other England – a land where thousands of young people join the dole queue each year, dispossessed of expectations and often desperate. We ignore them at our peril.

FAMILY AND KINSHIP IN EAST LONDON
Peter Willmott and Michael Young

The two authors of this most human of surveys are sociologists. They spent three years on 'field work' in Bethnal Green and on a new housing estate in Essex. The result is a fascinating study, made during a period of extensive rehousing, of family and community ties and the pull of the 'wider family' on working-class people.

'Probably not only the fullest, but virtually the only account of working-class family relationships in any country. The general reader will find it full of meat and free of jargon' – *New Statesman*

'This shrewd – and in places extremely amusing – book combines warmth of feeling with careful sociological method' – *Financial Times*

'Observant, tactful, sympathetic, humorous . . . I really feel that nobody who wants to know how our society is changing can afford not to read Young and Willmott' – Kingsley Amis in the *Spectator*

IMMIGRATION AND RACE
Maggie Wilson

Dealing with racial discrimination * Understanding the Nationality Act * Employment rights * State benefits * Dealing with the police and the law * Finding information in minority languages

Whether you are a recent immigrant or whether you were born in Britain into an 'ethnic minority', here is a handbook to guide you through your rights in a racially discriminating society. Set out in practical question-and-answer form, it provides you with the essential information for survival and to help you negotiate a better deal.

WOMEN'S RIGHTS IN THE WORKPLACE
Tess Gill and Larry Whitty

Women and training * Working part-time * Maternity rights * Women and new technology * Paid work at home * Women and employment law * Creches and child-care at work

Whether you're employed in an office, a factory or a school, *Women's Rights in the Workplace* is designed to arm you with the information – and the expertise and confidence – to get a better deal at work. Containing full, up-to-date information on women's jobs, pay and conditions, it is the essential handbook for all working women.

Other volumes in this new Penguin series *Know Your Rights: The Questions and the Answers* cover marital rights and claiming social security benefits.